CH £10

D1549762

Parallel Lives

Davina Jones

Appletree Press

First published in 2005
for Melissa Brownlow
by
Appletree Press Ltd
The Old Potato Station
14 Howard Street South
Belfast BT7 1AP
Tel: +44 (0) 28 90 24 30 74
Fax: +44 (0) 28 90 24 67 56
E-mail: reception@appletree.ie
Web Site: www.irelandseye.com

Desk & Marketing Editor: Jean Brown
Editor: Jim Black
Designer: Stuart Wilkinson
Production Manager: Paul McAvoy

Parallel Lives

ISBN: 0 86281 963 6

9 8 7 6 5 4 3 2 1
AP3227

Photographic Credits:
Melissa Brownlow and the publishers wish to thank the following for permission
to reproduce work in copyright:
© Sport & General (p 9) © Fox Photos Ltd (inside front flap and pp 25 and 32)
© The National Trust. Photograph by Roger Kinkead (p 35)
© British Army in the Rhine – Public Relations Section (p 134)
© Daily Mail (p 140)
© Mrs Yvonne Friers for the cartoon of William Brownlow by Rowel Boyd Friers (p 162)
© The Field (p 171)
© The Newtownards Chronicle (p 174)
© Belfast Telegraph (p174)
© Bobbie Hopkins (p 179)
© Healy Racing Photos (pp 182, 188)
© The Down Recorder (p 194)
© Bobbie Hanvey (pp 198, 199)

While every effort has been made to contact copyright holders, the publisher would welcome
information on any oversight which may have occurred.

Contents

Preface

Strangford Lough

THE VILLAGES of Strangford and Portaferry in County Down, Northern Ireland, stand 500 yards apart either side of the mouth of Strangford Lough. The small strait of water dividing them has the fastest tide in the British Isles with 400 million tons of water churning through it, filling and emptying the fifteen-mile long sea lough. As the tide rushes out to rejoin the Irish Sea it reveals immense mud flats which attract an abundance of bird species to the area. Its depths contain many forms of life from sea anemones and scallops to lobster, crabs, jellyfish, and even two breeds of seal. Sailing aficionados are also drawn to the area for its relatively protected climate and the pleasure of gliding through Strangford's waters and around its drumlin-shaped islands.

In 1921, the year a Peace Treaty with Britain set up the Irish Free State and Northern Ireland came into existence, two babies were born whose lives were to be linked by a large grey-stone house situated on a hill overlooking this lough. William, the first of the two born, would one day inherit this house and Agnes, the second-born, would come to work there. William was the eldest son of Jimmy and Elinor Brownlow and was born on 9th October in Winchester where his father was serving with his regiment. Agnes arrived a fortnight later on 21st October. The youngest daughter of Robert and Sarah Skillen, she was born in the Downpatrick Gate Lodge on the Castle Ward estate, close to Strangford on the other side of the lough.

William and Agnes were the first generation to know life in the new Northern Ireland, and their experiences through the turbulent decades of the twentieth century illustrate a picture of life quite contrary to the troubled one more often portrayed. Despite the occasional outbreak of politically motivated trouble in Portaferry the area was not known for it, "everyone's friendly, there's no problem," as Agnes says. Portaferry and Strangford are attractive villages populated by relaxed residents, "that wonderfully happy example of a well knit natural community," was how William would describe the neighbourhood towards the end of his life.

William and Agnes grew up in the years between the wars, at a time when the horror of the Great War was still tangible. The vast social changes put in motion by the next war had yet to entirely alter a way of life. They were an age-group that would know and understand the old order while watching it pass and in disparate ways, their lives were moulded by its existence.

The Brownlow family had moved to Ireland from England early in the seventeenth century and over the years went on to settle in various regions of Ulster. When William's grandmother died in 1938 his father concluded his military career in England and returned home to live in and manage Ballywhite, the family home overlooking Strangford Lough.

The Skillen family was established on the other side of the lough, with numerous members employed in the service of land-owning families in the area. Agnes' father had been born on the Myra Castle estate and later went on to work and live on the nearby Castle Ward estate where Agnes also found her first job. In 1939 at the age of 17 Agnes crossed the lough and, for the first time, pedalled her bike up the hill to Ballywhite to begin her work for the Brownlow family. It was the beginning of an association that has lasted over 60 years.

Acknowledgements

This dual memoir was the brainchild of William Brownlow's daughter, Melissa. It was borne from her love of both her father and Aggie and inspired by a desire to record the disappearing world they were born into. My own input has been to collate William's diaries, letters and piles of boxes and to sit down with Agnes and her husband Frank and listen to them talking about their lives. Their banter made 'research' a total joy.

My thanks go to Melissa, Agnes and Frank and to Eveleigh, Jamie, and Camilla, all of whom have made this a personal account of two very happy lives. It is almost impossible to acknowledge everyone who has assisted me with their time over the years but my thanks go to William's brother and sister, James and Anne, and to his extended family and many close friends for their detailed contributions. Thanks go in particular to my husband, Hume; as a brother officer of William's his help has been invaluable.

- DHJ 2005

Chapter One
William: Childhood

William Brownlow

WILLIAM BROWNLOW'S family dates its move from England to Ireland to 1610, when a forebear, John Brownlow of Nottingham and Lincolnshire with his son, William, moved to County Armagh.

Their move came as a result of the 'Flight of the Earls', the exile of Hugh O'Neill, Earl of Tyrone, and other Gaelic chieftains from Ulster in 1607, who opposed English rule and fled Ulster for the continent. Consequently their lands were declared the property of James I whose ministers divided them into plots of between 1,000 and 2,000 acres and handed them out to English and Scottish families prepared to settle in Ulster.

John and William Brownlow put themselves forward as 'undertakers' of this land and in 1610[i] they obtained two grants of land of 1,500 and 1,000 acres in the O'Neill area of County Armagh.

They arrived in County Armagh with an entourage of one freeholder, six tenants, six carpenters, one tailor, one mason and six workmen and made their settlement on the site of what is known today as Lurgan. Wolves were claimed to roam the area and the land was described at the time as 'woody and boggy country on the great Lough side'.[ii] A decade after their arrival 'Lurgan' was made up of 42 dwellings and by the end of the century it had developed into a linen manufacturing town. A Brownlow forebear is credited with designing the street plan. By the 1800s the Brownlow estate had enlarged greatly and also included land in Counties Monaghan and Louth. The family were a part of the Anglo-Irish Establishment with its members pursuing careers in the army, the church and politics; a number became MP for Armagh.

One forebear married an Irish girl, Eleanor O'Doherty of Inishowen, County Donegal and many believe this assisted the Brownlow family during troubled times. Their union led to the family secretly – because it was illegal – allowing Catholic tenants to retain their land. Another forebear was intrigued by ancient Irish manuscripts as Dr Thomas Molyneaux of Castledillon describes in his book *Journey to Ye North* written in 1708:

'This gentleman [William Brownlow] is more curious than ordinary and has by him several old Irish manuscripts which he can read and understand very well. He shewed me one in parchment of the Bible (as I remember) pretended to be written by St. Patrick's own hand but this must be a fable.[1]'

In 1839 Charles Brownlow, a retired MP for Armagh, was raised to the peerage 'for services to the Whig Party' becoming the first Lord Lurgan. He engaged an architect, W H Playfair, to design a large Elizabethan style house in Scottish sandstone and Brownlow House stands to this day, an imposing building, in the centre of Lurgan. The second Lord Lurgan owned the legendary greyhound, Master McGrath, the winner of the Waterloo cup in 1868, 1869 and 1871, whose successes are celebrated in a well-known Irish ballad.

In 1883 the Brownlow estate was recorded as being of 15,276 acres and worth £20,589 per annum[iii] but a family financial crisis combined with the changing political situation regarding land ownership saw the estates sold off. Despite no family members living in Lurgan today, a new town built close to Lurgan in the 1960s was given the name Brownlow. Unlike these antecedents, of whom one was fluent in Irish, William's own childhood was spent mostly in England. His first visits to Ireland were trips to see his grandmother and relations in County Down. His father was in the army and as a result William's childhood was nomadic; born in Winchester he grew up in four houses in southern England. It was not until his parents moved to County Down in 1938 that it became his real home.

Colonel Guy James Brownlow, William's father, had been brought up with his brother and five sisters in a late eighteenth-century house, Coolderry, near Carrickmacross in County Monaghan. 'Jimmy' or 'The Colonel', as he became known, had been sent to school in England, and on leaving Harrow in 1904 joined the Rifle Brigade. The political troubles in Ireland had escalated by the time of his father's[2] death in 1914, and he and his younger brother, Andrew, decided they must move their sisters and widowed mother, Georgina, away from County Monaghan. They found a house in a comparatively safe area in County Down. After the departure

Colonel and Mrs Brownlow

Elinor Brownlow on her wedding day, 1920

'Jimmy' Brownlow on joining the army

of the family from Coolderry it suffered arson attacks and has since been demolished.

Charlie Brownlow, William's great uncle, had settled in County Down on the Ards peninsula when he became land agent to the Londonderry family at Mount Stewart and the Nugent family at Portaferry House. Charlie, who lived on the sea front in the town of Portaferry, brought about the family's move to County Down when he advised his nephews that a house suitable to their mother and sisters' needs had come up for sale in his area. He worked from an office[3] in Ferry Street in Portaferry where he was in regular contact with Captain David Ker, one of the trustees of the Nugent Estate. Captain Ker owned a large Victorian house outside Portaferry which he had bought to let in 1911 and was considering selling on.

The house, Ballywhite, was built in 1890 by Mr Warnock, a solicitor from Downpatrick. It included large reception rooms as well as a ballroom and a conservatory. Georgina Brownlow arrived at Ballywhite in 1918 with her daughters[4], Marjorie, Geraldine and Nina[5]. Charlie Brownlow drove them there from Coolderry; it was a sedate journey much recalled by the girls as he failed to get out of second gear the entire way. Uncle Charlie was much loved by the family and when he retired unmarried he joined the family at Ballywhite.

William's father was unable to be at Ballywhite during the move owing to the Great War. His bravery was mentioned three times in despatches despite being wounded early in the war, and he later returned to France to work at an officer training school. After the war he was based in England where he was introduced to a young widow, Elinor Mitchell-Campbell. They continued to meet at tennis tournaments in Hampshire, close to where she lived and where he was stationed at the Rifle Depot, and in August 1920 they were married in Bembridge on the Isle of Wight. Her first husband had been an officer in the Connaught Rangers, Major Montagu Mitchell-Campbell, and had been killed in the early stages of the Battle of the Somme in September 1916. They had one daughter in 1915, Elinor, known as Nell.

Elinor Mitchell-Campbell was the daughter of Colonel George Scott who had served in the 18th Hussars. She and her sister, Esmie, were young when their mother died and their grandfather Joe Christy, and aunt Ethel Christy, brought them up at Upton Park, near Alresford in Hampshire. Colonel Scott did not marry again and lived for the most part in the Cavalry Club in London. He enjoyed his visits to his daughters and shortly after Elinor and Jimmy were married he died at their dining room table in Winchester.

In the first years of their marriage William's parents lived at Rotherly, a house near Winchester. Rotherly had been his mother's home after she was widowed. William was born there in 1921, his brother James arrived in 1922 and the following year the family moved to nearby Twyford House. Here the family settled into life with a household of a nanny, a butler, two housemaids, a cook, a kitchen maid, a chauffeur, a groom and two gardeners. Anne was born in 1927 at Twyford.

William, Nell, Anne and James

William with his first bird and Chubby

Anne and James with their much-loved governess
'Toad'

Elinor Brownlow loved horses and often drove her children to childhood parties in a pony and trap. James and Anne remember one particularly feisty pony called Snowdrop being used on such occasions.

The family spent Christmas near Salisbury with the Christy Millers, cousins of Mrs Brownlow's, at Clarendon Park. The large house seemed very grand to the children who were whisked away by servants. The tedious task of nursery meals was assigned to the third footman. William disgraced himself in the footman's presence when his least favourite pudding, tapioca, was served, taking a mouthful only to bring it back up again all over the table, much to his Nanny's horror and embarrassment. The young William had particular tastes and aside from tapioca he took against his mother's favourite pudding, junket. Not all puddings met with his disapproval and as a young boy he came across a treacle tart cooling before lunch and leaning his head over to smell it his sister Nell came up from behind pushed his head down into it. The tart was still warm and he was left red-nosed.

The family left Twyford in 1929 and moved to Dorset. Mrs Brownlow took on a governess, known to the children as 'Toad' after the character in *The Wind in the Willows*. Toad was popular with them, "when hounds came through during lessons we bolted out to see them," recalls James. Anne's first memory of her eldest brother was 'in pursuit' in the great outdoors. "He rescued me from an interesting rabbit hunt with our family dog Chubby: the latter and I were great friends and I tended to follow him everywhere. William discovered us, along with James, at the far end of a field. Chubby and I were peering down an interesting rabbit hole, the biggest of several others, and I had one shoe missing. It was found nearby." William had been given the terrier, Chubby, as a reward for stopping biting his fingernails.

When Anne was small James and William treated her almost as a toy. They would blindfold her and lead her through puddles and hedges until she begged for mercy. She was much the youngest and craved attention from the older three, as they had become quite a team.

Horses grew into a family passion: 'Mother resumed her love of hunting with the South and West Wiltshire Hunt and it was natural for me to ride with them also,' William told a sporting magazine[iv] later in life. The children started going to a Pony Club branch founded by their father and the well-known American huntsman Ikey Bell, Master of the S & W Wilts. Bell's daughter Di became the greatest of friends with Nell and her younger siblings. William's hunting career began at the age of eight in April 1929. He and James walked the hound puppies for the hunt; Harebell and Handicraft were two favourites whom they encouraged to gallop in the garden. William's first pony was called Trixie, (she had been Nell's before his), and he groomed her till her coat shone.

In 1930 William was sent away to board at a small prep school in Rottingdean on the East Sussex coast. The school, St Aubyn's, was situated in a Victorian town house,

William and Trixie at the SW and Wilts Show in 1936

William and Trixie with James and Felix (left)

Pupils at St Aubyn's, Rottingdean (William is 4th from left)

and its small façade was a front for a rabbit warren of buildings with terraced gardens behind, beyond which lay a large windswept sports pitch. He was an outgoing child and appeared happy there from the start. His brother James joined him there a year later. At school he made friends with Pat Nugent, the son of Sir Roly and Lady Nugent who lived beside his grandmother on the Ards peninsula. During William and James' time there the family moved from Dorset to Somerset.

School weekends were spent on the games pitch, gardening or watching Harold Lloyd films. William was given his first camera and aside from photographing his favourite pony or dog he took endless pictures of school friends larking about, capturing a happy, carefree existence. There was little vanity on his behalf – one school holidays he arrived home, his face appeared somewhat altered: "he was missing his eye lashes" remembers Anne. "He had cut them off with scissors as he was being teased about the length of them."

Sports day was a big event in the school calendar and the Brownlow family all travelled to Sussex to take part. The school band was paraded in front of the parents in military fashion with William proudly playing the drums. Everyone was expected to perform, and Colonel Brownlow was cheered on annually in the fathers' race. At the age of four Anne was persuaded to compete in the sisters' race. Her brothers were adamant she would win – they placed her so close to the finishing line they merely had to push her over it for her to win. As a result of their endeavours Anne become the owner of a silver napkin ring, complete with her initials and the St Aubyn's crest.

On the same occasion William thought of a prank he could play with his little sister. While his parents were talking to the teachers he dressed her in his pyjamas and put her in a spare bed in the dormitory. When the headmaster, Mr Lang, came to say goodnight to each boy he found an extra one, "close to tears, as I thought I was there to stay for the rest of the term." She was rescued by her parents.

William excelled in various sporting activities but his younger brother – 'Brownlow mi' – was by far the greater achiever in field games. The summer of 1931 was hot on the South Coast, 108 degrees on one occasion according to the school thermometer, but it did not hinder William on the athletics course. He and Beazley were first equal in the High Jump leaping to a height of 3ft 8½ inches and he won the Under 13 hurdles. He made it into the school cricket team and was good at squash. As a lightweight boxer his talents were written up in the school magazine in 1933: 'Curtis ma and Brownlow ma had two very even rounds, the former just winning.' While a keen shot he only came 7th in the 1st VIII in 1934, which the school magazine implied was an abysmal team: 'The scores for the St Patrick's [cup] were the lowest we have ever had, and the scores in the Imperial Challenge Shield were worse than last year.' William had taken part in both.

The school magazine of 1934 listed his departure: 'WS Brownlow goes to Eton (at very short notice); he was in the cricket eleven and was a sub-section commander.'

William had been expecting to go to Harrow but at the last minute his father changed his mind and sent him to Eton.

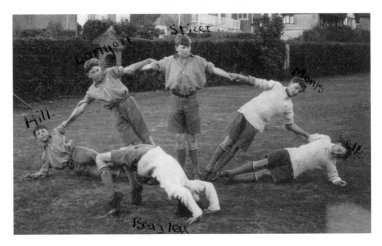

PT at St Aubyn's (William is on the far right)

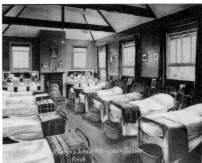

A classroom and pupil dormitory at St Aubyn's

Notes:
1 The Book of Armagh: the earliest existing specimen of continuous narrative in Irish prose; it came into the Brownlow family's ownership in the late 17th century and remained with them until 1853 when it was sold for £300; in 1858 it was presented to Trinity College, Dublin, where it remains.
2 Claude Brownlow
3 The building was bought by his great, great niece Melissa Brownlow, who converted it into The Port, an outdoor clothing shop.
4 Two sisters were living away by 1916: Gwen was working as a nurse and Eileen was married and living in Wimbledon.
5 Nina moved away when she married at St Philips Church, Portaferry with William, James and Nell as her attendants.

Chapter Two
Agnes: Childhood

Agnes Skillen

AGNES SKILLEN was born in the grounds of Castle Ward where her father and extended family worked on the estate in a variety of capacities for the sixth Viscount Bangor.

Agnes was her parents' fourth child: Hester was 10, Ida six and Albert four, when she was born. Her arrival was celebrated by her many aunts, uncles and cousins employed on the estate and also by Lady Bangor who took a keen interest in her naming. Lord Bangor had married Agnes Hamilton in 1905, and although they had not chosen her Christian name for any of their three daughters Lady Bangor suggested it to the Skillens: "Lady Bangor asked that I should be called after her, hence the name," says Agnes.

Castle Ward stands in a magnificent position above Strangford Lough and is well-known for its unconventional combination of gothic and classical styles in one architectural design. For four hundred years the estate was home to the Ward family and the present house, the third 'Castle Ward' to be built, was designed when Bernard Ward was elevated to the nobility in the eighteenth century becoming the first Viscount Bangor. He favoured a classical Palladian design, but his wife was adamant it should be built in the gothic style, which was fashionable in England at the time.

They compromised by building the north east front in Georgian gothic, the south west in the classical Palladian, and the rooms inside reflect their varying exteriors. The marriage did not last but the house stands, a testament to their differences; their idiosyncratic design is today a much-admired National Trust property.

The Skillen family lived in the Downpatrick Gate Lodge, one of the many cottages housing Lord Bangor's large staff: "there were Johnsons and Swails and Skillens living around Castle Ward, and we were all related, my father's sisters worked there, we were all cousins," remembers Agnes. At the time estates like Castle Ward were an important source of employment in the local community and generations of families followed each other into service in their households. A landowner such as Lord Bangor lived off the rents from his properties in Bangor, Killough and the area surrounding Castle Ward which paid for the upkeep of his large house and estate and the salaries of his large staff. His employees were housed either in these cottages or in the stable yard and members of the unmarried house staff were given rooms in the servants' quarters in Castle Ward itself.

"Nobody had to go out of the town for work then," Agnes' husband reflected many years later, "but death duties put them out of business, the government just grabbed everything."

Agnes' father, Robert Skillen, came from a large family, the 13th of 14 children. He was born in a gate lodge at Myra Castle, the neighbouring estate to Castle Ward, where his father worked as a coachman for the Wallace family. He and most of his siblings stayed in the area, married locally, and found work in a variety of capacities on estates such as Myra Castle and Castle Ward. A number of their marriages and forms of employment are chronicled in Ballyculter's church records[v] from the turn of the century: Samuel Skillen became a coachman like his father before him and married Charlotte McDowell, the daughter of a Strangford ferryman; Elizabeth Skillen married Robert Johnston, a gardener at Castle Ward. They lived and married in the area and many are also buried in the graveyard at Ballyculter.

Agnes' mother, Sarah Gain, was born in Scotland but she and her brother, Edward, moved to Ireland as children with their parents. Their father found work in the foundries in County Down and they settled a stone's throw from Castle Ward on a small plot of land just beyond the estate walls on the Audleystown Road. Their home was a two-roomed cottage, and when he was old enough Edward farmed the surrounding land. When Agnes was born both her grandfather and uncle[1] were dead and her grandmother lived in the cottage alone and let the land for grazing.

Sarah Gain and Robert Skillen were married in Christchurch, Ballyculter, on 15th September 1910. They were both employed at the time of their marriage and on their wedding certificate he describes himself as a 'labourer' and she as a 'servant'. They had found work at Castle Ward during the time of Henry Ward, fifth Viscount Bangor. He and his wife employed a huge staff both in and outside the house on a scale never

Sarah Skillen at Castle Ward

Robert Skillen

to be known again at Castle Ward. It consisted of a butler, two footmen, a personal valet, four housemaids, a personal maid, a cook, a kitchen maid, a scullery maid, laundry maids, a boot boy, a coachman and two grooms, a land steward and about 40 workmen who were mostly farm workers but also gardeners, gamekeepers, and boatmen. His wife, Mary King, is well known for writing and illustrating a book on the microscope as well as for her unfortunate death, falling from a steam train.

Robert Skillen was employed as a gardener and he was responsible for the upkeep of the sunken rose garden, which he had helped to create by digging out the beds and putting in the steps when he went to work there at the turn of the century. He was one of the gardeners kept on by Maxwell Ward, sixth Viscount Bangor, when he inherited Castle Ward on the death of his father in 1911. "He was in charge of the 'Little Garden' – which was about four acres – just beside Castle Ward house," recalls Sylvia Forde, a grandchild of the sixth Viscount. "It included the triangular and round beds between stone flags of the sunken Rose Garden as well as upper terraces of rose beds with clipped box edges. Also a sloped rockery made by my grandmother, herbaceous borders filled with perennials, agapanthus, large poppies and all the surrounding shrubs and lawns. He scythed the steep grassy banks between the different levels as close as the flat lawns cut by the motor mower."

The sixth Viscount was a military man who had spent his career on the south coast of England and in China. He was suited to life on the shores of Strangford Lough because his great passion in life was sailing. Like his father he maintained a large household at Castle Ward but he did not share his interest in farming and in 1912 he reduced the number of workmen on the estate to twenty. When the First World War came Lord Bangor's services were required on the south coast of England and the family were uprooted from Castle Ward for the duration of the war.

"Castle Ward was a big place with cattle, game and wood needing dealing with," Agnes recalls. "Aside from the rose garden there was a vegetable garden down below where my uncle worked and I had cousins who did the ploughing." Sarah Skillen did not work when her children were young but as they became self-sufficient she returned to work in the Castle Ward laundry. There was no electricity and clothes were scrubbed vigorously on washboards and pressed using flat irons.

While the wage was low Lord Bangor's staff paid him no rent and they were able to heat their homes with firewood taken from the woods on the estate. He paid for the upkeep of their homes (which were his property), and the estate account books note the money spent on general maintenance such as when new tiles were added to roofs and new ranges put into the kitchens. There were 20 houses on the estate and four gate lodges all of which were made use of by the families of farm, game and garden staff. The Downpatrick Gate Lodge consisted of two bedrooms, a hall, kitchen and scullery and was situated in a clearing in some woods at the end of the main drive leading to Downpatrick. The family earned themselves an extra half crown a week by opening and shutting the gate when Lord Bangor and his family swept in and out. Gate duty was one of Agnes' tasks: "You had to keep the gate closed all the time, two big gates, and whenever the horn tooted you ran across the grass, opened the gate and curtsied and they sailed on; they just nodded at you."

The position of the Downpatrick Gate Lodge was relatively isolated and there were not many children the same age as Agnes living on the estate. She enjoyed the camaraderie school brought and with Albert she walked the four miles to the nearest school at Ballyculter clasping bread, jam and milk for her lunch. Lord Bangor managed the school and paid for its upkeep, and local children as well as his employees' children attended it. Agnes and Albert collected the son of the chauffeur from the stable yard at Castle Ward on their way to school. Sometimes when they returned him home the boy's mother gave them a bit of cake, and Agnes remembers it always tasted of petrol fumes. In winter the walk home at the end of the day was long, cold and tedious. Agnes was shy of her parents' employers and on the odd occasion she spied Lord and Lady Bangor beetling home in their car she hid in the bushes to avoid their seeing her. Lady Bangor became used to seeing her hiding behind her mother's skirt and once expressed concern that the youngest Skillen child seemed "very backward."

Lord Bangor held a party for the school children once a year. "You'd have tea, biscuits and buns and then they'd give us an orange as we came out," says Agnes. "You could smell them in the boxes." The school itself was distinct by being an integrated school with both a Catholic and a Protestant teacher. "You did your religion and then you joined your classes." This was a good thing for relations in the local community and it had been this way since it was first opened in 1823. About two thirds of the pupils were Catholic and they were given their religious instruction by one of the teachers, Miss Mooney, while the Protestant third had their religious education with Mr McMurray. Lord Bangor was very pleased with the way it worked and became very agitated in the last year of his life when a Catholic priest from Strangford suggested that he stayed on as the school's owner but allowed the church to take over the management and its finances. 'I am in rather a difficulty about my school at Ballyculter,' he wrote in a letter to a Church of Ireland canon involved in educational issues, 'I have been manager of the school since 1912 and have never had any trouble … if I transfer it to the Education Authority he'll take his flock away.'[vi] There was never any religious conflict during Agnes' schooldays and the two schoolteachers bicycled to Ballyculter from Strangford, and educated between them about 100 children divided into two classes, depending on age.

Although the school did not organise any competitive games they were outside in the playground for all their breaks skipping and playing rounders and it was there they ate their pack lunches. The lavatories were to the back of the playground: "they were dry toilets, no flushing."

It gave Agnes a solid education and she was good at maths, "I could sort of count in my head and that sort of thing, we ran to school doing our tables and I know them off yet. I was not very good at writing, unless they gave us a sweet, then I was the best writer." Other lessons included needlework and cookery which proved to be her innate talents and stood her in good stead later at work: "I remember making swiss rolls and the jam pots, big heavy things." Agnes' favourite lesson was drawing, she was naturally gifted and went on to enjoy painting later in life. "I used to go and visit Aunt Annie Johnson[2] after school, Uncle George would be sleeping and she would be knitting and I would be drawing on a bit of paper."

Agnes made a lifelong friend, Annie Grey, at Ballyculter School. Annie was a few years younger but they attended the Girl Guides together and became friends. After school the two of them went on to find work in the big houses in the area and stayed in touch. Like Agnes' father Annie was born at Myra Castle. Annie's father worked as a chauffeur at Myra and when she left school she got her first job on the estate as a housemaid. Years later, when Agnes got married and needed to find someone to take on her work with the Brownlow family she suggested Annie as her replacement.

The Ward children were educated elsewhere: Edward Ward was sent away to public school in England before Agnes was born and a governess, Miss Harris, taught Mary, Helen and Margaret at home. Otherwise Miss Braine, a nanny who had come to the family when Edward was born, looked after the children. Miss Braine, or 'the Duchess' as Lord Bangor called her, was much loved by the family and stayed on at

Castle Ward until her death in 1939.

As a child Agnes was slightly in awe of the young Wards whom she knew as 'Master Edward', 'Miss Mary', 'Miss Helen' and 'Miss Margaret'. The differences in their positions and ages (the youngest was seven years older than her), meant that despite living alongside each other they remained distant figures. They were always charming to her, coming to visit when she was ill and offered her lifts on their ponies and she enjoyed following them when her father took them out in a boat collecting eggs from the islands.

In the summer the house was often full – Lady Bangor's sisters and their children came to stay, and they enjoyed themselves picnicking on the islands in the lough. 'Master Edward' was taken out onto the lough by Agnes' uncle, Harry Swail, the boatman, who berated him if he did not pay his full attention to the activity. Harry Swail also took Lord Bangor sailing and Edward Ward recalled his father's dealings with him in an autobiography.[vii]

'Yacht racing was always enlivened by my father's relationship with his boatman, Harry Swail, whom he had inherited from my grandfather. Harry was a small, spare man with a heavily lined face and a close-clipped grey moustache … [he] was a professional 'character' whose tall stories became proverbial. An old farmer called Mickey Press once said to my father:
'You know, M'Lord, there must be a lot of truth in Harry Swail.' My father was puzzled.
'How d'you make that out, Mickey?'
The old farmer chuckled. 'Well, he's never let any out yet!'

When young the Ward children enjoyed the company of Agnes' father and were happy to follow him about and live the country life. The sisters hunted and went to parties locally and when they came of age they were taken by their mother to London to do 'the season'. Lady Bangor was determined to launch her girls properly into society. Fearing her husband's lack of interest in spending money on such fripperies she kept sheep and used the profits to take them to London. She was delighted when they returned with their new London friends in tow for house parties. As the daughters grew into glamorous young women they became remoter yet to Agnes, but when two of them married in Ballyculter Church she was delighted because they asked her to come and throw rose petals at their weddings.

Lord Bangor funded Ballyculter Church and every week he took around the plate and brought it home afterwards to add it up. His son wrote in an autobiography:
'He never seemed to be able to balance the accounts with any facility. Moans and groans and curses could be heard coming from the study, punctuated by his favourite lamentation, 'I am the most unfortunate of men!'

Lord and Lady Bangor made their children walk with them to church on Sundays, and the Skillens too walked the distance from the Downpatrick Gate Lodge before taking their pew behind their employers. Lord Bangor read the lesson, looking up at intervals to check he had everyone's attention, and Agnes found it very difficult to behave herself beneath his watchful eye. When it came to Agnes' confirmation she dressed in white and was driven to church in one of the Bangor cars.

As a child Agnes enjoyed clambering up trees with her brother in the woods, or visiting her widowed grandmother at the farm on Audleystown Road. Her mother used to send her to the farm with food and when she was there she helped her grandmother gather sticks for her fire. "It was a simple sort of life, we just lived there down at the gate lodge and the nearest people were a long way away. I just played in the woods, and maybe on a Saturday night we went to the pictures, there was no entertainment in those days, we just made our own."

Her grandmother walked when she needed to go to the shops in Downpatrick and Agnes remembers going to meet her as she strode back clad in a black cape. Her mother cycled the distance and came back with her bags of shopping balancing on the handlebars. Even when a regular bus service made the journey easier there were no fridges, just a cold safe, and food shopping was a small scale affair. People would come around selling fruit and Agnes' parents kept hens and grew their own vegetables. Her Uncle George worked in the big greenhouses growing fruit and vegetables but he was meticulous about his job and never gave out any freebies to his extended family. At home they ate mostly fried food, eggs, bacon and sometimes steak. Meat was not an every day occurrence and often they would eat fried potatoes and onions which were easier to keep fresh.

Life in the gate lodge was happy and busy. In the evening Agnes helped her father with his woodwork hobby. Together they used glass and sandpaper to make violins and carve walking sticks. He also made model boats which they took out in the bay; Agnes' favourite was one she called Primrose. He cut out the bits of wood with a penknife and used glue to stick them together. He gave away some of his carvings, and Sylvia Forde recollects the exquisite detail of those he gave her: "Dodie [his nickname] carved birds from wood quite beautifully and painted them. I have a seagull he made for me which he said attracted lots of live gulls into his garden when he left it out. He also drew them equally well. One day he gave me a carved head with a long face, a moustache, beard and flowing woollen hair saying 'Shakespeare, a kind of a poet'. It was exactly him, a true portrait head, unmistakeable. I treasure it still along with the birds on delicate legs poised on flat pieces of wood, a terrier, a swimming duck, a 'sloth' – and indeterminate creations. And he also made lovely things from straw in autumn – like my intricate true lovers' knot and triangular harvest knot." She remembers by heart a rhyme he loved to recite about himself and his carving skills:

Agnes and Albert at Ballyculter School

Christchurch, Ballyculter, County Down

Some people call me Dodie, I'm a gardener to trade
I work down in Lord Bangor's where I'm great with grape and spade
I go to Down on Saturdays with the people there I'm thick
I presented Mr Hastings[3] with a beautiful walking stick
Mr Hastings took the stick he viewed it up and down
Said he, "the man who made that stick would be a credit to this town".

Lord Bangor enjoyed making things and had a workshop Robert Skillen loved, with tools neatly outlined in black on the wall where they hung, an idea he had copied from a prison he once visited. "Lord Bangor used to curse when he was down there," Agnes remembers of times she passed by the door. "There was always terrible shouting and he did all his work underneath a board on the wall where he had written, 'they say rats take soap – two-legged ones, I think'."

Robert Skillen's other passion was music and although untrained he learnt by ear and was a talented musician. He taught his children how to play the fiddle by putting his thumb on the strings as they played. Agnes loved to sing and play instruments; like her father she had a good ear and an innate musical ability. The family enjoyed jolly music evenings at home when old men came with their instruments to play. Agnes was a great observer, she watched and learned to make music with spoons and to play the fiddle and mouth organ and, without any training, she learned to play the piano using only the "black notes".

Notes:
1 Rifleman Edward Gain, 14th Bn, Royal Irish Rifles, died 18th January 1918 at the Battle of the Somme.
2 Her father's sister who lived on the estate also.
3 Mr Hastings was the 'monumental mason', responsible for the gravestones and the war memorial in Downpatrick.

Chapter Three
Eton College

William at Eton

COLONEL BROWNLOW drove William to Eton in his Daimler. 'How well I remember sitting in CJR's study with M & D!' he wrote in a diary ten years later recalling his arrival in his housemaster's study on 18th September 1934.

'I was shown my room by M'Dame [house matron], Miss Fagan, quite a good room for a new boy on the top floor where Norah was the boys' maid. I spent the first day, having been shown round the school by M'Dame, wandering about meeting the other 11 boys who had come from St Aubyn's all looking very strange and a little self conscious in their new clothes and top hats. David Colman was in the same house and had been at St Aubyn's.'

Eton appeared a huge and confusing place to its new boys, with almost 10 times the number of pupils of the average prep school and sprawled out across the town. 'The first evening of all was an ordeal as we had to have our voices tested for the choir, needless to say I did not impress … I got lost coming back in the dark opposite College Chapel.'

William became embroiled in the system of fagging for the older boys:

'I was assigned as a fag to Freddie Alhusen, who had huge feet and also won the steeplechase. I fagged for him with David Colman and Robin Janus, a little red-haired chap whose father was an admiral. He was a good fagmaster but had endless collars to keep straight! My worst worry was remembering when it was my turn for tea fagging. Fortunately for the fags it was only a question of boiling eggs or tinned stuff.'

Soon he understood the peculiar Etonian dialect: 'half' [term], 'long leave' [half term], 'divs' [classes], 'chambers' [break-time], 'beaks' [teachers]. His effortless manners endeared him to his housemaster, Mr CJ Rowlatt, who commented in letters to his father on his charge's 'sound and healthy' attitude to life and others. 'He is always cheerful and well-mannered,' he wrote at the end of his first term 'and (so far as I know) has not been guilty of any breach of the rules.' He wrote a year later in December 1935: 'If my estimate of him is right, he is a healthy-minded boy, happy in outlook, and keen on the right sort of things. In short, I think you may safely feel happy in mind about the way in which he is coming on.'

He was not inclined towards the world of academia and Mr Rowlatts had no qualms in writing frankly to William's parents: 'His work, judged by the standard appropriate to his abilities has been quite creditable. I must admit that he is slow and that he is not very accurate; but, in spite of a suggestion to the contrary in his mathematical report, I am convinced that he always does his best – and that, of course is the thing about which one minds the most.' Mr Rowlatts' bluntness is inimitable: 'Clearly he has no outstanding ability, but on the other hand he is not in any way a dunce, and he should be able to hold his own when competing with average boys.'

There were daily chapel services and William was confirmed in 1937. Foremost in his memory of the services were the blunders made over the ever-changing name of the King at the time of Edward VIII's abdication:

'How I remember the poor man's [Jackie Chute] difficulty after the Prince of Wales had abdicated and King George had taken over. He still had not got used to our Sovereign Lord King Edward. Now it was a question of our sovereign Lord King George as you were King Edward, as you were King George.'

Most afternoons were for sport and he enjoyed the school's annual cross-country race, the steeplechase, which he had first taken part in at junior level: 'I came in about 20th I think out of about 60 so was *well* pleased with myself.' In 1938 he came 4th and in 1939 he was third, an event he recorded in his diary: 'Maudsley led all the way and Ponsonby second. Had duel with Hugh Arbuthnot, but beat him for third place. I had stitch all the way round, very fast … find got only 10/- for 3rd, poor show!' Shortly before he left in 1940 he represented Eton in a 3-mile cross-country race against Gordonstoun. He found the Wall Game, a game unique to Eton, beyond his comprehension. 'M & D & Cam[1] came down for St Andrew's Day and watched our football, then we stared at the Wall Game listening to the unintelligible yells of the '*oppi-d-ans*' and '*coll-e-g-e*' from small boys perched precariously on the top of the wall. I felt M & D expected me to shout as well. I didn't, nor could I explain the game.'

In his first year field sports raised their head; he longed to be allowed to hunt hares with the college pack of beagles: 'My dearest wish was beagling. But M'Tutor would not allow lower boys to beagle.' Eton's pack, known as the Eton College Hunt, had been in existence since 1858 and was run by the boys and a kennel huntsman. He had been hunting with SW&W, and had shot his first pheasant at 13 when he was first allowed to use a shotgun: 'we went straight on to the farm from which we had rented some shooting. Suddenly an old cock got up and down he came, my first! I was using one of D's guns with both barrels loaded, very fortunate too as shortly after got a cock and a hen down they both came. My first right and left. What a day.' A few years earlier William had shot a robin, he was very proud of his first victim but his father was less impressed and made him pluck it and eat it. He diligently recorded his first achievements with a gun in a British Field Sports Society diary: 22nd December 1933 'went ferreting with nets, got one which D[addy] let go and I shot it (my 1st)'; 1st September 1934 'My first hare and hit rabbit and partridge.'

While William and James were at Eton their home was Somerset, but in 1938 their grandmother died and Ballywhite returned to their father and uncle. The Colonel left the army and made the move home to Ireland with his family. The children had spent many holidays at Ballywhite visiting their grandmother and had enjoyed themselves in boats on the lough and playing on the nearby beaches.

The Christmas holidays in 1938 were the last the Brownlows spent in Somerset. The children now aged between 10 and 23 continued shooting, rabbiting and mucking about on horses. William took Anne out on her first hunting excursions, he on Toreador and Anne on Trixie. They exercised the horses daily and William hunted right up to the last day of his holiday while the family prepared to move out. They spent New Year with Mrs Brownlow's Cousin Willie, at Watergate his home near Chichester in West Sussex and Anne went to her first party: 'Anne's first dance, *Doin' the Lambeth Walk* in fine style. I showed Mama some new things!'

William and James returned to Eton by train with two beagle puppies, Saxon and Savoury, which William insisted on bringing into the restaurant car before facing the sad prospect of returning them to the kennels at school. His passion to go beagling was at last realised when the Master, Ronnie Wallace, allowed him to step in as a whipper-in for the day in 1937. He considered Ronnie a 'hound god … who thought like a hound with perfect anticipation of his quarry' and he went on to become a whipper-in under him with Julian Holland-Hibbert and Hugh Arbuthnot.

William spent many hours at the kennels dreaming of being made the First Whip. If he was given the whip it was one step away from becoming Master, but he was confused as to whether Mike de Chair, the Master who had succeeded Ronnie

Riding at a gymkhana in 1937

Master of Eton College Hunt

Wallace, was going to appoint him. February 1939 was a depressing month as de Chair kept him on tenterhooks:

29th January: Everyone quite certain I shall get whip. *30th January:* very worked up about whip, longing to know. *1st February:* Very cold and beastly, feeling very dejected and convinced that I will not get whip, but hope still. *3rd February:* No one able to understand situation, everyone pro me! *14th February:* hope to hear something today but no! Getting very dejected about it. I feel there must be something very strange. *21st February:* Red-letter day. Got whip at long last so can only hope for next season.'

His parents' concern was the move to Ireland. Mrs Brownlow went to see Ballywhite at the end of January and wrote a letter to William to say she thought it was quite nicely done up. She returned to England for the final clearance and made the journey to Ireland on an overnight boat arriving in Belfast on 14th February. It was another two months before William made it over to Ballywhite. He stayed in England at the end of term spending Easter point-to-pointing with the Bells in Somerset. When he did arrive he recorded his impressions in his diary: *14th April 1939* 'It seems a very nice home, everything in good order. Much more formal than Charlton [the house they rented in Somerset]. Meadows, the butler, very funny.'

He enjoyed his stay spending happy hours pottering about in boats on Strangford Lough. He went over to Strangford in a 'punt' to visit his aunts and great uncle, and with his father made a frame for a lobster pot, which they put out and whiled away many hours checking. Pat Nugent and his brother John lived nearby at Portaferry House and came to Ballywhite often. Together the boys lifted lobster pots, went clay pigeon shooting and played badminton in the ballroom. On one occasion the Nugent boys arrived to find the entire Brownlow family in bed with food poisoning. Family and friends came to call on the new residents at Ballywhite, and William found himself invited to the local parties and 'to a dance with Musgraves in Belfast, scarcely knew a soul, but got on all right. Rather a dull sort of dance, everything too severe.' Not knowing anyone left him feeling gauche and when the Perceval-Maxwells invited him to another party he was delighted to find a familiar face, his school friend Dickie Ker. 'Still know so few people,' he complained in his diary. The prospect of war was raising its head and he logged the reaction of newspapers in a pocket diary. 'Hitler ruthless seizing country after country, but though war hanging heavy I do not think will be. *Times* not least excited. *Daily Mirror* even quietened.'

Back in England the threat of war did not hinder the social scene and William attended Ascot Week, although dull weather and the absence of the King and Queen, who were touring Canada, lessened the glamour. In Ireland terrorist activity was increasing, and William found light-hearted jokes made at his expense:

21st June 1939 IRA terrorists very busy - always accused of being one being Irish.'

Eton Days: *From top left:* Mike de Chair, William
Bottom from left: James Brownlow and Pat Nugent

William achieved his goal and took over as Master of the Eton College Beagles in May 1939. 'The average Etonian just thinks of the beagles as being a not much heard of part of Eton life,' William wrote disparagingly in a history of the Eton College Beagles. For him beagling had become his *raison d'etre*. As Master the beagles became his responsibility and he devoted himself to their welfare, the world of puppy shows and making all the necessary arrangements for hunting with local farmers. In the summer he arranged for a couple of the beagle puppies to be sent to Ballywhite for the school holiday and for the rest to go to kennels at Bicester in September. It was a difficult time to be in charge as the likelihood of war and food-shortages meant that the question arose, tentatively at first, of temporarily disbanding the beagles.

Because of his work with the beagles he was not able to spend long in Ireland over the summer holidays. He went over for August and joined in the Portaferry Regatta in the Nugent family team. William and James spent a relaxed month playing tennis with neighbouring families, the Lindsays, the Wickhams and the Nugents and whiling away hours dragging up lobster pots with Pat and John. They sailed, netted mullet and made trips out to sea to look at a wreck. The brothers Tommy and Frank White would take the boys out in boats and they gained a general knowledge of the area's wildlife from them. He was given his first experience of grouse shooting when Pat invited him to join him for a day[2]: 'We left at 8 o'clock and drove 90 miles, killed three grouse and one snipe in all to my gun, heavy walking and hot.'

He returned to England a month before term started with the intention of taking the beagles out cub hunting but world events changed his plans: *1st September 1939*, 'war almost definite. Hitler perfect curse.' His tutor, Dr Prescott, put him up at Eton and he found himself in the surreal position of assisting the staff's war effort: 'Hard work [sandbagging], lots of beaks at it, and the headmaster, very jolly parties,' he wrote in his diary. 'In the evening I collected and took bedding around to people having children. Hectic job. I had some boy who knew the district helping.' As the only pupil present he became sociable with the staff and was invited to dine with them all, including the Headmaster and Provost: 'Claud Elliot, the Headmaster, and I teamed up with an old van I had for the hounds, filling sandbags and resting with a cigarette each!' When war was officially announced he was with these new friends on the staff: *3rd September 1939*, 'war declared at 11 o'clock, Chamberlain spoke well. I was filling in the shelter at the time with T Lyon, we just went on working.' When he left Eton the following year it was on this period that Dr Prescott would reflect most fondly, 'I shall always remember our toiling together at the sandbags last September, Messrs Tindall and Holmes practically emptying your cigarette-case!'

During September he left Eton for a few days and went to stay at Watergate in West Sussex. It was a strange scenario as his mother's cousin, Willie, had died a month before and left Watergate to William's mother but for the interim the house was inhabited by 'Cousin Marion', a bridge-playing friend of Cousin Willie's. He had

William with the beagles

Perkins at the kennels

married her on his deathbed, and William's mother did not get on well with her.

He returned to school and resented going back to 'the schoolboy' and hiding the cigarettes he had so happily shared with the staff. He was elected to Pop, a prefect society selected by its peers, and as a member he was allowed to wear a white bow tie and coloured waistcoats to distinguish himself.

As the Master of Beagles in September 1939 his concern was what to do with the hounds during wartime. He was convinced he would be unable to keep a full pack of beagles and wrote numerous letters to see if anyone would consider taking them. He had already resorted to putting down the unnecessary hounds and this hit him hard: *13th September 1939* 'awful responsibility and strain for me having to deal with hounds. Everyone is sympathetic and kind, but awful and sad for Will [Perkins, the kennel huntsman].' The *Evening Standard* came to photograph the beagles for a series on 'how life continues in the ordinary way' and William was pictured with his established favourite, Miner. He could not put down Miner when the time came – he had sired half the Eton pack - and when William left in 1940 he brought him home with him as a pet. He did not mention this to his parents until they were both back in Ireland, 'D[addy] not too pleased with Miner, but he soon got to come straight into house and slept in my room and often on the bed.' James recalls their father's opposition, but admits that within a few weeks Miner was sharing their father's chair.

The hounds were sent temporarily to the Scottish Horse Garrison in Perthshire where they were needed for the land draft. William hated to see them go: 'took six couple of hounds to Slough [station] for Scotland. Awful parting with them, but hope and think it is not for long.' At the start of the last war the ECH Master had succeeded in keeping them going and was most put out when his time came to be sent to war. 'I think it is rather hard on Dill and I having to let the country come even before hunting,' he wrote before in the college hunting journal before going to France where he was killed. The hounds were not disbanded until December 1917, and the price of food made it difficult to get them back together immediately after the war.

William wrote to Mike de Chair to ask his views on reducing the numbers in the pack; Mike wrote back:

'I have given your problem considerable thought and have come to the following conclusions a) as there is unlikely to be any food shortage you would probably be able to keep 15 to 20 couple still in kennel and hunt from there. b) Why not take them all over to Eire – that would mean you leaving Eton. But you would have great fun hunting them there and would have plenty of grub for them. You could then return when this bloody war ended. c) If you *have* to farm them out I suggest you try all local farmers and supporters. I am *sure* they would all help.

I have tried for places here but it is hopeless. I shan't be here long as I shall very soon be a soldier – and I couldn't leave them with my mother as she has 5 dogs to cope with all ready!

Don't on any account disband them unless absolutely forced to … it is terribly bad luck on you and I feel very deeply about it. But make the best of it and hunt if God and reason will let you. Hunting must go on war or no war … Good luck and I hope good hunting, Mike. PS give my love to 'Will' and tell him I shall go into action with my old velvet coat on and blowing my horn!!'[3]

This was not the answer he was expecting, but he did succeed in keeping the beagle pack going during his time by reducing the pack and cancelling the annual puppy show. His actions attracted publicity from sporting magazines, and as Master he wrote up their activities for *Horse and Hound* and in a weekly column in the *Eton Chronicle*. Mike de Chair felt William had done the right thing in continuing hunting with a reduced pack:

'I assure you it was a pleasure to leave the hounds to so reliable a person. I was very glad to give you the opportunity. I must congratulate you very warmly on making the best in such difficult times. Besides the war you had the most impossible weather. How you managed to keep going I don't know. It was a great feat.'

It was difficult to feel optimistic about the future of the sport if the war continued, and William was concerned about Will Perkins, the kennel huntsman, and his employment. While he found the office of master a strain towards the end, he did not doubt the teamwork of those in the kennels: 'Perkins, one of the best men and last beagle kilts in England, we had hard times together but he was a colossal help to me and there was never a complaint.'

Following the outbreak of war the military training provided in the school Corps took on new significance, and William became involved. Following his birthday he was called to London for an army medical examination which he passed. In November he attended the funeral of the first old boy to be killed in action, in an air attack. He had been captain of his house, and in December 1939 the *Eton Chronicle* started to include a weekly list of names of old boys killed in action and the future seemed bleak.

He spent his last school holidays with the hounds at Watergate. His family joined him and they saw in the New Year there together. They went shooting and even attempted some beagling, Cam and Di Bell went out with him and he was delighted to be able to give them both a hare's pad as a trophy. The problem of the future of Watergate arose as it now belonged to William's mother:

'M wanting to keep Watergate but D very against it, so am I, as do not feel could keep up Ballywhite and Watergate decently. Nor do I really like Watergate though shooting grand so no wish to let M know this.'

The land at Watergate was more valuable than Ballywhite, but the house was not attractive, "hideous" is how Anne remembers it. The house had almost burnt down twice and had been rebuilt in Victorian times. During the Brownlow's stay the fire brigade were called out once when a chimney caught fire, and over their New Year stay another fire was narrowly avoided when a spark from the fire set alight William's mother's knitting. Anne and Cam both felt the house was spooky, and Anne had to have a maid sit with her until she went to sleep at night. Eventually a decision was reached to sell Watergate, and some of the furniture which Elinor wanted for Ireland was stored in a downstairs room but was all lost when a serious fire broke out. The fire was sparked by a smouldering cigarette – left by a soldier when the property was requisitioned – and the house burnt to the ground.

At Eton there is a leavers' tradition of giving away pictures of yourself to those you valued during your time there. William spent his last few weeks with his peers giving and receiving photographs, and he had carefully arranged photographs of himself both in Pop and ECH uniforms. He had made a good friend of Derek Bass and after he left Derek wrote to him in Ireland keeping him up-to-date with the goings-on, such as the landing of an aeroplane on a school playing field:

'It turned out to be Gubby Allen and a friend escaping from Dunkirk. They had landed there to enable Allen to visit his mother and tell her that his brother had been killed.'

Notes:
1 Nell became known as 'Cam' - a shortening of her surname.
2 Probably at Cleggan, near Broughshane with Lord Rathcavan.
3 He died from battle wounds in Algeria on 16th May 1943.

Chapter Four
Agnes Starts Work

Gothic exterior of Castle Ward

AGNES LEFT school at the age of 15. It was 1936 and for her the future was straightforward: "If you had the money you were sent to Queen's [University, Belfast] or somewhere else, if you had no money you had to go to work." She had gained a good, general education but had no funds to contemplate furthering it.

The big houses were an obvious source of employment locally and it never crossed Agnes' mind not to follow in her parents' footsteps. Her sisters and brother had all found their first jobs at Castle Ward, Ida and Hester as housemaids and Albert as a gamekeeper. Ida worked for Lady Bangor and Hester for her widowed sister-in-law, Mrs Hamilton, who lived at Terenichol, a house on the Castle Ward estate. As a young girl Agnes listened to their tales of life in the two houses and she never forgot the stories of Mrs Hamilton impressing upon her employees the fact she "was a cousin of the Queen[1]."

Both sisters moved on from Castle Ward to work in England. An agency in Belfast found them positions with families in Sussex and Leeds. Ida returned home from Sussex to marry Bob Barrett, a coal merchant, and to settle in his home town, Killyleagh, less than ten miles from Castle Ward. Hester went to Leeds and was followed there by Jack Hamilton, a plasterer from Castlewellan in County Down;

they married in England and some years later returned to County Down.

As a gamekeeper Albert lived at home with his parents and Agnes while she was still at school. In 1938 he left the world of game keeping for the army – he joined the Royal Ulster Rifles and was employed as a driver[2]. After the Second World War he left the army and found work as a lorry driver and settled in Belfast.

Lady Bangor enjoyed knowing Agnes had been called after her and was keen to secure her as a maid. Thus shortly after Agnes left school she was taken on the staff as an under housemaid. She was paid one pound a month and was given a half day off every week and every other Sunday she was allowed the afternoon off. When she arrived she had to provide two morning dresses and one black dress for the evening. Lady Bangor supplied the housemaids with collars, cuffs, a cap and some aprons and at Christmas they were given the makings of two morning dresses, which they made up themselves.

Despite the proximity of her parents' home house staff 'lived in' and she was given a room in Castle Ward itself. She shared her bedroom on the top floor with Jenny Turner, the head housemaid. Along the corridor there was a nursery and the room of Mrs Braine, the old nanny, and the Ward daughters' bedrooms, now grown up and moved away. Although some might have expected Lord and Lady Bangor to live in the grander bedrooms on the first floor only Edward Ward had a room there, and across the passage from Jenny and Agnes' bedroom were those of Lord and Lady Bangor. This created some confusion when Lord Bangor shouted "Aggie" to his wife and Agnes hearing her name would come running. They came to an arrangement by which Agnes would always be 'Agnes' and Lady Bangor 'Aggie'.

The Bangor's household was substantial and comprised of an under housemaid and a head housemaid, a lady's maid, a footman, a butler, a cook, a kitchen maid and a scullery maid. Whereas the housemaids lived at the top of the house the kitchen staff, footman and butler were housed at the end of 'the tunnel', a covered passage running from kitchen to the dairy, laundry and stable yard, supposedly built to prevent the family from having to watch their staff moving to and from the house. "I was working there at the same time as my father, my mother was working in the laundry with a cousin's wife, up the steps from her in the dairy was another cousin's wife, it was all family. I had some friends, but I was much the youngest." At the start of each week Agnes and other members of the household had to queue at the storeroom door for their cleaning stuffs. There Lady Bangor handed out tins filled with a home made scouring powder and a weekly supply of beeswax.

They cleaned and polished and brushed out the fireplaces before Lord and Lady Bangor awoke. In the darkness of an early winter morning the housemaids lived in fear of seeing the ghost of a lady dressed in red who was said to walk about the ground floor – Agnes never saw her but others said they had.

For all their dusting of delicate objects about the house there was only one memorable breakage during Agnes' tenure, and thankfully not at her hands. Three statues stood on the half-landing on the stairs and when a fellow housemaid dusted a certain part of the male statue's anatomy it came away in her hand. There was a panic as to what to do and the young housemaid quickly found some glue and stuck it back on. Lady Bangor noticed it immediately and called the offending housemaid in to see her. Lady Bangor explained that the reason she had detected the breakage was because the piece had been stuck back the wrong way up, the housemaid apologised remarking she had seen them before "that way round."

The household ate in a servant's hall in the basement, next to the kitchen and storerooms and beside the bells that summoned them upstairs when they were needed. The butler was in charge of the bells and letting everyone know of their required destination. Agnes' healing hands were made use of in the servant's hall, "I cured all the butler's warts, and the footman's too: the butler's hands were all covered in warts and I cured them with a potato which I'd put on them and then take away and bury in the garden for a while."

The cook, Mrs Foreman, had a short temper and used her authority to frighten the housemaids. She was miserly with their food rations and at lunchtime sheep's head broth was often on the menu. The staff were allowed half a pound of butter and half a pound of sugar a week each and when that ran out there was no more. Agnes and the other maids learnt their way about the rules and when butter was running low they would creep out of the house down the servants' tunnel to the dairy and persuade the dairymaid to spread a bit of butter on their bread. "We used to go down to Agnes[3] in the dairy with our slice of loaf and she used to put the butter on the bread herself."

When they were not busy they sat about on a little grassy hill outside the laundry reading or gossiping. Agnes enjoyed a good prank, and she succeeded in winding up the head laundry maid, who was "an awful cross cousin," by stuffing her newly-washed knickers with straw and leaving them to swing in the breeze on the washing line.

It was during Agnes' 18 months as a housemaid at Castle Ward House that her grandmother died. In a flurry Agnes rushed home for the funeral without asking for the time off and when she returned Lady Bangor called her into her imposing sitting room in the gothic side of the house to reprimand her for her flighty behaviour: "she was quite cross, 'you went without permission, you didn't ask me', she said to me."

Her parents inherited her grandmother's cottage, 'The Mallard', a bungalow with two bedrooms on the Audleystown Road, but they took their time to do it up and for some years they stayed on in the gate lodge. There was no rush to move while Agnes' father was employed by the estate and he intended to work as long as he could. He loved his job and felt great loyalty and affection towards the Ward family. He was good with children and Lord and Lady Bangor's children, and later

Agnes in a dress given to her by Miss
Margaret Ward.

Bob Skillen with Lord and Lady Bangor's
grandchildren, Patrick and Sylvia Forde.

their grandchildren, enjoyed his company. He entertained them with trips out to the islands in the lough looking for eggs. Sylvia Forde, daughter of 'Miss Margaret' and Desmond Forde, describes how she and her brother often spent time with him: "After working in the garden all week sometimes he would give up his entire Sunday afternoon to take us children nutting to look for hazelnuts in the lanes and hedges near his house at the Mallard and Myra where he knew the best places to go. Or birds' nesting there and on Chapel Island in the lough. After one of these expeditions he took us to his home, seized an apple pie from the larder and divided it between us. We asked if Mrs Skillen would mind or needed it and he said she was out and would never notice. He then got out his fiddle to play and sing *Pop Goes the Weasel* and plucked the strings to make the 'pop' sound."

Her memories of her grandparents' gardener portray a happy, genial character and emphasise the affectionate regard he was held in by the Ward family. "If we asked him the name of a plant he would bend down, put the flower head between his fingers, tilt his head to one side enquiringly and say, 'hey boy, what's your name? What's this they call you?' then as if he'd heard it whisper an answer he'd tell us what it was. We'd look at him in wonder and then all laugh together with him. He showed us how to cut faces on the poppy heads after folding down the petals like a dress round the stem, tie blades of grass as sashes, then pierce the stalks with stick arms and legs to make dolls. Each of us was given a strip of a flower bed to have as our own little garden where he helped us grow radishes, cress and sow flower seeds.

"American conifers, fashionable in the second half of the nineteenth century, stood beside the main lawn. Their canopies flowed to the ground like skirts and Dodie used to hide from us in them then suddenly appear and say 'I was just in the library' or 'the study'. One was huge which he called the 'Gothic room' after the sitting room, overlooking the lough, in the house.

"Hubert McGreavy was the garden 'boy' then and some extra help came from Mr Fitzpatrick. He had 17 children whose names Dodie often recited to us and we were always amazed he could remember them all.

"I cannot think of the Little Garden without picturing Dodie tending it and joking with us. Years later he would have been as horrified as Ernest Swail (who looked after the boats and was also an excellent gardener) who said 'Lupins! Lupins in her Ladyship's rose garden. Lupins!' had he lived to see them too."

Emma Escott, a nanny to the Forde grandchildren Patrick and Sylvia, told them of a time she was standing next to Dodie in the garden at Castle Ward when he saw Lady Bangor making her way towards them: "Hubert, Hubert, where's the wheelbarrow full of weeds?" Dodie shouted; to which Hubert replied, 'I've put them on the dump.' Quick as a flash Dodie exclaimed: "put them back at once her Ladyship's coming down'."

Agnes' uncle, George Johnson, worked in the vegetable garden and he too was fond of the grandchildren. He enjoyed showing them his growing crops. "He took us into the greenhouse and gave us a bunch of grapes," Sylvia Forde recalls one occasion, "and then he said, 'don't you be telling that grandmother of yours'."

Agnes made a friend to go into Strangford with on a Saturday night. "Mrs Hamilton had a girl Mary Downes working for her at Terenichol, and we would meet and go to the dances. That was my dance friend. We used to walk back through those dark trees, about 12 o'clock." If Agnes had a Sunday off she would walk on alone to the Downpatrick Gate Lodge. "I used to whistle. My mother used to hear me coming." The Smithy Brae, the road between Castle Ward and the farm, was a popular haunt where the unmarried estate staff and the house staff met up to promenade after work. During Agnes' short period of employment at Castle Ward she was much the youngest of the employees and she did not have a boyfriend there but it is most likely that her parents had met on the Smithy Brae years before.

At the age of 17 Agnes was diagnosed as suffering from 'housemaid's knee'. She had found it hard work polishing the vast floor of the Music Room in Castle Ward. This involved getting down on her knees and covering the floor in beeswax and then pulling along a vast iron contraption with a blanket attached to the bottom to polish it. The kneeling on the ground gave her an ache in the knees and was not assisted by her daily task of brushing the five flights of stairs. Ultimately this pain was caused by the endless housework and resulted in her cutting short her working days at Castle Ward. She resigned from her position at Castle Ward and moved back into the gate lodge with her parents until she recovered enough to look for more work. Lady Bangor wanted her to come and work for her again but she knew the same affliction would return with the daily cleaning of the flights of stairs and so she moved on.

She applied to Miss Gray's, an employment agency in Belfast, and they found her a position with the Ferguson family. They were an old couple who owned a linen mill and Agnes was happy working for them. She stayed for over a year, but her mother's ill health brought her back home. Her parents were still living in the Downpatrick Gate Lodge and she looked after her mother there while finding work locally for 2/6 a week with Dr Pooler. "My cousin, Elizabeth Swail, was the housekeeper there – she was much older than me. I wasn't there very long, he was bedridden, and it was too much. They lived at Old Court in Strangford, there was a room there and I stayed over sometimes but mostly I went down and back."

When her mother recovered properly she contacted Miss Gray's agency to ask for another permanent position. The agency came back to her in January 1939 with the message that a Mrs Brownlow would meet her for an interview in Strangford.

Notes:
1 Queen Elizabeth, the Queen Mother (1900-2002).
2 During the war he joined the Ulster Rifles and was Col. Panter's driver, the future Mrs William Brownlow's father.
3 Agnes Johnston, a cousin-in-law

Chapter Five
War: Early Days

Ballywhite

IN EUROPE war gathered momentum. By April 1940 Germany had overrun Denmark and invaded Norway, in Holland troops were on full alert along the German border and on France's northern border British and French troops were attempting to fight back.

During this period William was living with his parents at Ballywhite. 'Away from war and hardly affected by it in a lot of ways,' he wrote in his diary. 'Plenty of food and no lack of anything, except petrol and sugar.' In Northern Ireland eggs were not rationed until mid-1941 and milk, vegetables and pork remained available throughout the war. Most foodstuffs were obtainable across the border and smuggling was rife. 'Old Mrs McCauley never lets us go short of anything,' William wrote in amazement, 'hams up from the South when wanted.'

In the first stages of the war Northern Ireland did not react with the urgency and purpose on display in many other parts of the United Kingdom. This has been put down to its distance from Europe and the Government's decision not to bring in conscription. As late as 1942 the Mass Observation Organisation[viii] noted Northern Ireland remained unresponsive to the war effort:

'The lack of war urgency is most striking, the atmosphere in Ulster is entirely different … many of the things which are taken for granted by the average Englishman or Scotsman like clothes rationing or transport difficulties are still the source of considerable irritation or resentment.'

Sectarian division and the neutrality of the Free State meant Westminster feared unrest if they pressed conscription despite the Northern Irish Prime Minister[ix] urging its application. A senior Cardinal declared it would be a tyranny to impose conscription and Eamon De Valera said it would equate to 'an act of war against our nation.' Meanwhile, characters such as David Lindsay Kier, the vice-chancellor at Queen's University, created umbrage when he suggested all physically able staff and students should join up. By June the Netherlands were overrun, Belgium had surrendered and France was mostly occupied and on 4th June British troops evacuated from Dunkirk.

William planned to follow in his father's footsteps and become an officer in the Rifle Brigade, but he was not called-up until his 19th birthday which, despite the urgency of the hour left him a limbo-like summer at home pottering about on the lough with Pat Nugent. The horror of the evacuation of Dunkirk led the Government to announce that a Home Guard would be created from volunteers. It was to be made up of a series of local forces formed to defend the towns and villages of the United Kingdom should the Germans invade, and initially they were armed only with what could be cadged from local military bases and private weapons. It was not extended to Northern Ireland and in response the Inspector General of the Royal Ulster Constabulary offered the services of the Ulster Special Constabulary to fill the gap before they were reformed under military command.

William was eager to be involved and telephoned the local police station to put himself forward even before they had received any administrative details. In the second drill parade he was asked if he would take charge of the Cloughy district unit. It was a peculiar position to be in, being the youngest amongst men whose ages ranged from near his own to fifty, but they seemed to accept him and volunteer numbers rose from 22 to 32. 'Very nice lot of men,' William noted, 'but not over fond of too much work: like a lot of Orangemen very patriotic with flag waving but not too keen on too much action. Then came difficulty of RC and Protestants, one or two RCs joined and were not well received, they took no notice and soon it settled down.'

The Cloughy unit's duties included 'look out' patrols at night, for which they had to select hills that would serve as Observation Points. William chose Kirkistown Castle, an old turret and keep, which had a good view of the surrounding sea and countryside from the top. They fixed the old castle up comfortably with oil lamps and a dartboard. Night duty was the task of three volunteers:

'Some wanted to be on with each other and had to have men living near each other to see each other home as not safe to have single men with rifles about late at night as IRA always liable to try and take them.'

There was a general complacency about the German bombing campaign ever stretching to Northern Ireland and the British Government flaunted their belief that it was an improbable target when it evacuated over 1,000 children from England to 'safety' in Belfast. Air attack began in the skies above southern England in the late summer of 1940 but when a Unionist MP suggested Luftwaffe pilots could make it to Belfast in two and three quarter hours few took him seriously.

William opened his call-up papers when cutting up a poplar tree in the ballroom. He was requested to turn up in Winchester on 17th October 1940. 'Sorry to leave Ireland in some ways but too damned quiet.' He arrived flustered at the Rifle Depot in Winchester two hours late after catching the wrong train.

The recruits of A Squadron came from a variety of backgrounds and William found it impossible to place some of those sharing his dormitory in their civilian occupations. His diary records how everyone took time to relax with one another:

'Though a bit apprehensive, at first, of living at close quarters with the men, I soon found it all right and they are really amusing and most interesting. I soon realised, though I had most emphatically condemned Hore-Belisha's move of closing Sandhurst[1], that though officers were worked pretty hard, and far harder than ordinary men while training, that living with men you get to know their feelings and why they like so and so and dislike another.'

His dormitory had twelve occupants including a policeman, a garage hand from the Grosvenor Hotel in London, a gardener from Worthing, a factory worker from Swindon, a weightlifter turned taxidermist and a number of boys like himself straight out of public school. In many ways William thought it was easier for the potential officers than it was for the future soldiers to be flung together in this way. 'They are undoubtedly far more class conscious than us. They admitted later that at first they could not understand our humour, which is quite understandable, though after about a month they began to understand it!!' The potential officers included Hew Butler, Gilbert Talbot, Dawson Bates and Mike Welman who had all been at Winchester together and Dick McCaw, who had been at Marlborough and like William knew no one else.

For the first six weeks the training was intensive and interesting, but after the basics had been learned potential officers were keen only to learn when they were going to be selected for a place on an Officer Cadet Training Unit. Having been born in Winchester William was on home territory and the families he had grown up with entertained him generously, 'Winchester certainly is a good place to be, never wanting for anything to do, only trouble is fitting in dates with duties.'

As Christmas 1940 approached everyone was keen to get home but A Squadron was not given time off, instead it was handed details of its draft to Tidworth. They left Winchester station with the band on the platform playing *Old Lang Syne* making many on board feeling sentimental. The rail route to Tidworth took them through the dockyards at Southampton where the warehouses and surrounding buildings showed signs of air raid damage.

He and Hew Butler had become good friends:

'I went to Vic Turner's[2] one day with Hew … we went out shooting up a river for duck, quite a few at one place but some b_ put them up just before got there … good dinner and very good burgundy which had been over mulled and sent me to sleep going back to Tidworth in his car leaving Hew to carry on conversation in the front.'

A few were given Christmas off, but not William: 'Had great party in evening, starting at the 'Ram' and getting bottles of beer, which we got back to camp in our respirators! Then had great feast of various things sent us, I had stuff from Fortnum & Mason and other various things supplemented.' They amused themselves with the creation of a special menu for Christmas 1940 under the '*cuisinier et createur*' of Ivan Soboleff[3] and the management of '*Antone Butler and Francois Talbot*'.

Spirits were low as 1941 rolled in:

'Spent the first of New Year in a hard iron bed in an old wooden shack. In other words did not see New Year in. It brought nothing much in with it except continuation of war, though bucking up slightly, as far as war is going in Egypt and Libya. Wavell[4] ought to be a big figure in our grandchildren's history, though God knows what our grandchildren will be doing or what the world will be doing soon. May be buried under a sand hill or some such before war is over!'

At the end of January he was transferred to Droitwich to 168 Officer Cadet Training Unit. The officer in charge of the course there, Colonel Ralph Bingham, had recently been forced to move on. He had been much liked but had created a storm by writing a controversial letter to *The Times* about public school education making a great difference to the quality of officers. The course itself was intense and despite a map reading exam William enjoyed the work and made good friends. In March they moved to Lancashire and were given a few days leave to coincide with the move and as the Heysham ferry was close by William went home. On the crossing he found John Brooke, the son of Basil Brooke, and they ate breakfast without realising they had arrived in Belfast Docks and were keeping everyone waiting. At Ballywhite he spent time with Tommy White and his young family – he was godfather to his son William Thomas, then a toddler who amused him by rushing about with his twin sister, Elinor Anne. Cam made it home too; she had joined the women's branch of the army, the Auxiliary Territorial Service (ATS). He returned to Lancashire to finish his officer training.

Notes:
1 Leslie Hore-Belisha (Secretary of War until January 1940) replaced the Royal Military College with Officer Cadet Training Units
2 Vic Turner was an officer in the Rifle Brigade, and had served with William's father.
3 A well-travelled Russian who had been a Cossack lieutenant before going around the world on a motorbike.
4 General Archibald Wavell (1883-1950)

Chapter Six
Second Lieutenant Brownlow

William joins up

AT THE age of 19¹/₂ Second Lieutenant Brownlow arrived on the boat in Belfast with fellow officer Dawson Bates who was also going home on leave. He was annoyed to be improperly dressed on his first occasion out in uniform but his tailor in London had not got it to him in time: 'Left boat in battle dress with white pips on service cap, Dawson's shirt, very queer mixture, acknowledged first salutes through Belfast, kept meeting MPs[1] who gave colossal ones.'

It was the Spring of 1941 and the Luftwaffe finally made it to Belfast, Bangor and Newtownards, from their bases in France. William was at Ballywhite when the bombs came but his diary reveals that they failed to ruin his sleep: 'Number of Belfast Blitzes on when over there. Hell of a noise all night which never even woke me up. Mama and Cam went up onto mountain and watched.' Portaferry was unaffected by the bombings and William spent most of his time helping out with the potatoes and silage on the farm and attempting to net salmon in Strangford Lough.

On his return to England he went to stay with Hew Butler and his parents in Hampshire. Their home had been commandeered by the army but the house they were living in greatly impressed William with its history: 'I slept in room where

King Charles slept, there is a little cubby hole down below where he hid his horse.' On their way back to Tidworth they stopped off to see James, who had joined up under-age, and was going through the motions at the Rifle Depot in Winchester. William was proudly dressed in his uniform, properly this time, and found James being drilled on the parade ground, 'looking a great tough in battledress.' James asked the Sergeant if he could fall out to see his brother, the Sergeant said 'yes and remember to salute the officer', so he stood smartly to attention with his back to the Sergeant and saluted William all the while sticking out his tongue.

Life as an officer was a vast improvement and he enjoyed the perks such as a soldier servant to keep his uniform in immaculate condition but less so the hard graft of being sent on course after course. He wanted his own transport to get about and bought a little Morris for £15 which had its first proper outing to the South & West Wiltshire puppy show in Shaftsbury. He ran out of petrol on the way back, it was 11.30pm and it took him two hours to get a 'relief bus' to help him get some; that accomplished he discovered only one headlight worked and drove back very slowly. The Eton and Harrow cricket match was a great social event and a busload went from Tidworth to Eton to watch it. A rainstorm spoiled the cricket, but William noted the performance of one individual he thought had promise: 'hoped young Bramall[2] would do well, interesting fellow in many ways.' On their return journey they stopped in a pub in Camberley and enjoyed the novel experience of drinking Pimms by the pint.

The summer was hot and they all had the free time to enjoy it. One day a group of them jumped in the river outside The Crown in Salisbury: 'with Peggy Slater, our ATS officer, Tommy, another ATS, Pat Harrison & self in my car. Then met Hew & co in Amesbury for supper and ate on the riverbank.' When he did a course in Woolacombe, North Devon he swam in the sea every afternoon after work.

With his training finally complete he was ready to join a Rifle Brigade battalion. There were a number of battalions and he was keen on either 1st or 7th. He was not disappointed when he found himself in the latter but annoyed they were the only one still based in England; they were at Crowborough in Kent. He consoled himself with the thought that they would leave England soon as in Europe and Africa the war was intensifying. All the other Rifle Brigade battalions were in North Africa where British and Commonwealth troops were fighting the Italian forces in Libya and Abyssinia, as well as Germany's 'Afrika Korps' which had come to Libya in February 1941 to fight with the Italians.

Immediately before joining his battalion William went home on leave, which he spent helping out on the farm and coming from England the availability of food was especially noticeable: 'Great being back, eat much too much … it's awful in England, only one egg a month!'

When he arrived in Crowborough he was put in D Company. His company commander was Stephen Trappes-Lomax – 'very nice fellow and very young;' his second in command Dick Wintour, and fellow subalterns Ivan Corbie, Stanley Tibbets and Harry Prior. Along with Corbie, Tibbets and Prior he made up the company's platoon commanders. Their training was varied and included situations specific to the war they might fight and William did not enjoy learning how to cope with a gas explosion:

'We all went through for Chamber DM. Awful two minutes with respirator on and two [with it] off. Did not feel too bad in that but ran 200 yards when out and nearly burst, the gas cleared and felt awful kept sneezing and coughing and nose feeling terrible everyone feeling very cock eye.'

It did not take him long to find his confidence with the men. His first big exercise was in September near Lewes. William led his platoon into the Opera House at Glyndebourne, which was being used as a children's nursery at the time. This exercise was followed up immediately by the biggest exercise ever organised in Britain, codenamed 'Bumper'[3] it involved several armoured divisions acting out their reaction to a German invasion. The 'Germans', it was imagined, had landed on the East Coast of England and established themselves firmly across the country. William was on the British side and moved with his company from Leatherhead to Newbury where the Duke of Rutland of the Grenadier Guards was acting as umpire: 'We harboured in a wood in darkness, dripped all night.' Then on to Bicester where they came across vast crowds of foreign journalists and Stephen Trappes-Lomax spoke to them in Polish, Russian and French and discerned that the King was in the area. It was here that his platoon made their first capture of 'enemy' troops which they took back: 'I in scout car ahead with Bren gun, going along met other enemy armoured car sitting with head out so shot at him and he at me but no umpires … we took [a captured] map and we heard it was well received by the Brigadier.'

The next time he encountered the enemy was at Stowe School: 'Moved up through school who were doing PT, saw Gavin Maxwell … we went out with scout platoon to counter attack Stowe.' Then they were on to Bedford for the next round of action where he was captured in an ambush before discovering 'the battle' was over and the British had won. There had been 19 fatal casualties during the exercise, but the event had been unprecedented and considered a success. One Canadian soldier who had been involved wrote in a letter home, 'These Limeys don't fool around when they are playing these games.'[ix]

At the end of the exercise William was given a telegram to say Anne's condition had improved which was the first he had heard about her being unwell. He telephoned Ballywhite straight away: 'Got through in half hour. OK now but had been very bad, they had given up hope for a bit. Poor M sounded very upset and tired. They thought it was meningitis then pneumonia.' He returned to Kent and his company was moved to a new base at Groombridge, a few miles north of

From left: James, Nell and William in uniform at the start of the war

Crowborough and the rest of the battalion to East Grinstead.

In November he was given more time off and he travelled across England on the boat train north with his mother and James. They kept a seat free for Cam who joined them at Crewe: 'M in a flap all last part thinking she would not make it. However all together for dinner paid for by M!! … all well at home, Anne looking remarkably well after illness … J looking very new in service dress, had great photo of all three [of us taken] in Belfast, feeling very mad and foolish.'

They were not busy in Kent and he spent most of his time at parties: 'Went to another dance at Beacon with Rosemary Bromley, Dickie, Stanley Tibbets and Pamela Nunn who got most amorous by end of evening, and a very charming girl Ruth Watson with whom I was most delighted, very cheery and attractive person.' He spent the following months trying to pursue Ruth Watson, but she remained elusive and his admiration unrequited. One evening their band was playing locally when an orderly arrived with a note for Stephen: 'we all guessed what was included, which was for 50% of the battalion to go on embarkation leave the next day.' When William returned from a week in Ireland he was excited about finally leaving but it was a false alarm. 'Things going on as dull as ever,' he wrote in his diary. The Americans joined the war in December after the Japanese bombed Pearl Harbour but in Kent nothing seemed to change. Christmas came and went with no news of embarkation and in January they were given nine more days leave and William went home once again. On his return trip through London the Brown Hotel was full and he was forced to arrange a bunk in an air raid shelter. Fortunately for him he went back to the hotel for supper and a man came over and asked if he was a Lincolnshire Brownlow and offered him the spare bed in his room and he had a comfortable night.

William had established a small group of new friends, Chatty Bowar who was always on for a party and Peter Wolfe Taylor, a new Czech officer, who asked him to come with him to meet his fiancée's parents in Sevenoaks. When yet more leave came his way he met James and Cam at Eton to attend a service in College Chapel. The day was perfect, he had lunch with his brother and sister, found time to visit the kennels and bumped into John Nugent before having dinner with his housemaster. Afterwards James and he travelled home to Ballywhite and spent a few days out in the boat looking at wrecks at Knockinelder and Tara Bay.

By April they had been ready to embark for months and when they were given yet more leave William decided that rather than return to Ireland he would visit the Bells in Somerset and stay in London for Peter Wolfe Taylor's wedding to Molly. They got back from the wedding and were told to get ready to embark and this time it was for real. Final arrangements were made and everything became rather more certain when the King came to inspect them at nearby Brambletye in Sussex.

Notes:
1 Military policemen
2 The 'interesting fellow' went on to become Field Marshall the Lord Bramall.
3 29th September – 3rd October 1941

Chapter Seven
Under Housemaid at Ballywhite

Mrs Brownlow's order book

THE INTERVIEW with Mrs Brownlow went well and soon afterwards Agnes crossed the water from Strangford to Portaferry, hired a bicycle and pedalled her way up the hill to Ballywhite. When she reached the house it was surrounded by vans and removal men who were busily unloading furniture. Agnes was the first member of staff to be taken on by Mrs Brownlow, and when she reported for work as the under housemaid the two women were on their own together with the packing cases. "There was nobody else there when I arrived, just Granny Brownlow, we were the first, we got the beds up and got started."

The household quickly grew to five as Mrs Brownlow took on a cook, a butler, a head housemaid, and a kitchen maid. They were all unmarried or widowed and lived alone in the staff quarters at the back of the house reached by a separate staircase. In the evenings they ate together in a room behind the kitchen known as the servants' hall and afterwards went to their rooms or sat chatting together downstairs.

The butler, Meadows, did not live with the rest of the household upstairs, but had his own quarters downstairs beyond the servants' hall. A butler was an important figure in servant hierarchy and Meadows was an amusing character with curious looks: "He was a very thin, scraggy looking man whose ears stuck out," Agnes describes him. During the war he found his own way of coping with rationing: "he used to dry out the banana skins and the apples and then he'd smoke them. He was totally mad. He was a very good butler and he was there a good while." She learnt a lot from him by watching him at work and he taught her the correct way to lay a table and pour a drink. Later on another butler, Pratt, took to helping himself to the port in the decanter and the Brownlow children remember the waft of alcohol fumes as he served them their food. Colonel Brownlow, who took responsibility for the butlers, never commented on his behaviour, merely kept the key to his wine cellar. Eventually his behaviour meant he lost his job. There were two other butlers, Dunn, who threatened to leave on a weekly basis and had to be sweet-talked by Mrs McCauley into staying and Craig who remained with the family for many years.

At 17 Agnes was the youngest on the staff by some years. She was allowed one half-day a week off and one Sunday a fortnight. The hours were the same as Castle Ward but the wage was higher: "When I went to Ballywhite I had £30 a year less a stamp, but I had a pound a month when I went up to Lady Bangor's, so that was a big rise." She reported to Lily Erskine, the head housemaid, who had worked in other households across Northern Ireland, and came originally from Larne. Together they were responsible for all the cleaning in the house. The housemaids wore a uniform; 'morning dress' was a blue and white spotted dress which Agnes was very fond of and 'afternoon dress' was a more formal black dress with white collar and cuffs: "a wee white square apron with a bib and a bow at the back," remembers Agnes. Mrs Brownlow had done away with housemaids wearing hats with 'afternoon dress' which was new to Agnes who was used to wearing them at Castle Ward.

It did not take long for everyone's domestic duties to fall into a daily routine. Mrs Brownlow was a stickler for things being done properly and she was not disappointed by her new household as Anne remembers: "The five staff fitted into the ways of Mama's organised schedules with little fuss." Lily and Agnes' day began at 7am when together they drew all the curtains and cleaned out the fires with black lead and re-laid them, they also prepared morning tea for Mrs Brownlow which Lily carried to her in her room, later Agnes took it to her. The tea was weak China tea and with it came very thin slices of white bread and butter cut diagonally with the crusts cut off. When Anne was young she rushed to her parents' big four poster bed and squeezed in before the tea and bread arrived. Agnes carried in the hot water for Anne and Mrs Brownlow to wash with in great big brass jugs, and the butler brought it for the boys and Colonel Brownlow. Lily and Agnes made sure all their tidying was done by the time Colonel and Mrs Brownlow emerged for breakfast at the sound of the gong. "There was nobody to be seen when they came down at nine, and then when they went to the dining room for breakfast you went up the stairs and started up there and put the clothes away," says Agnes.

Breakfast was no small affair, first there was porridge which Colonel Brownlow ate walking around the table, then fried bacon, sausages and eggs which was put out on the sideboard in silver entrée dishes, and occasionally there was kedgeree or kippers. Butter was rolled into balls and toast was always white and without crusts. Also on the sideboard there was a ham, which was only to be carved by Colonel Brownlow.

Every morning Mrs Brownlow made her visit to the kitchen at 10 o'clock to see the cook, plan meals and order the food. The kitchen was always spotless and the table scrubbed. Anne loved joining her mother on these visits as the kitchen was forbidden territory to her, as indeed it was to Agnes and Lily. "Mama would have the menu book, a pencil on a side table with a chair put ready for her. She made the decisions on the meals for the day, for both sides of the green baize door … a large sirloin of roast beef would be the Sunday roast – the filet kept for the dining room and the sirloin for the servants' hall. Mama would always know, never having cooked a thing in her life, if a recipe was not quite right – and the next morning she would tell the cook if too much or too little of anything was in the final taste."

The food came mostly from Portaferry, although the fish came down on the bus from Sawyer's in Belfast once a week, and Willie, the chauffeur went to collect it from the bus in Portaferry. Provisions were delivered by the Grocers, Arthur Gracey, meat came from the butcher, Tommy Ferris, and bakers all came round with their vans. There were no fridges and instead a slate shelved larder facing north kept things cool with wire mesh to keep the flies out. Specialist provisions arrived at Ballywhite direct from the supplier in London – Mrs Brownlow's Balkan cigarettes came from Harrods, Colonel Brownlow's cigars and Turkish cigarettes from Fox's of St James's Street and coffee beans came from Bells in Wigmore Street. At Christmas time hampers arrived from Fortnum & Mason filled with special treats: pineapple rings, morello cherries, crystallised fruit, chocolates and mature cheddar and stilton cheeses.

Mrs Brownlow disappeared most mornings into her much-loved garden. She returned to the house with flowers arranging them herself and leaving the plant debris for Agnes to clear away. She was passionate about flowers and most tables had a flower arrangement, sweet peas in summer and dahlias in the autumn, and rhododendrons in great big vases. She especially loved her rockery which matured and blossomed under her supervision.

The two housemaids spent their mornings dusting, polishing and cleaning, stopping for a cup of tea at eleven with the rest of the household. After lunch they washed and ironed, mended the linen, darned and generally busied themselves with any necessary household chores. Tea was laid out in the window of the dining room

Agnes and Frank White during their courting days

overlooking the paved garden, the tea was served from a silver kettle kept warm by a methylated spirit flame, and there were usually scones which were served by either Agnes or Lily.

In the early evening Agnes went to Mrs Brownlow's bedroom and laid out her clothes for dinner. Then at 7.15pm a member of staff rang the gong to announce that it was time to change, they did this every night whether or not they had guests. "You rung the gong and that was dressing time and they went up and dressed, but you had everything left out for her, and then when they went down to dinner you went up and turned down the beds, left the night-dresses and slippers and all that." The family congregated in the drawing room by 7.45pm for a drink and at 8pm the gong was rung to call them to dinner. There were three courses and Anne remembers wonderful soufflés and delicious fruit fools made from their own cows' cream.

After their work everyone sat together in a room at the back of the house, playing cards and sewing. From the outbuildings behind the house – just beyond the servants' quarters – came a constant battle with vermin: "Rats kept coming up through the floor boards. The place was alive with them," says Agnes. "I remember a cross cook, Miss Sharp[1], sat at the stove and one ran out from behind her and she ran for her life."

The Brownlows also employed a number of men outside the house to do the work in the garden, farm and on the cars and boats and one to help with the horses. In Agnes' early days at Ballywhite these men were Walter Reed, the garden boy, the White brothers and Mr Keogh, the groom. Tommy was the elder of the White brothers; he had begun working at Ballywhite even before the Brownlows lived there; his brother Frank began work there under William's grandmother. By the time William knew them Tommy was married and living in the gate lodge at

Ballywhite with his family and Frank with his mother at their farm a few miles away. When Tommy's eldest son, Jimmy, found work as a mechanic in Greyabbey – a village closer to the White farm than Ballywhite – Tommy suggested the uncle and nephew swapped houses for their own convenience, and thus for a time both brothers lived at Ballywhite.

Agnes had not been working long at Ballywhite before Frank caught her eye. Frank was regularly found outside the laundry singing, "little sir echo, how do you do" to which Agnes would reply, "Hello, hello, hello," and for many years Agnes was teased by the Brownlow family about their courting by song. Their romance began gradually and both were happy with its steady progression, Agnes was some years younger than Frank and in no rush to get married. "He was working there when I got there. We would go to the dances at Portaferry, the hunt balls and dances and things in the Waring Room, it was really a sort of factory and there was a big cinema and they had dances downstairs. We used to go over in a boat from Ballywhite to see my parents, many times – everyone expected us to get married, we didn't rush into it."

Anne was the only young Brownlow to be brought up at Ballywhite; she was ten when they arrived and the others were already away at school and beyond by the time the family moved to Ireland. Agnes was only seven years older than Anne and they took to each other at once. For Anne she is one of her first memories of Ballywhite as she remembers her standing on the doorstep the day she arrived at her new home. The two became great allies, Agnes was full of ideas and Anne loved spending time with her. As the youngest sibling Anne was often on her own and quite lonely at Ballywhite, she loved the camaraderie of her friendship with Agnes. "We were great conspirators, she and I," recalls Anne. "I was the youngest by far and always marooned upstairs while all the fun was to be heard going on downstairs. Agnes' head would appear around my bedroom door, laughing blue eyes and infectious laugh, she would come in and say, 'now don't be telling your Mummy but would you like a wee story?' "

Anne enjoyed following Agnes about listening to her stories and watching her work. On occasions Agnes would let Anne come up to her room, "where I would clop about in her shoes and she would allow me to pat my nose with her powder puff," remembers Anne. It was entirely out of bounds for Anne to go up the stairs at the servants' end of the house – the reason being she may wake up one of them getting their hard earned rest – but she so enjoyed her times in Agnes' room she often tiptoed quietly up the stairs terrified she might get caught by the cook or butler.

They spent happy days together and sometimes Agnes took Anne with her to pick blackberries and visit Frank's family on a nearby farm. Anne watched the romance growing between Agnes and Frank and loved going to his mother's house.

"The greatest treat of all was when she would take me down to visit Frank's and Tommy's mother in her cottage at Bishop Mills. There I would be sat down and given the lovely fresh scones off the griddle and soda bread farls – the smell would tantalise you till it reached the mouth dripping in butter."

Car-ownership was on the increase in the 1930s, but to most families they remained an expensive luxury. Agnes and her friends travelled by bus or bicycle. When Anne was eleven she was given a Raleigh bicycle for her birthday and Agnes and she often escaped together. Anne was thrilled by their trips, sitting in Portaferry eating ice cream in cones with Agnes was the epitome of freedom. Agnes was only allowed to do this on her afternoon off – between 2pm and 4pm – but she was very good at bending the rules and Anne remembers rushing back with her so Agnes could avoid getting 'tongued' or 'catching it' as she put it. It was shortly after Anne was given her new bike that the two of them took themselves off an a memorable ride in the Belfast direction: "I flying on my new bike with speed control for up the hills, the wind on our faces and not a care in the world," says Anne. The pure enjoyment of the ride distracted them both from the time and when they turned about they were beyond Kircubbin and Greyabbey, some fifteen miles each way. The corner the girls turned around at to make for home became known as 'Aggie and Anne's Corner' in the Brownlow household. Agnes went everywhere by bicycle and when visiting her family the other side of the lough, she took it with her in the small fishing boats and peddled home from Strangford.

Mrs Brownlow employed a governess, Margaret Dickie, to educate Anne at home. Miss Dickie was from London and lived in the house with the family. A little school at Ballywhite was set up and attended by other children whose parents were friends of Mrs Brownlow, including Sally Percival Maxwell and Lizanne Musgrave. Later Anne was sent to a local boarding school at Castlewellan and when she was fourteen and a half she was sent to Downham, a girls' boarding school in England. Later Anne was sent to The House of Citizenship, a finishing school which aspired to giving girls the right skills to train them to become an efficient secretary to an MP or other such suitable careers. When Anne completed the course Mrs Brownlow was advised that the "best solution" for Anne was to get married and not to chase a career, and so she returned happily to her family in Ireland and did just that.

Agnes and Anne whiled away many happy hours together at Ballywhite – it seemed they were natural companions from the start. Anne was the first of many friends Agnes made amongst the Brownlow family.

Notes:
1 Miss Sharp replaced Mrs McCauley

Chapter Eight
To Africa

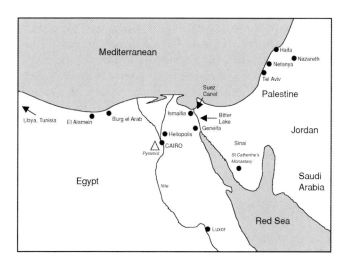

Egypt 1943-44

LATE IN the evening of 5th May 1942 William's battalion left Kent by train. They were given no idea of their destination, but the following afternoon they arrived in Glasgow and boarded *HMS Mooltan*. Conditions on board were cramped as it was built to carry 800 passengers and it had to transport 3,000 servicemen. For a few days they sat in the harbour waiting to depart and for one man who could see his house in Helensburgh it was too much – he jumped overboard and swam home.

When they set sail on 11th May the sea was rough but the scene memorable: 'very red sky behind hills great sight for possible last look at England … just missed seeing Irish coast as I got up too late.' There were 15 ships in the convoy as well as a naval escort of destroyers. The only stipulated physical activity on board was 20 minutes PT and otherwise they lived a lazy life. After about a week at sea it began to get warmer and as it did tropical uniforms came out and a new rule allowed them to sleep on deck one in three nights.

During the voyage William was asked to defend four soldiers who were court-martialled for handing letters to a porter to post at a port. In an attempt to excuse them he used the argument that they had been in quarantine for twelve days before leaving and therefore had never had a lecture on sea orders. He managed to get three of them off, but not a corporal who had written in his letter home that he knew he should not be doing it. It was not that they were not allowed to write letters home but that every one written had to be censored before being sent. William was tasked with becoming one of the censors: 'Very hard work and very boring after a bit as all say same thing 'Darling', 'Sweetest' etc. every other word.'

After almost a fortnight at sea they saw land for the first time and on 27th May they docked in the port of Freetown in Liberia. In early June they arrived in South Africa and everyone was given 'shore leave'. Cape Town was swimming in troops and they were put up in a tented camp outside the city at Retreat for four days. Although it was drizzling William decided to take his platoon for a walk up Table Mountain to see the view, one rifleman found a lizard, another a tortoise, and everyone was very impressed by the strange shrubs and rocky terrain. On his return he found his brother James in the bar in the Officer's Mess and with Hew Butler, John Ford and Dick Bird they went into Cape Town for dinner: 'No black out was a great joy, lights blazing everywhere. A pleasant town, a colour ban meant no worrying from natives!'

When they set sail again everyone returned to work and most seemed the happier for it. As the temperature rose speculation began as to their ultimate destination: 'some boats off to Bombay, we are going to Aden and then Bombay, and then? Syria, Iran, India or Egypt, probably India or Iran.' They soon found out. The German General Rommel had launched an offensive in May 1942 which resulted in his troops pushing into Egypt. The 7th Battalion were amongst the many shipped into Egypt to help the Allies push them back out again.

In Aden they did not disembark, they refuelled and journeyed on towards Suez. 'Wonder if we will get there in time … men seem quite happy at thought of action at last. It is certainly good after our long training.' During their last few nights on board they were allowed to sleep on the deck. They travelled up the Red Sea and two months after they left Glasgow they arrived in Suez.

They were taken to a transit camp at the town of Ismailia and two days later they were taken to a 'preparation camp' where they were not even given time to acclimatise before being called into action. The historian, Arthur Bryant, concludes that a decision to use troops who had been in Egypt for ten days only reflected the depth of the crisis:

'Less than two weeks after the 7th Battalion landed at Suez in the desperate emergency of the hour, it was moved to Burg el Arab in the desert and, three days later, into the front line with the rest of the 23rd Armoured Brigade.'[x]

William came in from a navigating exercise to find everyone packing up. On hearing they were going straight to the desert he rushed to the town of Ismailia with Stephen Trappes-Lomax and Peter Wolfe Taylor to buy the much in demand desert boots. Meanwhile James' regiment, the King's Royal Rifle Corps, had arrived in Egypt minus their equipment ship which had been sunk on the way. Their lack of transport meant they could not join the Rifle Brigade on the frontline which William felt was just as well from his mother's point of view.

The riflemen were excited to be joining the fight at last: 'They are longing to go and have a crack at someone … can hear several tents singing away,' William wrote in his diary. They drove to the front through Alexandria and Amirya arriving at the concentration area at Burg el Arab in a duststorm. D Company were split from the rest of the battalion and told to join 60 Royal Tank Regiment working with the Australians further north.

'I went off in scout car ahead to reconnoitre leaguer[1] area just below the coast road about seven miles east of El Alamein – we were now separated from battalion and brigade. Next day we had a look at the 'Battle Field', there was a bit of shelling going on the Australian position which gave us quite a good first taste!

Next day heard the plan of action. Tanks were to attack Ruweisat Ridge, which was to be consolidated by an Australian infantry battalion. We were reserve to exploit … a fiasco, the Australians never got there. We went to their leaguer behind minefield at night to find 15 tanks out of the whole Regiment returned. Each platoon commander took out a patrol to look for wounded, tanks etc., to bring back through mines. I found nothing but walked through an Australian position thinking they were reserve troops and wandered about, not till got back found had been well in front of forward positions!'

For the next few days they faced problems with tanks breaking down:
'Lot of Fordsons broke back axles, including two of mine, so other platoons equipped with them went and I was left to wave them goodbye. We moved up by night to leaguer area. Early morning shelled and dive-bombed, Ingram[2] killed, Corporal Phipps wounded, when shell hit their front wheel. Dennis Bowers hit in the leg. Sergeant Blackstone shell-shocked, also Shepherd. I came up in evening to leaguer and got shelled going down track, quite alarming and very close! …The remainder of the battalion had moved off to be on start line in centre seats by 0800, but got lost by night a lot rain on mines. Peter Coryton[3] killed in scout car, John Francis blown up in jeep but OK. John Ford blown up but wounded, about 5 ORs [other ranks] killed, a few more wounded. A fiasco of the worst degree. *Ought never to have been* undertaken on so small scale especially by troops only in Egypt fortnight or so.'

It has since been accepted that it was a disastrous move to put 23rd Armoured Brigade (of which 7th Battalion, Rifle Brigade was a part) into action so shortly after it had arrived in the desert. About five days after this 'fiasco' they moved back from El Alamein to defend gaps in a minefield. After which William went with D Company to help the 2nd Batallion, Rifle Brigade commanded by Lt-Col Vic Turner and the 2nd Battalion, King's Royal Rifle Corps:

'My platoon attached to them for few days on forward minefield, saw lot of Peter Curtis, Geoffrey Jameson and Roly Gibbs, also a few Eton masters – no excitement there, odd man over to shoot at but little shelling.'

In the larger picture of the battle for North Africa General Montgomery was called out from England to replace General 'Strafer' Gott, the Commander of the Eighth Army who had been killed on 7th August. Montgomery arrived in the desert on 13th August with great plans for a fast reorganisation of troops. He believed Rommel would make another push with the next full moon and he was right. On 29th August Rommel announced to his troops that they would be in Alexandria in a few days.

William was given a fortnight to rest after suffering from desert sores and a poisoned thumb and on the day he returned to work on August 31st Rommel made his attack. His diary records the battle:

'I had been watching some Royal Army Supply Corps being dive-bombed a short distance away when ME4 turned and came straight at me and my group. I lay flat and prayed, luckily he failed to press button or this would not be written! … I was sent out with two trucks to see what was south of us and had lunch next door to burnt out armoured car with nicely done corpse inside, the flies were awful!! We sat around in these positions for several days … I spent the night as 'listening patrol' on the minefield with Jerry 2,000 yards away, surrounded by 19 of our compressor sets could hear little!!'

The battle of Alam Halfa, as it became known, was a disaster for Rommel and gave great heart to the Allied troops. 'I think that this battle has never received the interest or attention it deserves,' Montgomery wrote after the war. 'It was a vital action, because had we lost it, we might well have lost Egypt.'xi

With four days leave allotted to him William went to Cairo for the first time only to find all the hotels full: '*Saturday 8th September*: found a room in Hotel de Pain funny little hole but not too bad, spent time shopping, eating, drinking in Shepheards and Gezheriah Sporting Club … played golf then rode round Pyramids on Arab pony hirelings, very bored by them.' Shepheards Hotel had been the centre of colonial life for British ex-pats living in Cairo and during the war it was a focal point for off-duty officers. 'I met hundreds of old friends in Shepheards, everyone is out here now.'

When he returned to work he learned that in his absence there had been great reorganisation and the platoons had been reformed to give them specific functions: carrier platoon, mortar platoon, machine gun platoon and anti-tank gun platoon. He was given command of carrier platoon which meant he was in charge of transportation.

They moved to a new camp but William was diagnosed with jaundice. The doctor sent him to 9 General Hospital in Heliopolis from where he wrote to his parents enthusing that everyone thought North Africa was almost won: 'Optimism as to a speedy end to the war is terrific out here, I can certainly see it in this theatre very soon, but in other places it is more difficult.'

After nine days in hospital he was released to work in Brigade Headquarters in Geneifa rather than to his battalion. He recorded:

'First night a bad 'khamsin'[5] brought down my tent at about 100 miles an hour then it started to rain … everything, including a locked suitcase, full of sand the next day," he writes. He went to Cairo to celebrate his 21st birthday, hitchhiking there with Peter Wolfe Taylor: "We met Eric Tibbetts and Henry Beckwith[6] there. Gezireh in the afternoon we started drinking in Shepheards, starting with their 'Suffering Bastards' a sort of Rye Whiskey, Pimms, then a lot more very potent specials outside on the veranda, on to the Continental for dinner and cabaret where we had a rare good evening, staying at Shepheards.'

The outbreak of jaundice meant that there were other friends about waiting to go back to their battalions. 'I am leading a very lazy life for once,' he wrote to his parents on 12th October. 'Cairo is quite amusing now, we meet an enormous number of people by just sitting in the veranda place at Shepheards where everyone drops in some time of the day.' The 'lazy life' came to an abrupt end with an order for everyone to return to the desert immediately and there was a great flap as they all tried to do so at the same time.

Notes:
1 Assembly area
2 Rifleman Douglas Ingram died 27th July 1942 aged 22.
3 Peter Coryton (1920-42) joined Rifle Brigade after Eton; he died in a minefield.
4 Messerschmitt, Axis aeroplane
5 A hot wind which brings on a sandstorm.
6 Henry Beckwith (1916-43) was killed trying to recover some broken down carriers in Tunisia.

Chapter Nine
El Alamein

*"Before Alamein we never had a victory,
after Alamein we never had a defeat"*
Winston Churchill

To the battlefield

THE ORDERS for all troops to return to the front heralded the start of the next phase of fighting. The Battle of El Alamein, as this fortnight of combat has famously become known, was to be the decisive battle in North Africa and Montgomery knew that everything depended on its success. The preparations for battle had been well concealed and on October 23rd William arrived at the Amirya camp at 9.30pm and had dinner: 'Told in the bar the battle was due to open at 22.20 hrs!!! We went outside and heard the barrage open 50 miles away! Then German aircraft came over dropping their bombs by the station.'

Montgomery knew that the enemy would be expecting an attack, and so the plan was to surprise them through its direction. His strategy was to use the light of the full moon of October 24th. He had 164,000 men under his command; Rommel had 50,000 German and 50,000 Italian troops. The Eighth Army was also better equipped with over double the number of tanks and anti-tank guns and 500 attack aircraft to their 350. The RAF sank a German equipment ship, and a report back to Berlin implied the enemy had only enough fuel for eleven days in the desert without re-supplies[xii]. Less encouraging was that since the enemy's withdrawal at Alam Halfa it had established a line of deep defences and planted half a million mines.

The Rifle Brigade's 2nd Battalion went straight into battle. To William listening to the action but not being a part of it was frustrating:

'We spent all day kicking our heels unable to get on. So I went with James Lees to Alexandria where we had a very good lunch at the Union Bar, in my opinion the best food in the Middle East. The next day we moved on to a reinforcement point and spent a 'sandy' day there. Then we listened with awe to the tremendous barrage and watched flight after flight of Bostons in groups of 18 and fighters going to join the battle. A great pall of dust hung over Alamein and dust was flying all day. Little or no news of how things were going as is always the case without civilian papers.'

He wrote to his parents in the morning of 25th October venting his disappointment at not being in the thick of it all: 'It is sickening not to have been able to get away a few days earlier if you think of the news. However daresay I shall not miss all the fun.' The call came to move forward in the afternoon of 25th October:

'We moved off to join the echelons, reached them after dark and spent the night with 'Cherub' (RL Angel). Vague rumour there of casualties from drivers who had been up with rations. We moved off the next day with the echelon from near Hamman. Found Stanley Tibbetts and the HQ Transport near Alamein where we heard Tony Miall[1] had been killed, Hugh with us at the time. Then on via the 'Sun and Moon' tracks, everything much altered since were last up north in July, new tracks laid with tarmac along the railway, all marked as sun, moon or star. Obviously vast planning had gone on well ahead this time.'

Their advance was made between the Australian and Highland Divisions:

'We then moved up through the gaps in the three minefields, two British and one German taken in the first push. In the middle of the 3rd met CSM[2] Grose returning with B Company carriers saying the battalion had been given 20 minutes to get out. We were amongst the guns here and the noise was unbelievable, as we were much bunched and there was a bright moon I very much feared dive-bombing. We got word at length to move on with mixed feelings! Eventually we reached the battalion, shells dropping intermittently, got off and found Eric Tibbets and Kenneth Hick. Kyrle Simond had been wounded already, also Hew B waiting to go back as much shaken. I spent the night in an old Jerry slit trench with Denis Bowen, a lot of stuff flying about and very noisy.

Kenneth asked me to join B Company as they were especially short. Eddie Gibbon was in charge, John Frances having been wounded, with him Mike Bird. Took over a platoon, shelling going on the whole time but little else, about six knocked out German tanks, and one Churchill knocked out by an Aussie tank's six-pounder … slightly left was a carrier from D Company which had been knocked out the first morning and several lives were lost trying to see if the driver was still alive. D Company was on our right and I soon made contact with Stephen and Ivan, also Frank White. They had had hell's own time and had moved up in the dark and on reaching the place had to jam all the transport together then with two fixed line machine guns firing into them! Still digging when the light came and being shelled and sniped the whole time, a lot of casualties from snipers including Peter Lockwood-Wingate wounded and CSM Burgen. Eventually we got dug in and transport back a bit. Only three D Company vehicles knocked out, about 13 casualties in D Company to date.'

During breakfast William heard about the extraordinary bravery and success of the 2nd Battalion the previous day at Kidney Ridge (known as the 'snipe' position) under the command of Lt-Col Vic Turner: '2RB had done a great job at 'Snipe'.' William recorded later in his diary, 'tremendous effort.' The success of the action on the 'Snipe' position was crucial to the course of the battle, but also significant in the positive effect it had on morale, effectively proving the infantry could counter tank-attack. Many in the Second Battalion were awarded medals that day and Vic Turner was given a VC.

William spent another morning in the battle before being sent back to rest. 'There was only one infantry attack on the battalion position by Italians who drew off again. Some trying to surrender to the Aussies but being fired on and withdrew, prisoners were wandering through everywhere. The snipers were the greatest curse hiding in knocked out tanks; the air burst of shrapnel annoying but not very effective. Few enemy aircraft about though RAF strafing the whole time. About midday we moved back to beyond El Alamein station to rest and refit, nearly got hit by a stray when we stopped between mine fields! We sat back for a week refitting and resting, and I rejoined D Company with joy. We had a great dinner party with the commanding officer in an ex HQ dugout which we blacked out. 2RB equipped at great speed up to full strength again, amazing work as lost nearly all their six-pounders. Heard via James Lees that James [Brownlow] was still OK, my only news of him. Thank God he was not in my battalion, I think that is far worse.'

The disturbing casualty rate, the slow course of the battle and the few advantages taken, alarmed both Downing Street and the War Office and Churchill began to question why every general sent to fight Rommel ultimately came off badly. In Egypt Montgomery was confident of what he was doing; he was busy regrouping troops for the next offensive. William was certainly not negative about the way the fighting was going and wrote a letter home during the rest period:

'D[addy] will probably be able to imagine what our task was like if you compare it with the last war, the only difference being all in our favour. The staff work was absolutely incredibly efficient, the supplies never failing, the RAF quite magnificent and the Bosche tough but unhappy … the battalion has now got itself recognised as being well up to the Rifle Brigade standard and that says a lot considering our reputation out here, so we are all very bucked with life.'

When they returned to the battle the Italians and Germans seemed weakened by the continuing barrage and morale was high.

'We moved up again, leaving about 0200 hours [on 31st October] in the rain, boring journey up. We were to move up through the New Zealanders who were to have done a 4000 yard advance and then sit out in front forming a box with the tanks to try and draw the jerry armour into battle. We did this, counting thousands of prisoners winding their way back, and getting vaguely shelled and shot at. We arrived at the position and the shelling started in earnest. Had a 60th[3] subaltern with us as we have run out of our own reserves, this was his first action and looking very green! Stanley Tibbetts hit just after we arrived, we have lost about seven officers to date, George Russell[4] among others killed.

'Got into a position with support of three six-pounders and got dug in, the transport moving back. Surrounded on all sides by tanks firing away at invisible (to us) enemy tanks. I had to liaise with the 60th on our left, 14 Platoon being on the left flank of the battalion. I wandered about for three-quarters of an hour looking for the 60th but could find no trace, shelling hard now and feeling very lonely wandering around among unknown regiments. When I started to go back found I had little idea of my position having not bothered to take compass bearings (fatal). However found them at length and very glad I was too! Then I had a great job to find Company HQ although only about 200 yards away. Found Frank there as well and happy as a lark as usual.

'Getting quite used to near misses now, though still find it difficult not to duck at 'overs'. The 88mm make such a row. Found Stephen in a big hole with an old Italian truck. Talked there for a bit with him, the Commanding Officer and the anti-tank gun Battery Commander when a shell fell five yards away bursting towards us but no one was hit. A miracle, I was nearest it! Sat around all day being shelled and tanks firing away, occasionally one getting hit and burning up, things did not seem to be going too well. Lot of 210 shells falling round position hell of an explosion and huge black column of smoke and vast splinters. Lance Corporal Doggett[5] hit by a splinter in back of the head sent him back but no hope for him as brain exposed. O'Brien hit in leg, then a mortar platoon fellow. Sgt Wood absolutely grand all through, often had to order him into his truck when shelling heavy, he got hit slightly in leg and arm but carried on. Men very browned off with nothing to do but be shelled. I lay around reading in my trench and wandering around. We got word of 60 enemy tanks coming from south but they never arrived. It was a grand sight watching the Boston bombers coming over in faultless formation, the bombs sprouting like a huge forest in the sand.'

The second phase of the fighting, Operation Supercharge as Montgomery named this big push forward began that evening. The 7th Battalion's role was to force a gap in the enemy line for tanks to get through. They planned to send D Company and B Company to attack and clear Tel El Aqqaqir Ridge and Sidi Rahman Track so the anti-tank C Company could advance and the tank battle begin. The 2nd New Zealand Division had tried the night before but failed to break through to the Rahman track.

William noted, 'that evening we were told to attack with the Brigade on three points: 7RB centre, 2RB right and 2KRRC[6] left. They were not sure if there were stragglers of the Sherwood Foresters on our objective so I was sent out to reconnoitre. Took out Sgt Wood and about eight men, we ran into men shouting and driving tanks about, about three-quarters of a mile away. We could not tell if German or Italian, but listened to them for some time.' He decided they were German accents and returned to tell his company commander. Sergeant Main of D Company recalls the patrol in *The Imperial War Museum's Book of the Desert War*[xiii]:

'We had sent out a patrol which could only hear enemy rations being distributed and we were unaware whether the enemy positions were Italian or German.'

The story of the subsequent attack is told by William in a diary written some months after the event:

'Attacked about 2400 hours, D Company leading, 14 Platoon leading them as I knew the way. Found no enemy where I had first located them, but just short of the objective saw men jumping into trenches just ahead. I was ahead of platoon at time so moved back and lay down not knowing whether enemy or own troops – soon knew when they opened [fire]. Then they hit me in hip and foot almost immediately. I yelled at the platoon to charge but was unable to get up myself; hearing curses and screams I rightly concluded others had been hit. Trying to open with my Tommy Gun I found it had jammed, then I heard Stephen rallying the company to my right, they charged in, and I heard Ivan [D Company Second in Command] calling my name but did not answer as he would have come and got killed. I had been hit again by now in my back and was lying very close hoping for the bullets to go over. After the company charged all became quiet, I did not know what had happened or where the rest of the battalion were.'

The rest of the company charged forward and Sergeant Main's recollections continue the battle where William left off:

'Above the noise of the explosion I heard the company commander, Major Trappes-Lomax, shout: 'Up the Rifle Brigade! Charge!' Trappes-Lomax disappeared through a hail of tracer bullets. I felt he couldn't go in by himself and I gave the order to charge. I went through the enfilade fire and I couldn't understand how I had not been hit. It was like daylight with the flares and mortar explosions … I had been advancing in a series of rushes, firing my rifle at the hip … we now acquired two German prisoners who had been hiding under a truck. A little later we met up with Major Trappes-Lomax and found that only 22 of the company were left. We now received orders to withdraw. On our return just before daylight a roll-call revealed that D Company had thirteen men left. My platoon consisted of Corporal Sandford, myself and a rifleman who had stayed back because of a scorpion bite.'

William lay wounded where he fell:

'When all was quietened down the Jerries came out and looked us over. They gave us some water. One gave me some foul coffee. I had got my own water bottle [lid] off, only found the bullet had gone through it as well and empty. Tried to get my field dressing on, had hell of a job to get it open and then could not fix it myself. The Jerries did not touch our wounds or move us. Sgt Wood was also wounded and in great pain, also King, and five others lying dead. The rest had disappeared. The Jerries pinched my glasses [binoculars] and compass but left everything else intact including my pistol. Roger then appeared having been captured and gave me his Great Coat. Wood was given a blanket; it was very cold. There we remained for the rest of the night. I could still sit up with difficulty and crawl a little. The Bosche disappeared in the morning, and I must have slept or fainted as I did not see them go. Sgt Wood died[7], so King and self left. We lay all day, the ridge being shelled but unable to crawl to a trench, it was only a miracle we were not killed by splinters. I got two small splinters, also bits of grenade in my ear from one, which had exploded just in front of me when I was first hit. Luckily I had my tin hat tilted over. I also found a bullet had gone clean through my hat, another close shave. Very hot lying there and the flies were awful. King got very thirsty and I spent a long time trying to reach a dead man's water bottle, even trying to stand with aid of rifle, I got on my feet but fainted. About 1630 saw some men waving a flag in a hole about 200 yards away. Thought they were Jerries but I yelled for water, and then saw they were British. Later two Dingoes appeared and drove up to them, 'did I yell'. They drove over, and found out it was Sgt Guy and Cpl Keen waving their pants on a rifle. We were piled onto the bonnets and drove off without being shot at. They were two 'Bays' scout cars. We went to a Regimental Aid Post (RAP) where I was given morphine and my wounds dressed, also I had a cig. I had cigs and matches with me but matches soaked with blood.'

While still lying wounded he had laid his matches out in the sun to dry in the hope of being able to smoke a cigarette.

'Put into ambulance and slept all the way back to the Australian Casualty Clearing Station (CCS) at Burgh El Arab where given tea and my wounds were dressed properly. Slept till morning and then taken to airfield where put on plane and back to Heliopolis. The stretcher being fixed on racks, the plane carrying 13 men. Taken to No 9 General where I had been when I had jaundice in October. I heard later King[8] died from bad wounds in stomach. I was afraid he would as heaving blood.

Looking back on this experience it seems appalling but at the time it seemed

William shortly before he was wounded

William revisits the scene where he nearly died

Rifleman King's grave

fairly natural. When I was first wounded it did not hurt just made me jump and gasp as if winded, and then I wondered for a moment if this was dying! I wondered what the next step was, hoping it would be to get picked up by the battalion. Then it was all puzzling not knowing what was going on. I was rather dubious about what the Germans would do when they came out but they were all right except one ardent fellow who would wave a pistol in my face, so I asked him to point it the other way! He did!! I was mainly angry with them for giving us no medical aid, but I don't think they had any. Then I wondered which way I would go back – with the Germans? Or back to Cairo? I did not mind much at the time but I am glad now. The shelling was bloody and trying to get water for King was heartbreaking. Wood just faded out as King shouted that he thought he was looking worse.

Then we lay watching the tanks a mile away wondering whose they were as I now had no glasses and always thinking they were coming nearer and hoping to be picked up. When we were I gave over to Sgt Gray who held me onto the car, I was weak now and tired though fully conscious. Once or twice I thought I was going to faint. He was grand and keen. King had a lot of pain from the jolting, so had I! I was thankful to those Bays. At the hospital I was redressed and plaster put on my foot. I sent off a cable and wrote home, also a report to Stephen, hearing later from him they thought I had been killed. Then Gray reported what had happened but that he thought I would not live! My wounds were extensive but not dangerous.'

His efforts were noted in a regimental chronicle: 'The Hun had withheld his fire until the very last minute and cover was very scarce. A truly uncomfortable position at first but eased by the speed at which D Company went for them. Bill Brownlow and Frank White led their platoons with great effect.'[xiv]

He had been shot at one o'clock in the morning and had gone through the extremes of night and day in the desert. The final thrust came the following evening: troops made it south of Tel el Aqqaqir and by dawn the enemy had been forced back and the armoured divisions broke through, in Montgomery's words: 'the Battle of El Alamein had been won. Everywhere the enemy was in full retreat.' The Eighth Army had 13,500 troops killed or wounded in the battle but a great victory had been won. 55,000 of the Axis troops were killed and 30,000 taken prisoner before Hitler could be finally persuaded to permit Rommel to pull his army back. The triumph was received with jubilation in Britain and Montgomery's name was made. After El Alamein it was one long push westward for the Eighth Army who reached Tripoli in Libya in January 1943. Rommel retreated into Tunisia but in May 1943 the Allies captured Tunis and Germany was forced to accept defeat in North Africa.

Notes:
1 AN Miall (1916-42) joined the London Rifle Brigade at the beginning of the war.   2 Company Sergeant Major
3 60th Rifles, King's Royal Rifle Corps, a regiment with close links to the Rifle Brigade.
4. Second Lieutenant GA Russell died aged 21.   5 Corporal LG Doggett died aged 21.
6 7th Battalion, Rifle Brigade, 2nd Battalion, Rifle Brigade, 2nd Battalion, King's Royal Rifle Corps.
7 Lance Sergeant GWC Wood died 3 November aged 29.   8 Rifleman James King died 3 November aged 29.

Chapter Ten
The Patient

William recovers from his wounds

THE TELEGRAM William sent made it back home before the War Office's, it reached Ballywhite on 15th November: 'In hospital with flesh wounds shoulder thigh foot comfortable nothing damaged heard James was well about week ago.' It was not until a fortnight later that his father received the official notification: 'Regret to inform you of report dated 25th Nov 1942 received from Middle East that 2nd Lieut. W S Brownlow The Rifle Brigade has been wounded in action stop letter follows shortly.' The letter that followed stated he had 'sustained gunshot wounds in the thigh and back' and that if he became 'seriously ill' further reports would be sent via telegram. For the first few weeks William was at the No 9 General Hospital in Heliopolis:

'Vic Turner came in, just out from the 15th Scottish, also Kit Tatham Water who heard by chance I was in. Then we were sent by ambulance train to Palestine 23rd Scottish General Hospital near Sarasand. The train journey was more comfortable than expected as my back was very painful for lying on, but every comfort on board.'

James went to No 9 General in Heliopolis only to find William had been moved to Sarasand, it was impossible to get there without leave as it was an overnight journey on the train. He heard Vic Turner had been in and managed to get to talk to him and learnt first hand that his brother's life was not in danger. Vic Turner was very good at visiting men from the Rifle Brigade in hospital, and after his first visit he sent Ballywhite an airgraph saying William, 'was really very cheerful and getting on well.' William tried to alleviate his parent's worry by keeping them regularly informed. He sent telegrams home suggesting he was better than he was, such as the one he wrote a few weeks after the battle which arrived in Portaferry on 4th December: 'getting on fine now in all quarters hope not worrying no need should not be long before up.'

On his arrival in Palestine in the middle of November he wrote:

'They have moved us to Palestine now, which is much better for quick recovery, and very pleasant. The 'holes' are going on nicely, the one in my left thigh just went through fleshy part so no trouble, the one in my left shoulder I got after the others and was lying on my back, the bullet I think struck the ground underneath so went through nothing, but just cut the flesh – it is the most painful as have to lie on it but used to it now. The foot is OK just wants the bone to mend. I live off huge Jaffa oranges here, there is a grove just outside my window. It is a hutted hospital and very comfortable, nice sisters and doctors, good food. I sit up in a chair sometimes but cannot walk about yet.'

Stephen Trappes-Lomax wrote him a letter on 7th November expressing his huge relief in discovering he was alive and filling him in on the rest of the battle:

'I can't tell you how relieved I was to see Corporal Keen and Sergeant Gray the night after the battle and to learn that they had found you and brought you in. I am very sorry to hear of all your wounds and hope very much you have not suffered too great pain though I fear you must. Keen was most impressed with your courage throughout and I would like to offer my congratulations both on that and on your performance throughout which was first class. When we charged I could find no trace of you or your platoon, though I shouted for you time after time. I can't say how relieved I was to hear you were back after all, for I had almost convinced myself of the worst. Your patrol was excellently done and the information you produced was invaluable in preparing us for what happened.

I'm afraid your platoon suffered badly (as you may know), Sergeant Wood was killed. What a loss. How excellent he was and the perfect gentleman and a first class soldier. About 20 of us got to the objective and joined up with 2RB. However the anti-tank guns could not get up and we had to get out – they successfully in their carriers, but we with no alternative to our feet. I tried the way we went in but we caught a lot of fire – machine gun, mortar and grenade and only nine got out of whom two (Hart and Mallory) were wounded in the process. The others were Butch, Powe, Sergeant Finch, Corporal Main, Lance Corporal Sandford, Underwood J and myself. Two had got out earlier (including Dopey who pending your return is batting for me); and as you know Gray and Keen returned later with the glad news about you. I can't sufficiently emphasize what a joy and relief that was after rather a trying time … you can rest assured that no one could have led them better than you did and I'm sure there is no one by whom they would rather have been led. And I *mean* that.'

His wounds were not recovering well and he was in a lot of pain. 'After about three weeks I had violent pain in the buttock which lasted three days, then they operated and let off pus. I was very weak after this and given a blood transfusion. Very thin and weak by now, but did not realise how serious I was,' he recorded later in his diary.

It was some time before James was allowed the leave to visit Palestine. When he arrived at the hospital he walked the length of his ward without finding him, but walking back through the beds he came upon him. It was not merely the new moustache that made him unrecognisable; his features were skeletal and James saw that he was gravely ill. He found the doctor in charge of his case and was told his leg was septic and there was a very real chance that if he did not respond to the drugs they were using they may have to resort to amputation. James reasoned that his mother was strong enough to take the news and he decided that he must write and explain why amputation was a possibility and that the doctor believed his life would not be in danger if it were done.

Christmas in the hospital was a jolly affair with turkey and beer on offer although William ate little. His parents sent him a thermos flask and the Ward Sister gave him a toy wooden donkey, a gesture he was very touched by. On New Year's Eve he was operated on again and it was discovered his hip joint was infected. He was given another blood transfusion and put in plaster from above his left knee to his chest which he found uncomfortable as it stuck into his back and made breathing difficult. He was weak and the blood transfusion helped him, although he loathed the six hour process.

'They hang the bottle upside down over the bed with a long rubber tube leading from it. In the tube is a glass filter, then a glass dropper regulated by a small tap. A curved needle is then pushed into your vein (in the arm or leg) and connected to the tube and strapped down tight to keep it still. The blood then runs down the tube, drips through the dripper and into your arm. This is inclined to give one the rigors, which I got with a vengeance, shaking and shivering, one's teeth chattering, and no means of controlling them.'

It was decided to give him another operation to relieve pus near his spine and his parents received another War Office telegram: 'Your son WS Brownlow sustained bullet wounds foot and chest 3 November satisfactory except last produced Osteomyelitis of Iliceum still discharging.'

His wounds began to heal but Osteomyelitis (bone inflammation) kept him in

Telegrams charting William's recovery

bed longer than anyone else in the ward. He made many friends who helped him during his more difficult days although the longevity of his recovery meant he saw them come and go: 'I saw the ward with everyone up but me about five separate times.' Amongst those who became friends were Barry Holt-Wilson from the Rifle Brigade's 2nd Battalion, who came in with a burnt foot in January, and another Rifle Brigade officer, George Burrows Smith, whose leg had been broken at El Alamein. His longest-serving ally was Ralph Gamage of the Durham Light Infantry who had been wounded in the arm at El Alamein the same night as William; the failure of his arm to recover meant the two men remained on the ward almost as long as each other.

He remained fascinated by the events of the night he was wounded. 'I cannot remember if I told you,' he wrote home in January, 'one of our company sergeants was in this hospital, so I got him to come in to see me and tell me details of what I had not heard from the company commander. The officers were very lucky for once, only two wounded in that attack, me and 2nd i/c, though two wounded earlier on in battle … Stephen Lommax got the MC; he had no business to be OK with all the grenades flung at him as they went through.'

Sister Paddy Lush was his favourite nurse and he described her in letters home, 'she is absolutely marvellous value, she makes me yell with laughter … she makes me and another chap [Gamage] who has been in a long time special sandwiches, yesterday she brought in some violets she had found as I had said how I liked them.' She watched him writing his letters and decided to write to his mother to tell her how he was getting on:

'I have been looking after your son for a long time now and although he writes frequently I thought I'd write and tell you how he was as men are so vague about illness. His brother came to see him about a month ago and thought he looked very pale and thin as he then did but he has improved tremendously recently and looks much better now. When the weather was fine we carried his bed outside and he got quite sunburnt. His appetite is better now and his face looks much fatter. I can't tell you what a terribly good patient he has been through a long and tiring illness because he'll probably read this! But he is exhibit No 1 in the ward and everyone comes to see him. I was born in Co Down so we talk about home sometimes.'

As his condition improved his bed was often moved outside. 'I used to have great fun lying outside the ward in the sun in my bed just watching the 'goings on'. A lovely view of rolling orange groves and masses of flowers, punctuated by donkeys and foals and goats and small boys, stocks, bee-eater birds, camels and Arabs wandering about their various ways,' he reflected in his diary. 'Watching Arabs working is an endless pastime as they jabber, stroll off, lie down and smoke and even occasionally work, but never all together!' Convalescing officers were allowed a tot of whiskey in the evening and William later recalled he would not have pulled through without this small luxury.

There were numerous visitors, Colonel Geoffrey Hunt, Ivan Corbie, Stephen Trappes-Lommax and James who visited him again while on a course at Gaza. Everyone was amazed by how much he had improved and no one more than his surgeon. He wrote to his parents on 25th March:

'I had a long talk with the surgeon this evening and I have only just lately realised the scare I have been raising now that I am OK. Apparently they normally fear the worst when that os? (I can't remember the name!) sets in. However as I told you they have not only saved that but it looks as if I shall have full use of my joint

Father Christmas visits the patients

Back on his feet – almost six months after he was wounded

as well … the great thing now is to get about again. He told me today, much to my consternation, that originally they had visualised my returning to England and being invalided out! That shook even me a bit, however I have done so fantastically well that they will have another pow-wow to think things over.'

His first step on the road to recovery was when he got out of bed in April. 'I started getting up after $5^1/_2$ months in bed, once I was entirely healed – by dangling my legs over the bed. Then I stood with the Medical Orderly holding me and my first day took six steps, very wobbly, my main trouble being no sense of balance.'

He was soon eating in the mess, and going to the officers club at Sarasand and even visiting Tel Aviv. His letters home were cheery, telling them about the life the troops were leading in Cairo, and how he was already planning his return to the Rifle Brigade. His mother wrote back frequently, filling him in on life at Ballywhite and often to let him know of his friends' deaths: in one letter she enclosed a published tribute to his school friend David Coleman, who had been killed at El Alamein on 5th November 1942; and in another she told him Pat Nugent, a Lieutenant in the Grenadier Guards, had been killed on 27th April in the final push towards Tunis.

In May the Axis forces surrendered and William considered:
'It seems strange now that the war in North Africa is over. Great excitement over our victory though nobody doubted it would come we did not expect it quite so suddenly. I wish I had been up there – what looting! I might have made up my binoculars that were pinched by the Bosche! Montgomery has undoubtedly done well but what an untidy little devil – talking to Winston C with his hands in his pockets.'

He was moved to a convalescent depot at Nethanya on the Palestinian coast north of Tel Aviv where he strengthened his muscles swimming. Vic Turner came to visit him and he wrote to Mrs Brownlow to keep her in the picture:
'He was walking about without any limp at all and looking quite a different person to the white faced person I saw last December … it was delightful seeing him and finding him so well, he told me about his awful experiences, laying out from 1am till 6pm after he was hit, he must have gone through a very bad time.'

He shared a room with Alastair McCleod of the Seaforth Highlanders: 'An absolute open forthright Scottish character … Probably the only fellow I could tolerate sharing a room with, being of about the same untidy habits and so entirely affable even in the early morning.' They kept themselves amused with cards, swimming or croquet and on a trip to Tel Aviv he proved slicker than William with the ladies: 'he met a girl off the bus and had everything fixed within a few minutes. The fastest work I have seen for some time!' One of their croquet partners, an Irish Guards officer Tom Langton, impressed them greatly with his war tales.

'He had had an interesting time having been on a long distance desert patrol and failing to get picked up by the naval launches found himself with three other men well behind the Jerry lines. So he started trekking. If anyone knows German or Italian it is amazing what they can get away with. I have heard of people who have gone up to enemy sentries and sussed them to hell, walked on or even commandeered enemy transport by bluff. Langton spent a long time with the friendly Arabs finding there an Indian who had escaped four times from the Italians and was living in a cave. He eventually cut south down the desert and met our troops as the advance from Alamein started. He was out I think about two months.'

On one Tel Aviv trip he saw the film *Desert Victory* with Ralph Gamage: 'very good, the noises especially being most realistic, shells coming over nearly sent us to the ground below our seats and the tank noises reminded one of night leaguers.' He noticed the Jews' unpopularity and the friction between them and the Arabs:

'Presumably after the war there will be hell's own bust up as both Jews and Arabs lying in arms as fast as possible, pinching some and buying others from the Australians who will sell anything. Even ten carriers and six-pounders being found buried under village streets! On the whole I think the troops are on the Arabs' side. The Jews are training quite an army by their police, which do about six months each. The British police are good but tied by the all powerful Jewish Agency.'

He returned to the hospital to be signed off and the doctors and nurses took him out to say farewell:

'Camel hock at dinner and some *French brandy* after, a great rarity now! Danced a bit after dinner, then decided to have 'midnight bathe' … rather romantic, dried ourselves on our handkerchiefs. I had to walk back, they accompanied me quarter of the way. It was the best evening I have had since coming out here.'

Chapter Eleven
Back to Work

William reports back to duty

IN JUNE 1943 the doctor gave William the all-clear to do a base job at Ismailia near the Suez Canal. On the overnight train back to Egypt he ran into his friend Ivan Soboleff, the Russian he had met when joining the army. Soboleff had joined another Rifle Brigade battalion and had been awarded the Military Cross for 'conspicuous bravery' in June 1942.

In Ismailia he found Stephen Trappes-Lomax in the Officers' Mess. 'Nothing much going on here except work, we go down to the Lido on the Bitter Lake and bathe most days.' The American Air Force was stationed nearby and British soldiers took advantage of their naivety as they had just arrived:

'Americans incredible our men were selling them Luger pistols for outrageous sums … one Sergeant had a lot of sandbags in the bottom of the jeep, as usual against blast of mines, the yank asked what they were for so he told him. The Yank then said, 'Gosh is that real Alamein sand?' – 'Yes' said the Sergeant who had filled them that moment, 'all the way from Alamein to Tunis' and sold him two bags for 10/-!'

In the middle of the July heat James came from Syria to visit and they spent a few days together in Cairo. Wartime Cairo was full of off duty troops, but most spent only a few days there biding their time shopping and socialising at the hotels and sporting clubs. The officers had fixed haunts and tended to congregate at Shepheards, the Continental and the Turf Club. Most European women in Cairo were ATS officers or medical sisters and although the majority of 'peace-time' wives from regiments stationed in Cairo before the outbreak of war had gone home, a few remained working for institutions such as the Red Cross. In August he took more time off to see James and they stayed in Shepheards the most popular hotel in Cairo. In September he was sent to do a course in Palestine: 'Good bathe yesterday, lovely stretch of beach just lie around in sun and bathe and eat huge grapes … I have never enjoyed a course more.' While there he went to Tel Aviv to see his nurse and doctor, Paddy Lush and Major Wilson and they met at the Jaffa Club. 'Both delighted at my disgusting good health.'

Everyone supposed the next arena of war to be Southern Europe, possibly Italy where support for continuing the war was wavering. When Mussolini fell from power at the end of July Italy seemed set for surrender and in the beginning of September his successor, Marshall Pietro Badoglio, held secret meetings with Dwight Eisenhower, the Allied Commander. Hitler, fearing an Italian surrender sent German troops into Northern Italy. When the surrender came on 7th September 1943 Allied troops had already taken Sicily. The Germans moved south and took Rome and by the end of the month the Allies were in Naples.

William was in Palestine when he heard the news about the Italian surrender. 'A news flash came onto wireless programme announcing that Italy had surrendered unconditionally. There were about seven of us in the mess. The reactions were amusing: some, South Africans mostly, rushed to the bar, some looked up smiled, pondered it and went on doing what they were at, one fellow coming in later on being greeted with news just said 'good, but what's the beer situation like tonight'. The main topic of

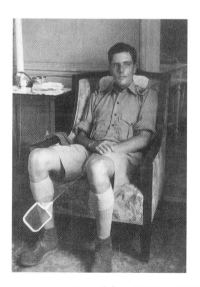 

James (left) and William (right) enjoy a few day's leave in Cairo

interest was what will happen to our POWs … a big party ensued till 1.30am – everyone in great form, unfortunately only local brandy so many sore heads next morning.' He was excited by the prospect of re-engaging with Rommel's troops in Italy: 'No doubt there will be heavy fight to expel the Hun as lots of reformed Afrika Corps there. I have not had feelings against the Afrika Corps. They were good clean fighters and Rommel a great General.'

He was put forward for a job with an Officer Cadet Training Unit which he was keen to do as a captaincy came with it. He travelled to Cairo to be interviewed for it.

'Lots of black buttons as usual in Shepheards … John Frances practically opened the door of our taxi as we arrived … no hotel to charge more than £1 per day, which means food rather unvaried as always full so do not care … Had big row and sent for manager at Maxims one day at lunch as only water melon for fruit two days running when Egypt stiff with grapes, figs etc.

'Frank [White] and Tim [Dewhurst] in great form, great bit of luck their being there as had not seen either since I was wounded, had some good parties. Peter Wolfe Taylor, back at Maadi with his intelligence unit, told me of a very good little Indian tailor near Soliman Pasha Square who I got to make me a pair of whipcord jodhpurs, very good at that. We stuffed ourselves at Groppios then went and bathed at Heliopolis Club with Ivan [Soboleff] at last a captain in a photographic intelligence unit. Went round the Musqi Bazaar again, Dick and Tim had never been, bought nothing in end but all shopkeepers greeted me like an old friend, how they remember I do not know.'

He remained in Cairo at the headquarters while waiting to be assigned to the next training unit. 'What the hell they find to do with all those people in GHQ 'I do not know' (in D[addy]'s words) … some were working hard others making jobs to employ themselves and all covered in mysterious initials and numbers and a vast pretence of the terrible 'hush hush' jobs.' General Sir Henry Maitland 'Jumbo' Wilson had become Commander in Chief, Middle East, Cairo and Gilbert Talbot[1] who William knew through the Rifle Brigade was his ADC: 'quite a pleasant life for people like Gilbert Talbot, when I went to see him everything all laid on, he just rings a bell for drinks etc.'

The OCTU was north of Haifa so he returned to Palestine once again. He enjoyed the job and made the most of the horses there. 'Ride most afternoons after tea, grand country out in the plain between us and the hills, though keep getting chased off the runways of the local RAF Station!' They lived fairly independently aside from a visit by General Jumbo for a passing out parade.

He had been annoyed to leave Cairo just as his battalion moved there – to Mena by the Pyramids – and was pleased when he was called to give evidence in the trial of a corporal and came briefly back to the battalion.

'Lot of new faces in the mess, the two most outstanding younger one's being Peter Bowring, as charming as ever, and Johnnie Persse, two first class subalterns, feel quite

Instructing an Officer Cadet Training Unit

Charles Mott-Radclyffe

General Sir Henry 'Jumbo' Maitland Wilson visits the 7th Battalion, Rifle Brigade

old and senior now! Charles Mott-Radclyffe, MP, and Bill Beecher two new company commanders; Colonel Douglas in good form and long chat about Charlton days and very keen to get me back [to the battalion] if I can get up graded. Big inspection by Jumbo on Monday, the battalion incredibly smart, Douglas asked me to meet the old boy on the Mena Road and escort him to camp as we were expecting King Farouk and Eden as well. Nearly got caught napping when standing on the corner with a Military Policeman as first Jumbo came with no outriders and in an ordinary staff car, whistled him down only to find a big flap on as Secretary of State wanted to speak to him urgently on the phone. The battalion signaller on the exchange was quite overwhelmed by such vast requests. Parade was a grand sight, the march past for the '95 excellent, the double past and advance in review even more impressive. Cairo Area Band playing having a Rifle Brigade band master.'

In October the Italian Government officially declared war on Germany, effectively making a foe a friend: 'Latest horror is Italian officers will be admitted to officers clubs … must be polite to them – let me meet a blighter!' In Lebanon there were riots against French rule: 'Lots of people's leave mucked up by riots in the Lebanon … slight repercussions amongst the Arabs in Haifa.' He enjoyed exploring Palestine the area and at the end of one course he took his cadets on a tour of Nazareth. At the end of November they were given leave and he travelled to Jerusalem with friends and stayed in an attractive villa in the German Colony, an area of the city built in the 1800s. 'Mooched around the old city looking at the views from the walls visiting the mosque of Omar, which is very gaudy but quite fine … Another day, we were walking up the hill where Mary visited Elizabeth before St John was born and near the top we found a maternity home, full of Polish ATS, and an old English woman who has built a chapel for all religions.' In Jerusalem armed guards surrounded the King David Hotel as service chiefs were there on a sightseeing trip. William got excited believing the VIPs to be Stalin, Churchill and Roosevelt holding a conference. He was right that they were in the region at the time, but Churchill, Roosevelt and Chiang Kai Chek met in Mena, Cairo and Churchill and Roosevelt flew on to meet Stalin in Tehran.

On Christmas Eve William travelled to Cairo on the same train as John Brooke and they went together to Shepheards arriving in time to take the last room. 'Christmas Eve party in Colonel Douglas' flat, very hectic, and on to Shepheards with Dick Southby (2i/c), Tim Dewhurst (adjutant), Dick Adams, Ted Eccles and self; Dick and Ted returned ill during dinner. We blew Christmas in on the horn having sung the [Eton] Boating Song all the way down Kasr El Aini in the jeep.' On Christmas morning he travelled to the Pyramids to meet up with the rest of the battalion for a day of organised activities. 'Starting with donkey racing, donkeys supplied by the Pyramid wallahs … Race cards and Tote Steward, Colonel Darling and Major Dick Southby judges Captain RB Adams, C RSM Warboys, Clerk of the course Lieutenant J Persse, Whipper in Lt P Bowring. The names and breeding of the donkeys were generally some

Celebrating Christmas in Cairo with camel and donkey-racing.

reflection on the jockey's character, e.g. Scruffy Downing who arrived out just in time to get the Africa Star, donkey's name Africa Star by Scruffy – 'just in time'.' There were celebrations all day long and after a reunion with the officers and soldiers of D Company he and Dick Adams slipped off to an evening service in the Anglican cathedral in Cairo. There were more celebrations on New Year's Eve and William 'saw in' 1944 in Cairo: 'blew the New Year in on the horn with Douglas at the Americans' New Year Party.'

He was declared fit and returned to his battalion to fill in for Bill Beecher as company commander of D Company. 'CSM Keen very pleased at my return.' He enjoyed life back with his company and spent most evenings up in Cairo. The battalion's training included launching an attack on the ancient site of Memphis[2] 15 miles south west of Cairo: 'All ruins now, but incredible with a great statue of Rameses lying about.' At the end of January they moved to Ataka, near Suez and said farewell to Cairo with a party at the British Embassy: 'Lady Lampson[3] managed to sit down while dancing, which caused a flutter of ADCs.'

The move to Ataka was not popular, the camp itself was desolate and Suez and the surrounding towns had been put out of bounds following an outbreak of bubonic plague. When Bill Beecher returned to take over D Company Tim Dewhurst, the adjutant became ill with jaundice and William took over from him. There were terrible sandstorms and he returned from one exercise in the desert to discover much of the tented camp down: 'Sergeant Reynolds had his glasses blown off his nose ... my own tent was down and my last batch of photos blown away, also a couple of M[ummy] and Anne I had just framed.'

Larry Fyffe, James Keith and William took time off at the beginning of March to go sightseeing. They caught a sleeper from Cairo and booked themselves into Luxor's famous Winter Palace Hotel.

'It was hotter than Cairo, only wore grey flannel trousers and silk shirt, seemed funny going out without a hat. Put on service dress in evening. The hotel was not crowded, there were only about 20 people there, civilians and a few army, Poles and Armenians. Very lazy time, sailed down river in Felucca … to the Valley of the Kings, where Kings were buried, about eight tombs in all, some recently found such as Tutankhamen. Very interesting as the colouring is as if it was done yesterday, all underground carved out of solid rock and carvings of their life and hobbies on the walls, some bigger than others as they could only be made while king alive, slaves worked six days a week for the king, one for their own tomb, it seems to have been their only interest in life. Went to Valley of Queens, much the same and on to old temple built to some old queen[4], good pictures of ducks. …Visited Luxor Temple which was rather boring, going by gharry I drove myself and raced the other gharry back, the driver getting highly excited and seizing the whip to whip the old horse up!

'Went out one day taking Mohamed Ali, the snake man, it is supposed his whole family can find and handle snakes. Went to an orange grove and he first found a scorpion which nearly stung him once or twice. Then a serpent, about 18", then two cobras in some brambles, had windy time getting them out. He wanders along chanting bits of Koran then says he smells snakes; whether planted or not I do not know, but very amusing. The town of Luxor itself is mostly native except for stretch along the Nile where hotels (3) are and few tourist type shops, good views, very good on the whole and service excellent. On the last day we got up at 0500 hours and went up river in sailing boat to shoot duck … I got one Mallard and four widgeon.'

In their absence the battalion had moved to Burg El Arab on the Mediterranean coast close to El Alamein. While there William took the opportunity to revisit the battlefield. The sand storms were terrible, and he attempted to write up his diary during one: 'God this storm is hell, my tent is reaching loose and sand whipping the whole time, spent the afternoon reinforcing pegs … visibility at four yards.'

'This storm continued for about three days,' he wrote subsequently. 'After my tent had gone I had my white scout car brought over which is fairly sand proof and had my bed put up there. Went into Alexandria and had a bath at the Union Club, terrific queue, mainly Household Cavalry, what joy to be away from the permanent whipping sand and flapping canvas … Every other letter I censored had some remark about Lady Astor's statement about troops in the Middle East having a Mediterranean holiday[5]. Wish she had been in that storm, the wind reached 95mph.'

The whole Brigade was at Burg El Arab ready to be put on ships for Italy. At the beginning of April many officers travelled to Cairo for Mike Bird's[6] wedding to Yvonne followed by a cricket match and a regimental dance in the evening. They left Burg El Arab early in the morning of 1st April and made it to the wedding just in time: 'Flew

Left: Mohamed Ali – the snake man with two cobras
Right: William enjoys a trip on a felucca

Luxor, March 1944. Shooting duck from a felucca on the Nile with Larry Fyffe (left) and Keith James (far right).

on down that long straight road steady 52mph with my heel on the accelerator … changed and shaved and on to the cathedral to find Colonel Douglas and Yvonne standing on the steps. Good wedding, about 50 people, Mike looking petrified! On to a flat where there was first class scoff and rare old party.' They stayed in Shepheards and had lunch at the Turf Club the following day, before leaving the social whirl of Cairo for the last time. Shepheards itself later burnt down in the 1950s.

Before they left North Africa they had to assist militarily with one last spell of activity in North Africa. Two mutinies had broken out on political grounds among the Greek forces: they had been settled but when a third broke out in April 1944 just as they were expected to embark for Europe the Commander-in-Chief of the Middle East Forces, General Sir Bernard Paget, took it seriously.

'In the middle of an officers' football match with Warwick Yeomanry we got word that the Greeks were mutinying in Alexandria,' William wrote in his diary.

'We stood to but nothing happened till about 0300 hours when a Greek Sgt Guard Commander arrived to say they had arrested their officers and were drawing their army. The next day we moved off to Alexandria … General Paget ordered the arrest of the chief of merchant navy who had barricaded himself in a flat in Mohammed Ali Square. At 1500 hrs he was due to be arrested and fearing shooting we were called out to assist. B Company threw a cordon round the house two deep, there was a large crowd but it was fairly quiet, at 5 minutes past the Chief of Police entered with the Provost Marshall, Douglas Darling and a section of D Company and some MPs. After a pause he came out and was popped into a car and whisked off after a lot of jabbering and raising of fists with his companions on the veranda.'

The battalion was relieved from Alexandria in time to clamber on board a ship bound for Italy. As the time came to depart William reflected on all the school friends injured, captured or killed during his days in North Africa: '… I wonder if I can run through them: Oliver Steel, was RNVR, David Dickson, POW?, David W, RAF, Michael Hargreaves, Grenadier Guards, Mark Phipps, Coldstream Guards, Hugh Arbuthnot, Welsh Guards, Porchy, Household Cavalry, Tony Lyttleton, Humphrey Fitzroy, Coldstream Guards, Mike de Chair, killed Tunis[7], 18th Lancers, Julian Holland Hibbert, Coldstream Guards, badly wounded and paralysed, David Colman, KRRC, killed Alamein, Pat Nugent, Grenadier Guards, killed Tunis and how many others whom one cannot reel straight off the list owing to this memory destroying 'middle east'?' He left Egypt in April with B Company, of which he was now second-in-command, travelling as the advance party. 'Away from sandstorms now!'

Notes:
1 Gilbert Talbot was killed in France in June 1944 aged 22.
2 3100 BC
3 Wife of the Ambassador, Sir Miles Lampson.
4 Hatshepsut
5 Nancy Astor had asserted that the Eighth Army was 'dodging D-Day'.
6 Captain Mike Bird, C Company, 7th Battalion.
7 William found out details of de Chair's death later: "Mike de Chair was only slightly wounded in the leg and developed rheumatic fever which killed him."

Chapter Twelve
Agnes' War

Mrs Brownlow writes to her children

WAR BROKE out not long after Agnes began her work at Ballywhite, but it did not disrupt the household as none of the staff joined the army. Without conscription nobody was made to enlist, although Frank and Tommy White's brother Jim did join the army and they did not see him for a decade.

When Civil Defence Units were set up across the country in 1940 Frank put himself forward to help out. He started out in the Cloughy Unit with William who had just left Eton. Frank also drove William's father 'the Colonel', who was in charge of several such units, to his meetings across Northern Ireland. Frank remembers that some of the men in the Cloughy Unit needed help with William's English accent, 'they didn't know what he said … our work was up at the castle [Kirkistown], you went up for an hour or two and the other boys slept and then they went up. We were looking out for invasion.' Frank spent evenings up at the castle as 'watch keeper' but he never saw any action on his guard.

With the war came a variety of changes, noticeably the blackout curtains to ensure no light at all could be seen from the outside. Mrs Brownlow arranged for curtains to be made on roller blinds to ease their nightly use. The rule was that every window that would show light was covered with black cloth. In many houses the shutters were nailed in so the cloths could hang permanently. Agnes particularly remembers the great black curtains outside the cloakroom at Ballywhite at the servants' entrance to the house.

Ballywhite was relatively self-sufficient, milk came from their own cows and butter and cream was churned in their own dairy, and with two gardeners most of the vegetables eaten were grown at home. Mrs Brownlow had hens and they pickled eggs and fruit, such as pears and apples, which were stored in large jars so that they could use them as treats for guests or on special occasions. Agnes hated the eggs, "ugh they had an awful taste."

"We'd want for nothing in those days," said Frank. Obviously with war everybody took on extra jobs, and Agnes found herself helping out in the hayfields, using pitch forks to put the hay into stooks. "It was heavy work but great fun to be outside." The other job Agnes and others took on was to knit socks, gloves and hats for the troops which would go into Portaferry and be sent off in packages together with blankets made from any scraps of material. Everything was used: there was no wastage at this time. "Everyone was knitting and working and making things," recalls Agnes who willingly did her bit of extra work.

There were also evacuees, some from England and others from Belfast. A family called Herdman came to live at Ballywhite when they were evacuated from Belfast. The three children moved with their mother into a small flat intended for a driver and lived quite separately from everyone in the house.

Colonel Brownlow tried to do his bit for the war effort by removing the iron gates to Ballywhite and offering them as scrap metal to make weapons. He replaced them with wooden ones but his handing over of his iron gates proved to be a pointless gesture. They were never used but they were not returned and after the war they had them remade by a local blacksmith.

With war came rationing which was organised via coupons for petrol and clothes and there was an allowance of half a pound of butter and sugar per household per week. The Irish Free State[1] remained neutral in the Second World War and although nobody was allowed to make trips across the border for the purpose of bringing back food it did not stop anyone and smuggling was commonplace. "It was illegal to do it, but a lot of them did it," remembers Frank. "They searched you on the way into the Free State and the way out. I went on a bus, there was another boy from down the road here, Gerry Porter, a good bit older than me, and we bought stuff, a whole lot of stuff, and we were on the bus and pushed the stuff in below the seat. We sat there and they asked us if we had anything to declare, and we certainly had." Clothes coupons were arranged along with food rationing and everyone had to conform, there were no tights or stockings and clothes were scarce. Petrol was rationed to one gallon per week and trips to Portaferry were ideally made by bicycle to save petrol. Frank drove Mrs Brownlow

Anne driving the tractor on the farm

Col. Brownlow with Anne

when necessary but she stayed at home mostly and spent a lot of her time gardening. The visits of William, Cam and James in the early days of the war made their parents very happy.

As war continued the barrage balloons were put in place and to many people's disbelief the *Luftwaffe* eventually made it to Northern Ireland. "When it did come we could hear them and see them, one of the housemaids at Ballywhite woke me up, I thought it was thunder," remembers Agnes. 'That's German planes,' she told me. They all went up to the top of the mountain and watched them bombing Belfast, all the flames going up, Mrs Brownlow, everybody." Agnes went over to the lodge, to Frank's brother Tommy and his wife; their twins William (Billy) and Elinor were got out of bed and taken outside across the drive to the gateway overlooking the lough to see the action. "The planes came over the bar with a sort of drumming noise. When Belfast was bombed the sky lit up, it was like a fireworks display."

Frank recalls how Bangor was also bombed, "I knew two people killed in it, two Taggarts killed in it, they are buried in the Abbacy. There were instances when bombs were disposed of on the aircraft's way home to lighten the load: "There was one dropped in Alan's Brae, a field near Kircubbin, luckily no-one was hurt!"

"After the bombing I went down to the Albert Bridge in Belfast, and there was a row of houses and the first two or three weren't there, they were blown to pieces, and the beds and sofas were sitting there," recalls Frank who drove Mrs Brownlow and some of the staff, including Agnes, to Belfast to see Queen Elizabeth who had come to witness the bomb damage. For her visit they lined the route in Shaftesbury

Square, which was seriously damaged, and waved frantically when the Queen went past.

In many ways day-to-day life at Ballywhite continued almost as normal during the war. There were less visitors but the family and close friends continued to be entertained. 'Today the Bangors came to lunch and Juggler and Harry [dogs] were found having a glorious tug of war with his hat, which was a complete wreck – Lord Bangor was wonderful and said it was a very old hat and already had holes in it from a bonfire he had been making the other day which I am sure was not the case,' Mrs Brownlow wrote in a letter to William. 'Would you believe it, that pair who must be over 70 and over 60 rowed themselves from Castle Ward to Portaferry and back to have lunch with us. I wish you could have seen them they were a grand sight.' Agnes remembers their visits, "but I would be away in the background, I would have seen them coming and hidden, I was always like that."

But for those back home the war brought worry, separation and tragedy. Mrs Brownlow, who had lost her first husband in battle, was desperately concerned for her sons' safety. "The Colonel sat in the smoking room, and Mrs Brownlow sat in the drawing room writing letters and that. She worried a lot about her sons. I used to see her out feeding the hens, she would be crying coming in and I would ask her what was wrong. She'd say it was 'those blessed boys, they are a worry'. She was in an awful state when William was shot. They were both in an awful state about that. She worried about them all the time." Mrs Brownlow managed to get hold of a few hives and during the war she started to keep bees. Anne saw her tending to them as a form of therapy which helped her deal with the all the uncertainties of war. "If she was worried by the news bulletins, or heard the fighting was bad, she would go out to her bees and talk to them; in her bee hat, veil and gloves, they were a source of great comfort to her."

Mrs Brownlow's anxiety escalated when witnessing the very real suffering of their neighbours. Lord and Lady Bangor's son, Edward, was working as a war correspondent for the BBC when he was taken a Prisoner of War. 'They have not heard anything from their son for four or five months,' (Edward Ward who used to broadcast at the beginning of the war) 'he is a POW in Italy, was taken during the retreat back to Egypt I think,' Mrs Brownlow wrote to William. 'They are worrying a bit with all the bombing of Italy and whether he is getting enough food.'

The tragedy of their neighbouring family, the Nugents, was heartbreaking and affected Mrs Brownlow deeply. Sir Roly and Lady Nugent had three children, Pat, John and Elizabeth, and by 1944 both boys had been killed in action. William's friend from St Aubyn's, Eton and Ireland, Pat, was killed in Tunisia and his brother, John, the following year in Italy: they were 22 and 19. "When the Nugents were killed she [Mrs Brownlow] thought that something would happen to her boys then," recalls Agnes.

Agnes watched Mrs Brownlow try to come to terms with the tragedy of Pat Nugent's death, and saw her at her desk writing to her sons giving them the details and hoping they might have heard more for her to tell Sir Roly.

'He seems to have done extraordinarily well, from a letter Roly has just received from his Colonel who says that in the fighting the previous day his company commander was either killed or badly wounded and the company 2 i/c went up to take over for the assault on the hill that day and shortly before the time to start he was hit in the hand and bleeding so much had to go back to dressing station and the Colonel gave the command of the Company to Pat and had very little time to explain the details with him, but he went off and that was the last he saw of him, racing off to his company. They achieved their objective with only 20 men left and no one seems to know where Pat was wounded or killed. He was found in a field which had been long corn and grass at the time of the battle with two guardsmen, who had also only been reported wounded at first, too – it sounds as though there had been a bit of slackness being so long finding he was missing not in hospital and having another search, almost two and a half months.'

Agnes' brother, Albert, had joined the Ulster Rifles and was employed as a driver for Colonel Panter[2] who lived near Newcastle in County Down. There were a number of men from Portaferry who went away to fight, but Agnes lost no friends in the fighting and the deaths of the familiar faces of the Nugent brothers were the greatest tragedy she can recall. The new cook at Ballywhite, Miss Sharp ("and she was sharp"), knew all about the sadness the Nugent family had to bear at Portaferry House, "she was great with the cook over there so we heard it all. Lots of people went away, a lot of Portaferry people went – but it was the Nugents that died. I remember them both coming up to the house before, John had glasses and a thin face, Patrick was fat and tall, a lovely good looking fella, just a pity."

Notes:
1 The Irish Free State became the Irish Republic in 1949.
2 The father of the future Mrs William Brownlow

Chapter Thirteen
Cassino to Florence

"And then the hot rake of War was slowly drawn up the length of Italy"

Winston Churchill

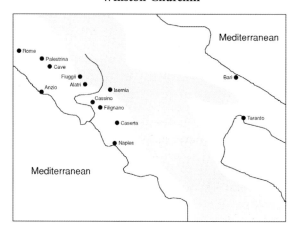

Italy: April-June 1944

AN ITALIAN front had become inevitable and General Sir Harold Alexander[1], a Northern Irishman, was put in charge of Allied Armies in Italy. Under his command two armies fought their way the length of Italy: the British and Commonwealth Eighth Army under the command of Lieutenant-General Oliver Leese[2] and the US Fifth Army, under General Mark Clark.

When William arrived in Taranto in April 1944 the biggest problem on the road ahead was the German held town of Cassino. From January the Allies had fought and failed to get the Germans out of Cassino and a monastery strategically placed 1703 feet above sea level at Monte Cassino, half a mile outside the town. If Cassino was taken it would enable an advance to Rome but it was proving extremely difficult and in May another assault on the town was planned.

Charles Mott-Radclyffe, William's company commander, was fluent in Italian having spent two years before the war working in the Italian Embassy. On arrival he used his language skills in the docks in Taranto to arrange for a driver to take him and William to their transit camp, avoiding an eight-mile march. He was a Conservative MP for Windsor doing his war service with the Rifle Brigade. Along the road out of Taranto William took pleasure in the green European countryside.

He wrote in his diary:

'As one got into the country it was unbelievably grand to see trees, corn grain and stone walls. The green of the [Nile] Delta was far too lush, though grand after the desert … Interesting looking at the Iti army and navy disporting themselves. On the [sea] front women nearly all wearing smartish shoes but with thick cork soles to save leather. The army are unshaved and very dirty. There are some pretty slummy areas outside, little better than the Egyptian [slums], and as dirty. Don't look too hungry – one sees American tinned food in shops.'

The rest of the battalion arrived in early May and together they set off stopping when they reached the mountains east of Cassino.

'We stopped just beyond Isernia where a bridge across the ravine had been beautifully blown and waited till dark to move on. Went on up to Filignano after dark as part of the road was under observation. Very steep and tricky road up, afraid some of our drivers might go over but all right, two New Zealand colonels had been killed the night before. Put ourselves into a little field near all the New Zealand workshops and camouflaged like mad. Quite a nice spot out of observation, surrounded by wooded hills … we sit on reverse slope of one hill by day and forward by night, likewise the Bosche. He has Monte Croce, which overlooks us, but the Itis have captured a very high mountain on our right, which dominates all, a very great feat.'

As they waited outside Cassino the planned assault swung into action: 'The Colonel informed the battalion that the big attack would start in Italy that night at 2300 hours. The Polish Corps[3] attacking Cassino from the north since the line runs North East. The Indian Division attacking up the coast and the French left of Cassino.' The BBC time check at 2300 hours on May 11th was the signal for the guns to open fire.

'I went over to C Company to have a sharpener where there were Larry Fyffe, Mike Bird, Dick Adams, self, later Charles M-R, all except C had heard our opening battle in Egypt. At exactly 2300 hours the sky lit up and I looked at my watch by it, for 40 minutes the sky was permanently lit, though the noise here was not great for 2,000 guns. This barrage was fixed counter battery to knock out as many guns as possible. Our planes droned about otherwise we heard little but the dull booming and nightingales singing like mad.'

The attack caught the Germans by surprise and the following day some British forces pushed their way beyond the town into the Liri valley. The battle was fought by land and air, the RAF concentrating on disrupting German communications and the American Air Force in full attack.

'The sound of 300 bombers going over early this morning was most impressive, thank heaven they are not letting the Americans bomb targets near our lines. They did a wonderful raid on Cassino but they emptied all their bombs on Isernia

James (left) and William meet at Caserta

(about 25 miles out) knocked Isernia to bits and hit Corps HQ knocking out most of the Corps Commander's Caravan!'

Their role in the attack was to deceive the Germans into believing there were many troops behind their lines. It was vital that the Germans did not notice the disappearance from Italy to England of the many troops needed for the forthcoming invasion. 'Our part of the line,' William wrote, 'will put on a 'mock up' to contain as many troops as possible this end, troops being very thin here at the best of times.' After watching the opening battle he got an hour's sleep before being called to carry out this 'mock up': 'Firing everything for 30 minutes while eight tanks swooned down the road with their silencers off as if an attack were coming in from us, then 30 minutes of nothing, then another shoot though no infantry involved.' They then took over positions on Monte Croce from the Parachute Regiment. The ground battle was bloody; utterly determined Polish forces fought on under heavy fire and eventually captured the monastery but at a great cost, 1,000 Poles were killed and thousands more were wounded. The German Field Marshal ordered a German retreat and by 17th May German troops on Monte Cassino had withdrawn.

The battalion was moved to Allied Headquarters at Caserta on 17th May where it set up camp in a peach orchard[4]. James passed through Caserta returning from sitting the Regular Commission Selection Board in Naples and stayed the night. 'He was in good form though only just out of CCS with a poisoned finger,' William wrote in his diary. 'He is not enjoying the role at the moment, holding six miles of front patrolling and shooting.'

It was a considerable advantage to the Rifle Brigade that the Allied Supreme Commander in the Mediterranean was General Jumbo Wilson, a Rifle Brigade man. General Jumbo gave Colonel Douglas the news at GHQ in Caserta that three Rifle Brigade battalions would join together to form the 61st Infantry Brigade[5] with another Rifle Brigade man in charge, Brigadier Adrian Gore: 'Douglas was so excited that he made me drive him home.' It was the first time in the Rifle Brigade's

Passing through a village

A burnt out tank by the side of the road

Peter Wolfe Taylor with an Italian soldier

history that a brigade composed entirely of its battalions had existed. The news was not all good as it was thought that their role as motorised infantry would have to be reconsidered in light of the mountainous Italian terrain and most of their vehicles were taken away.

Ahead of them the push towards Rome seemed to be going according to plan. 'The news from here is very satisfactory,' William wrote in a letter home on 25th May, 'In fact it looks as if we shall have to hurry up if we are going to get employment in this area.' He assuaged any fears his parents might have by letting them know that the only deaths to date were accidents, 'one signaller was walking to latrine at night and went over the quarry and died, Colonel Douglas' driver died too, he fell over a cliff top.' Spirits remained good and one night they had a 'vino party': 'Great discussion during dinner whether it is possible to fall flat on one's face – Peter Shepherd-Cross tried first but put his arms out. Then Douglas with a crash! Then Ted Eccles said that's 'mush', fell flat and nearly broke his nose.'

He began to take an interest in the locals' way of life and began to understand how much they disliked the Germans. 'A lot of people slaughtered by the Germans here,' he reflected. 'Found one little village where their main industry seems to be making ropes from rush stuff, having a sort of wheel which turns it while the children go along putting wisp of rushes in like making a straw rope. This goes on all along the village street … three old women have taken a great liking to Charles and self as he talks Italian and they say I look like a brother of theirs who is a POW in England.'

The 61st Infantry Brigade set off from Caserta in a slow-moving convoy. 'I am sitting at the moment in my vehicle looking at Monastery Hill with Cassino behind,' he wrote on 29th May, 'what a place to hold, sheer cliff with the monastery on top, now of course absolute ruins. Everything is flat here, all the farmhouses, trees topped off and battered crops torn up, the birds of course still sing.' In the Liri Valley their role was to give cover to engineers rebuilding bridges:

'There is really nothing about though there are small parties of Germans in the valley who have been cut off and are getting hold of civilian clothes. Thousands of flies and no doubt bugs but our room looks fairly clean. The inhabitants started turning up again this afternoon with their bundles of bedding and two cows and about five sheep and a donkey. I suppose they had moved off during the fighting. However, they are lucky to have a farm left, crops still standing and a lot of farmers spraying vines as usual, the Germans only left two days ago.'

Close to the town of Alatri the 7th Battalion moved into the advance guard position in the convoy, which meant little sleep and often travelling by moonlight. There was no sight of the enemy until an officer[6] was killed. His death sparked immediate firing from both sides, and brought the battalion back into action for the first time in over a year. It was only the beginning as the *Rifle Brigade Chronicle* for

1945 notes: 'We were to remain in action with hardly a break for more than twelve months and until the end of the war.' They took prisoners – 'filthy dirty, half undressed' – and discovered there were more Germans in the surrounding hills.

With his men William climbed the terraced olive groves and took more prisoners, but as he neared the crest of one hill their communication sets started to fail and Colonel Douglas gave an order for them to return. It was fortunate as they had come within thirty yards of the enemy's main position. His job was to interrogate prisoners. 'An Austrian Special Alpine, very willing to talk … battalion pleased with the information – not bad as none could speak English or I German.'

'Scruffy Downing[7] went further up hill with Sergeant Roberts to see what was there, and when guns opened fire Sergeant Roberts lost touch with him. They ran into some Germans at about 15 yards, he has not yet returned so do not know what has happened to him. Two men wounded by snipers coming down and one killed, 14 German POW.' Scruffy Downing, who at 20 was the youngest officer in the battalion, had been shot in the head. His body was found and brought down off the hill a couple of days later and he and a Rifleman were buried by the side of the road.

In the days that followed they made good progress and by 4th June 1944 the Fifth Army marched into Rome. Before he even heard the news William was in celebratory mode as he had gathered some Etonians to celebrate 'The Fourth of June'[8]:

'We celebrated 4th June in fairly historic way as we were standing by to move off but got Larry Fyffe, James Keith, Maxie Pemberton, Charles Radclyffe to come over and drink to *alma mater*. Standing there drinking vino as scotch getting low when a Grenadier Guards Major pulled up in a jeep. He had come through from the Anzio beachhead one of the first men right through Route 6. Asked him if he was an OE and he was – more sharpeners!'

On 6th June the D-day landings were made in Normandy and spirits were high as they travelled on towards Palestrina, a town to the west of Rome. 'INVASION OF EUROPE,' William wrote the following evening in his diary.

'We heard the German news agency report that Allied troops had landed in France over the 19 Set this morning and since on the BBC news. What a great coincidence it actually hitting the same day Rome was captured. We are now sitting about 5 Kilometres from Rome waiting for a position to be cleared the other side of the Tiber … The King spoke … we all gathered round the company wireless and listened. Rather disappointed with too much sermon aspect to it … We are in an extraordinary situation as we are right up and some [other Allied troops] beyond the Tiber yet still behind us on the route we came through are the Herman Goering Division, 3 Panzer Grenadier Regiments, 90th Light and an Infantry Div! I suppose somebody is dealing with them.'

From Rome the race was on towards Florence, and in the early hours of 9th June they set off north of Rome travelling along the Tiber. Their first objective was to push the Germans out of Terni. Timing the pace forward was difficult and they had to pull up when the road ahead was blocked by troops running behind schedule. While they were waiting for the road to clear ahead they were attacked:

'Then all hell was let lose, we must have been well in view of an Observation Post as they started shelling us about 1100 hours, thank heaven we had time to get slit trenches dug. The shelling continued for about three hours, some of the most intensive we have had including Alamein … our area was bad enough one landed four yards from our company headquarter slits … Peter S-C wounded, Peter Bowring, Sandy Brigstocke, total in battalion about five killed including Corporal Cann[9], A Company Medical Orderly, battalion photographer and Sergeant Conus[10], the Intelligence Sergeant, and about 30 wounded, very shattering casualties when not even fighting. Why on earth they couldn't have left us until the Guards had made further progress I cannot think.'

The following morning the Padre held a moving service, which despite pouring rain was attended by a large number of riflemen. They reached Terni on 13th June, the day the town fell to the Allies, and William described the capture of the town in his diary as it was happening in front of him:

'The Germans are moving out the other side [of Terni] with some sitting on a bridge trying to blow it. I can see a lot of demolition going up and machine gun fire, think it is our Bren guns. Hashell has just come back in Colonel's jeep for a truck to take back the prisoners. We hear the bridge is blown but we do not know how it is going, it is all quiet now, no firing.'

They took the town and moved in:

'Terrific welcome from Itis, yelling, clapping, throwing flowers, [they hand me] a woman who they say was working for the Germans on telegraph. I do not know what to do with her so tell CSM Roberts to put her in a top room of the house beside which I have my HQ where there is a bed. She promptly has hysterics and pleads and paws me, I just send her up with Chucky Ball and leave her all night! Get to bed about 0200 hrs, wake up at 0500 … find Tim Dewhurst and Hugh Meldrum in bed, Tim reading *The Times* and drinking tea! Colonel comes in on his way to a bath! What a war!'

They moved on until they were north of Todi where they met 'thousands of hysterical refugees coming back over the river' Tiber telling tales of drunken German troops and of fascists creating trouble in the villages beyond. The local population treated the Allies as saviours:

'I was met by vast crowds at entrance to a village [in the hills near Todi] where I found the Germans gone but people very worried, two families had been killed in reprisals and several women mauled … A few Germans still supposed to be in a farm nearby, so I take a party out but they have gone leaving a trail of misery, old

Johnnie Persse (left) and Keith Egglestone

The cost of war - Persse's grave among the many in Perugia.

man having a stroke, women and men hysterical with fear, wish we had found them as would have shot them out of hand. We took another German prisoner and had to protect him from Itis, one old man with a scythe prowling around trying to get at him.'

When they arrived outside Perugia the battle to take it had begun and they were sent straight away to their fighting positions a few miles south west of the town. The strength of the German resistance was great and on the battalion's first day two officers, Johnnie Persse[11] and Cripps Whitehead[12] were killed. William recorded: 'Keith Egglestone came up and got Johnnie Persse in after dark … such a loss … still trying to get the dead down to bury centrally.' After two days of fighting one company alone had 22 casualties of whom 16 were killed; the Colonel was also injured, hit in the shoulder by a large shell splinter. The company set up headquarters in a farmhouse: 'In a little room with Charles, plaster falls every time a gun goes. Some of the civilians returned, and women with babies in rooms either side, just one more maddening noise!'

The 16/5 Lancer and the Rifle Brigade were the first regiments into Perugia on 19th June. *The Eighth Army News* of 22nd June noted the Rifle Brigade's contribution to the taking of the town itself:

'The battle of Perugia lasted several days, with the Hun fighting hard for ground dominating the town. These positions were taken, one by one, by the Rifle Brigade and as they took the westerly road in the area of the railway station infantry advanced into the town.'

Charles Mott-Radclyffe and Max Pemberton went into Perugia with William on 24th June:

'The town is still well intact. We went to a hotel where there was a hall porter with frock coat. Charles had stayed there before and managed to persuade them to carry some buckets of water to a room and we had a bath and lounged on lovely beds with sheets, what luxury. I was looking out of the window to a lovely view when I was disturbed by a few bashes as some shells landed on the football field where tanks were leaguered … Charles met two English women who had been in the embassy at Rome and married Itis, had terrible time as interned and gulled by Gestapo. There is also a Colonel Roche, late of the Irish Guards, who has been living there and welcomed 10RB [10th Battalion, Rifle Brigade] in uniform.'

They returned to casualties from the many mines in the area. The Perugia losses took their toll and with invasions planned for France there were no replacements coming from England. It was decided to work with three companies instead of four. William wrote to his parents on 25th June:

'I am still going strong as no doubt you will be worried by us being mentioned as being in the van at Perugia. We had a fairly tricky time but sorted out now and hope to be quiet for a bit. Poor young Johnnie Persse was killed though – his

Fun at Regimental Birthday celebrations in Faella.

Faella

family will be desperately upset, especially as he is an only child.'

At the beginning of July they were sent to a 'rest area' south of Lake Trasimeno. William took a quiet moment to describe his nomadic existence in his diary:

'One lives almost entirely in and around your vehicle, it is your home and that of your crew so you are never far distant from them … When we are continually on the move as we were a few weeks ago it was very difficult to get settled at any time as one was nearly always at half hour notice to move. But when we know we shall have a static day then can get settled in. I have a bivvy [tent] fixed and rolled to the side of the vehicles which unrolls out from the side. My bed goes in the lowest part and my table (a roll up one) and chair go near the side of the truck where there is just room to sit up properly. We feed normally off the mobile cooker the same as the troops as not really possible to have a mess going. Though if we know we are safe from a move I get the rations collected and cooked by the servant.

Charles and I normally feed together and also the subalterns have their stuff brought over to my vehicle and have a drink. In the evenings if we are static Dick Adams, Larry Fyffe and Mike Bird normally forgather at one of our vehicles and have a chat and drink till about 2200hrs … It is really not a bad life, but the worst part is never knowing how long we will be static.'

By 10th July they were beyond Cortona in foothills when the attack on Arrezzo was launched: 'There were about 70 casualties in all including, I think, about eight dead. One extraordinary incident was when C Company stretcher-bearers were out collecting in dead they nearly fell into a hole which turned out to be two well concealed spandau gun posts. The Germans gave them cigs etc. – they came back![13]' Arrezzo fell to the Allies on 15th July.

Charles Mott-Radclyffe returned to his constituency and while Dick Adams, his replacement, was still recovering from wounds William stood in temporarily as company commander. He saw action for his first time in charge of a company when the battalion was sent from their base at San Leo, west of Arezzo, to take Castiglion Fibocchi. He was leading the company as they went towards Castiglion: 'We got to within 1000 yards of village when spandaus opened all round. Bill Raynor's platoon was pinned in the ditch as were the rest behind. After some difficulty I got two platoons back to go round the north and come into them there. It was very dark and the ground terrible, Bob Jones' platoon leading and Max's platoon behind. We got down near a sniper when a spandau opened up into our flank at about 30 yards range and grenades started landing in the midst of everybody. The machine guns were ripping the grass all round. I saw that in the dark nothing could be done so ordered the company to get back as best as they could. We got out with only three casualties, amazed there were not more … All through the day we were shelled and mortared, very unpleasant lying in the hot sun in slits … We spent an anxious evening wondering if we should be relieved or have another day there. Thank goodness we were told to move out at last light. Total casualties in B Company four wounded and only two killed and twelve wounded in battalion. The two [dead] had a direct hit in their slit trench – a fearsome sight, half a thumb lying on one side a leg on another.'

From San Leo they were allowed a short stint at an official rest area at Laterina. Even in the rest areas accidents happened which senselessly reduced their numbers. 'Had an annoying accident when a Rifleman was cleaning his Bren in the back of a truck and it went off going through the back of a Rifleman in front, piercing his lung. He has since died.' While there they heard on radio that an attempt had been made on Hitler's life and Churchill broadcast saying war might be over sooner than anyone dared to hope.

Florence was the next goal, but the situation there was peculiar because it was not held by the Allies nor ceded by the Germans: 'apparently we gaily send people in to shop in the south half and the Bosche do the same in the north,' he wrote to his parents, '[Brigadier] Adrian Gore sent a liaison officer up to try and find a villa he knew and see how it is.' Sheer cliffs surrounded the Arno valley leading to Florence and when William sent out his first recce patrol it was fired on from all sides and two men disappeared and neither they nor their bodies were found. Dick Adams returned to take over B Company and William reverted to second in command. They tried to continue their way along the Arno valley but under continuous fire their progress forward was minimal. He noted:

'Company getting bomb happy … wonderful peaches and plums around here, huge orchards of them, I've eaten thousands. Cook knocked up an open peach tart last night, very good! Oh for the end of the war and getting relieved for a rest … had a comfortable day lying on a bed reading with odd people dropping in from 10RB. Charles Calistan[14], DCM, was killed a great loss, he loved war.'

They moved forward slowly, carrying out attacks on the enemy on the opposite slopes and sleeping in farmhouses and on one occasion a monastery. One of William's platoons ran into an ambush while out patrolling:

'The rear section was ambushed in Pieve … Corporal Tetlow was very bad, his right leg half off from a grenade and his left foot half gone, I hear his left foot was amputated. Howarth's right leg had a big hole and Wilson was badly wounded on his left side and he died, we buried him in the cemetery with help of local priest, he was such a nice boy and so young.'

During the shelling on Pieve they were given a lot of help from locals who were happy to keep them updated on the Germans movements:

'One sad thing is the priest from Pieve who helped with the wounded and took them into his house, went to another village to see if it was clear and if so to ring the church bells unfortunately four Germans came back to pick up a telephone and took him away. He had been very good helping us with this landlord and also looking after his people – he even lent the altar cloth as a pillow for Corporal Tetlow. We sent a cross up to young Wilson's grave, and found they have put flowers on it and are looking after it.'

The number of dead and the very few replacements available for operations in Italy were taking their toll. Dick Worsley[15], a friend of William's who served as an officer in the 2nd battalion, reflected almost 60 years later on the tragic 'wastage rate' of young officers in Italy.

'It was something like one a month – from any battalion in action – twelve officers a year were being either wounded or brought out of battle or being killed sadly. It was tough from that point of view – very – and one forgets that. The advancing was not quick, it was a slog. All the bridges were destroyed and everywhere you came to a bridge had to be rebuilt and you had to capture the ground to do that and so on and so on. It was not spectacular to the extent that there were great armoured pushes it was a grind.'

Allied troops took Florence on 13th August and from France the news reached them that Paris had fallen:

'I am not banking my hopes on too early an end, these Germans are such strange creatures, why is the army still fighting? Granted a lot of POWs coming in do not know France has been invaded. They are like machines – if told to do a thing they do it. Just like these atrocities, a POW on being asked how he could take part said we were told to and that was that, they would go fighting even if they knew they were beaten.'

From their positions in the Arno valley they were given a rest period to be taken at Faella, the timing of which coincided with the Regiment's birthday on 25th August. While there they received orders to move immediately to Leccio where they would be taken temporarily under the command of the Fifth Army. Everyone was handed a *Personal Message from the Army Commander*, Lieutenant-General Oliver Leese, congratulating them on their efforts so far:

'You have won great victories. To advance 220 miles from Cassino to Florence in three months is a notable achievement in the Eighth Army's history – to each one of you in the Eighth Army and in the Desert Air Force, my grateful thanks…

To those who go temporarily under command of the great Fifth Army – Your role is vital to our success.'

Notes:

1 Son of the Earl of Caledon.

2 He replaced Montgomery who had left to plan the invasion of NW Europe; he was also the godfather of Patrick Forde, the future Mrs William Brownlow's step-brother.

3 Polish Corps with the Eighth Army; the French Expeditionary Corps with the Fifth.

4 It may have been here that he discovered booby-trapped peach trees, his family recall he never trusted Italians after this.

5 2nd, 7th and 10th Battalions.

6 Lieutenant 'Larry' FJ Lowrison (1916-1944).

7 Lieutenant 'Scruffy' SJ Downing (1923-1944).

8 Eton College's open day for parents; the date commemorates King George III's birthday.

9 Corporal HEJ Cann of Stockwell died aged 31.

10 Sergeant CF Conus of South Ruislip died aged 24.

11 Lieutenant J H Persse (1922-1944), the only son of a racing trainer.

12 Lieutenant Robin Christopher John Whitehead (1923-44).

13 They were told that the wounded men they had been out looking for had been taken prisoner.

14 Lieutenant CV Calistan (1918-44) received his Distinguished Conduct Medal for his bravery at the Snipe position.

15 He went on to become General Sir Richard Worsley, GCB, OBE.

Chapter Fourteen
The Apennines

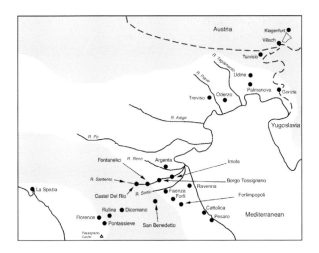

Italy: September 1944 - May 1945

THE NEXT goal was to drive the Germans behind 'The Gothic Line' which ran from La Spezia across the mountains north of Florence to the East coast of Italy. The Fifth Army's remit was to push through the Apennine range, a rugged 50 mile wide barrier of mountains.

The 7th Battalion joined the rest of their Brigade at Pontassieve near Florence and travelled on east into the mountains. Within days they were back in the action: a platoon out patrolling ran into about forty Germans and was surrounded before it realised. William helped dress their wounds on their return. He took over Headquarter Company temporarily when John Brooke was wounded. Although this brought with it the responsibility of 360 men he lived in comparative ease at the base camp. The number of enemy surrenders locally was encouraging, with some walking into platoon positions unwittingly and others coming forward to give themselves up: 'D Company Sergeant looked round coming back and noticed he had two extra men, they were Germans walking along with their hands up.' It was the beginning of September and William felt encouraged by the direction of the war: 'Most of France seems to have fallen, things are moving in Italy as well, the Gothic Line is said to have been breached, and the Germans opposite us have pulled back as well.'

Colonel Douglas Darling had recovered from his wounds and was back in charge. During a lull in activities in the mountains he asked William and Mike Bird to come into Florence with him. They stopped on their way to look at the view across the city from the Piazza Michelangelo. Florence in September 1944 was full of barbed wire and sandbagged pillboxes, and fascists acting for the enemy as snipers were still busy in the north part of the city. The residents complained that the city had been flattened but William felt that aside from the bridges ('except the one with shops on, Ponte Veccio, which has the buildings either end blown') there was remarkably little damage. In fact General Alexander had gone to considerable effort to prevent the destruction of the attractive cities and towns of Italy and Perugia, Sienna and Florence were not destroyed in the fighting. Some of the shops were open selling leather goods, umbrellas, hats and silk stockings and they found a bookshop selling English titles. Colonel Douglas took them to lunch in a large house in the Florentine hills. The Villa Capponi[1], built in 1572, was owned by a family known to Brigadier Adrian Gore and he arranged for it to be run as a leave centre for officers from his brigade. William recorded:

'It is run by an old 60th chap, Teddy Voules, who does it very well having run some hotel in peacetime, several guests: a marquesa, an American woman and her brother-in-law, a late chamberlain to King Victor E[2] and one or two others. Very amusing standing on the terrace after lunch looking at the view and drinking coffee seeing shells landing about 400 yards way.'

It was only a brief vision of civilisation and they were fast back into the hills and the fighting. Torrential rain made William's job of keeping rations supplied via heavily shelled tracks doubly treacherous. Colonel Douglas decided to relieve William of his toils with the rations and make him his adjutant. 'I saw a gratifying thing on Douglas' desk today recommending various officers for a regular commission in which D said [of me] 'I recommend this officer far above any officer I know in any of the battalions'. We are getting on very well together.' He was slightly in awe of the 30 year old Colonel Douglas and after hearing that their mothers had met in London he wrote home inquisitively, 'What's she like? He is the sort of chap you expect not to have one, but just to have happened.'

They lived in the hills behind the heavily shelled town of Rufina. They were busy taking prisoners, on one occasion finding 11 in the cellar of a church. They and the Germans were living in close quarters in the hills and often patrols wandered into enemy held territory. Their work involved helping the engineers rebuild bridges and making hill roads passable. From Rufina they took the nearby village of Perucci without much resistance and to everyone's pleasure set up their headquarters in an attractive villa complete with running water and a geyser. After a hot bath and an evening by a log fire drinking whiskey William felt perfectly content.

With the rain came mud!

1944: Villa Capponi, Florence

Rufina, to the east of Florence

Military success elsewhere in Italy and in North West Europe during the course of September meant everyone began seriously to consider an end to the war and a life beyond it. To amuse themselves the soldiers organised a sweep: 'We're holding a big sweep in the battalion on the day of peace, 50 lire tickets going well, November 11th is very popular. We had to submit names of all people who came out before 30th June 42, so a great uprising of spirits in the battalion. Very good news today on the wireless about demobilization and raising of pay. Very good show, it may help the government in the next election with any luck.'

They moved north to Dicomano and at the end of September travelled on with the rest of the Brigade to tackle the St Benedetto mountain pass. 'We did a spectacular advance into the Gothic Line, right up through a 3,000 foot pass, nine miles on foot to San Benedetto – little German reaction.' Behind them tanks and guns were moved up secretly into the hills: 'We are going to drive through the mountain in a most unexpected manner … but guns not allowed to fire, only guns a long way back to make Bosche think that no guns have been moved up, they will not even know a regiment of tanks are here!'

There was huge excitement at getting so far forward and a lack of belief in Churchill's warning – after Allied failure at Arnhem in Holland – that war could continue into the following year. 'Incredible country for fighting … we are through the middle of the Gothic Line and Portico the last stronghold is not far in front. The eyes of the Eighth Army are on us! … Churchill says he thinks war may go on two or three months into next year. Heaven forbid.' In fact the Allies failure to take Arnhem had left Germany's frontiers intact, renewed the resolve of German troops everywhere, and made another winter of fighting inevitable.

High in the Apennines winter came early and it was unseasonably cold at altitude in late September. 'Spanner thrown in the works when Colonel arrived down from C Company, he found them frozen cold, one man had died, and of the remainder several had to be carried into houses. He had moved the company back to two small houses on Monte Collina where rum, hot food etc. was dished out and came down to tell the divisional commander in no uncompromising way that he was not going to kill off his battalion by taking them up there.'

While the weather left their assault static General Kesselring encouraged German troops to cling tightly to their positions. The shelling and mortaring seemed never ending and it was with difficulty they used mules to remove the wounded from the slopes by night. They stayed slogging it out against a constant barrage well into October. In all the ugliness and tedium of the fighting the beauty of the area was not lost on William and he enjoyed the changing seasons. He was amused when two German soldiers were discovered picking blackberries and on 1st October his mind was firmly off military matters and on the start of the pheasant-shooting season. His role as adjutant tied him to a desk at battalion Headquarters

On the road through Florence

and his free time was spent in an officers' mess which had been set up for the three battalions.

'Peter Bowring and I behave like children really but is good relaxation, wish we had more like him – another chap is Balbo, the Italian Liaison Officer, who used to be in Iti Cavalry Regiment with one of their Armoured Divisions in North Africa so twit him the whole time, very nice chap and very amusing getting the other side of the picture.'

His 23rd birthday came and went unmarked but during October he escaped to Florence for a four day break with Peter Bowring, Colonel Douglas and Dick Adams. 'I shan't be sorry to get away as have been in this room almost solidly for a fortnight, total time spent outside probably three hours until today!'

'Two girls to dinner,' he writes of an evening at the Villa Capponi, 'very pleasant, had English governesses so were fairly anglicised. Duc and Duchessa Schwarza staying again, she has a Scottish mother and is highly vivacious getting off with everybody, Brigadier Adrian, Colonel Chris and subalterns all included. Antonio, the husband, is very quiet and pleasant and very elegant but completely ruled – though he stands no nonsense and when she disappears he goes to see what is going on as happened when she and Adrian disappeared into the library after dinner!!'

The battalion moved back to Dicomano with Divisional and Brigade Headquarters. 'Wonderful sight of caravans churning out, traffic … Mess being packed up, chicken, turkeys and geese being rounded up by their respective messes, tearing in and out of the traffic, everybody from Brigadier down trying to field them.'

William received a telegram from his mother saying that Pat Nugent's 19-year-old brother, John, was missing from the Grenadier Guards who were fighting alongside him in Italy. Everyone at Ballywhite was keen to know if he had heard anything about his death. He learnt he had been killed on 2nd October in the mountains north of Castiglione dei Pepoli, a town north of Florence. He felt extremely sad and sorry for Sir Roly and Lady Nugent who had lost both of their sons to the war. 'Poor Roly and Cynthia,' he wrote home. 'I heard from John's battalion, though they will have heard the details by now, I will send extracts of it to them as it may interest them. I wrote to them saying I was trying to get news.'

At the end of October they were redirected to a different section of the mountains, this time further north around Castel del Rio on the eastern edge of the Apennines. It rained and the mud made conditions yet more challenging. Colonel Douglas and William went about their company visits in the hills by horse. The Germans continued to hold on and the fighting was a never-ending ding-dong battle. The casualty rate was high and there were no reinforcements arriving as any new recruits were needed in France. In two direct hits from mortar bombs in one morning there were 25 casualties: 'Terribly unlucky, daren't think how long it will take to get them down, even on the track people are walking on hands and knees in mud to get up.' The weather prevented the Colonel from getting down the tracks to a lunch with the Foreign Secretary, Anthony Eden, at Brigade Headquarters in Dicomano. 'However he [Eden] sent a very nice signal saying he was well aware of our conditions,' William wrote in a letter to his parents, 'and what we'd been doing and sending best wishes to all his brother riflemen.' The rain brought with it the additional danger of landslides: 'I asked which landslide had killed the B Company chap as we passed over one,' William writes in his diary of a conversation with his new battalion Second-in-Command, Vivian Street. 'He said 'I think this one,' and then said, 'here he is,' and sure enough the rain had washed some of earth away leaving his boots sticking out.'

They left the hills with snow falling all around them on 11th November and travelled to Passignano Castle, the official rest area south of Florence. Every few weeks during the winter they were withdrawn back to this area for a rest and refit: 'Vivian went off to Bari to get some drink he knows of, having a liqueur sent over by plane from Yugoslavia!3… Colonel and I do our evening duet on our hunting horns, sharing the music! (Some calls taken from a book of Vivian's called *Fox Hunter Weekend Book*) we hear the rifleman yapping and barking downstairs!' They returned to seemingly never-ending shelling at Castel del Rio but towards the end of November things changed and there was only light opposition at Fontanelice in the foothills of the Santerno valley. At last it seemed they might be about to break out beyond the mountains. The news from the numerous war fronts struck everyone as positive. 'I wonder,' William wrote hopefully on 28th November, 'if Churchill's speeches about the war lasting till next year were a cover plan for this push.'

William was moved to become company commander of D Company and

Mules and their Italian drivers loading up

'Digging in'

Peter Bowring

temporarily promoted; 'makes up for losing adjutancy' the 23-year-old major wrote in his diary. D Company moved to Fontanelice and from there took out patrols to Tossignano, a village perched on a cliff a few miles beyond. With the snow little action was possible although vigorous patrolling continued along the entire front. If they could take Tossignano they would open the road to the plain beyond. It was decided that the 2nd Battalion would attack Tossignano and the 7th Battalion would attempt to take the surrounding positions and offer a diversionary attack. 'People seem to think Tossignano is not strongly held but I doubt that as it is the hinge of their present line with the 8th Army.' He moved one platoon into nearby Siepe when the shelling began in earnest. Communications between the platoons was difficult as the lines were down and a number of mules transporting rations were killed in the crossfire. 'We had about 12 casualties, all wounded and only five stretcher cases.'

In fact both the attack on Tossignano and the subsequent street fighting proved a failure and disastrous for the 2nd Battalion whose casualties totalled 13 officers and 207 riflemen. As a result of no reinforcements it was decided to amalgamate the 2nd and 10th Battalions, keeping the name the 2nd. The 61st Brigade was allocated another battalion to maintain numbers, the 1st Battalion, Kings Royal Rifle Corps.

During their next rest period at Passignano Castle Colonel Douglas took all the company commanders on a trip to the Villa Capponi. 'Good dinner helped along by some of the champagne and sherry, Kimmel got from Jumbo's cellar when he moved! It was a great sight to see the great families of Italy trying to learn to dance reels under Douglas' tuition.' News of the failure of the attack on Tossignano reached them at Passignano and they received orders to move back to the area early. An early Christmas celebration was hurriedly arranged much to everyone's disappointment as they had thought they were getting Christmas out. They had a dangerous journey back through snow and ice and when they got there the attack was delayed a week. All was not quiet and William had a near miss with a shell when out in a jeep near the village of San Maguerita. New Year's Eve prompted a sad diary entry: 'to think that this time last year we were blowing the New Year in at one of Colonel Douglas' parties in Cairo. It does not seem so long – or does it? It seems a lifetime ago to the one before when I was awaiting – or rather recovering – from my second operation in hospital.' Others stayed up and drank to the health of 1945:

'Those who did witnessed a strange sense of humour by the enemy who at two minutes to twelve opened up into the air with everything, spandaus firing, tracer and Verey lights along his whole line, continuing for about five minutes. We replied with a sharp reply from the guns into his lines.'

The snow fell again in early January and on one night alone there was an additional eight inches making it difficult to get supplies delivered and paths had to be re-dug for the mules as the snow balled up beneath their feet. The army winter issue clothing was put into good use: 'The army has excelled itself for once ... white snowsuits much in demand, people wandering round in white smock and hoods, quite impossible to recognise. One rifleman in the streets of Fontanelice looked at me and said 'peekaboo!' I hadn't got an answer ready for that!'

There was no end to the enemy's shelling and it got to the point when William found it safer to walk than drive so he could hear them coming. Brigade Headquarters planned another attack on Tossignano but after a series of postponements it was eventually called off and the town remained in German hands.

With the attack abandoned their role was to hold their line and wait for the Eighth Army to get into the right position for them to move on. Their Officers' Mess was established in a farmhouse where evenings were spent playing roulette or entertaining other regiments positioned nearby.

He wrote home in the middle of January assuring his mother that his existence was not tough: 'You say you feel guilty living in a warm house while we shiver in Italy. If you could see us I do not think you would feel quite so sorry for us.' He thought often of his siblings; Cam was doing well in the ATS, James had been sent to Greece and Anne had turned 16, something he could not imagine. However, despite the brave spirits life was not easy and most difficult of all was the deaths of friends and colleagues. Following the death of a soldier William often entered into correspondence with a grieving relative for whom personal contact with someone who had been close to their son in war was all important. He kept a letter from the mother of one of his soldiers – Rifleman Vodden[4], who died from wounds sustained at Castiglione Fibocchi – as a reminder of the many he had received over the years:

'*Devon, 12th September 1944.* Dear Sir, No words can ever express my gratitude to you for the letter I received from you yesterday telling me about my dear son Kenneth. It is indeed a comfort to me to know all you told me and yet it upset me so much to know it all and it is so kind of you to send me that sister's letter by sea mail. I hope I did not give you too much worry and bother when I asked you so much about my son. Your letters were so nice I felt sure you would do all I asked you to and you did. … He must have been badly hurt and I feel I must try to take some comfort in the hope that he is better off where he is now than to have come home perhaps be an invalid for life – I would have loved to see his dear smiling face again and would have nursed him untiringly or even given my life for his, but he wouldn't have liked it as he was so active and full of life; sport was part of his life. The whole village loved him just as much as I did. I hope and pray you will be spared to come back to England and that one day I shall meet you. I am only a poor working-class mother who dearly loved her boy and is grateful to you for all you have done for me, and if I knew where you lived I would come to your house if you would allow me to. Sir, is there any thing you need out there that I could get you, such as soup or tooth paste or anything you cannot get. If so please

San Bennedetto

Vivian Street

Passignamo Castle – Used by the regiment as a rest area

tell me and I will send it to you. You are a kind and noble gentleman and I thank you so very much.'

In early February the thaw set in and conditions improved. William was wanted in Naples to appear before the Regular Commissions Board. The Board was to decide whether or not he remained an officer when the war was over. His journey took him across ravaged countryside. 'All along the route are skeletons of German troop carriers and tanks, in many places there are up to 50 or 60 all head to tail on the sides of the roads where no doubt the RAF had had a field day as the enemy pulled back. The bridges are slowly being rebuilt though few are quite finished with Indian sappers assisting the civilian labour. The shell holes are being ploughed in and vehicle tracks turning into normal fields again.'

In Rome he succeeded in getting a room in the Hotel Eden, meant to be reserved for senior officers, and bumped into an acquaintance who had been married that morning and invited him to join her wedding celebrations that night. 'Good party with a few people and all very pleasant. Had a shock though when I found myself being introduced to people as Ronnie Denton! Apparently my double and it was not until the end of the evening I was able to clear the matter up!' He was much taken by the clean wide streets and buildings of Rome and went touring the Vatican and St Peters.

'I spent the morning going around the church and the Vatican Museum, where there are lovely pictures though the place I liked best was the hall of animals, sculptures of all sorts of animals of all ages, best of all was one of a very large lobster! Just like a huge one we got at Ballywhite. Sent Anne a picture postcard from the Vatican post office complete with Vatican stamp, you can send to any country from there but only five words. I wish I could have remembered Hew Butler's address and sent one to POW camp.'

The run-down city of Naples was a shock after the grandeur of Rome, 'probably the foulest place on earth, worse than Suez … Vesuvius in the clouds so cannot see it though only just above us.' He made it into the regular army and spent a leisurely week at Passignano Castle drinking Vino Santo 1933 with the Count who owned the castle who took him to see olives being pressed.

'All the locals bring their olives in for crushing … put olives in a big basin thing in which there are two upright mill wheels, which revolve round an axle crushing the olives as they go, a scraper also revolves placing the olives in their path and stirring them up. Their oil then runs away to a big tank later to be sorted in huge earthenware jars.'

In Florence he was invited to other regiments' parties and discovered the riding schools:

'In order to make it more interesting I decided to try and get a line on the Italian style of riding. I found it most uncomfortable and not very practical, riding as one does with legs right back, toes up as far as they will go riding on your crutch, with your backside sticking out and leaning forward of necessity, reins short and hands right down. I think the Italians were rather surprised at my English style of riding though flattered at my asking to learn theirs!'

When he returned to Fontanelice there was shelling from both sides but the 7ᵗʰ Battalion was preparing to pull out and hand over to the Italians. 'Murray Hunter turning out operation orders in Italian,' William wrote in his diary. 'I took the Iti Colonel out to look up the ground; luckily he talks English, very voluble. He had been opposite us at Alamein and took part in the September break through, very interesting to hear the other side of the story.'

They left the mountains for Passignano Castle and while they were there great celebrations for Vivian Street's wedding to Anette on 6ᵗʰ March were held in Florence. It was a great affair with virtually all the officers in the Brigade there the night before for a huge dance. William was an usher at the wedding: 'My job was to escort people from the entrance through the cloister to the chapel, instructing them meanwhile on the drill – it being a mixed RC one and nobody knowing the form. Quite simple stand up as the music starts, sit down as she reaches the altar and stand up as go out!' The reception was held back at the Villa Capponi in grand style with everyone drifting about on the lawn overlooking Florence and drinking champagne, 'a miracle to get it.'

Winter in the mountains – near Fontanelice

Notes:
1 Queen Elizabeth (1900-2002) made her first trip abroad to stay here in 1911.
2 King Victor Emmanuel; the last King of Italy.
3 Vivian Street had worked on Tito's staff before joining the 7th Battalion.
4 Rifleman KV Vodden died on 25th July 1944 aged 20.

Chapter Fifteen
The War is Won

William talking to Lt-Gen. McCreery

THEY LEFT Passignano Castle for the last time on 9th March 1945 and travelled through Dicomano, Benedetto, Forli and Rimini to re-join the Eighth Army on the Adriatic Coast at Cattolica, a small fishing village.

For the rest of the month they lived in villas along the coast and were busy training for the final push up through Italy. There was great rejoicing when they were given transport and returned to their role as motor battalions. William's rank, which went up and down depending on who was away at a particular time, was confirmed as a 'temporary major and substantive captain – so come what may I cannot come down less than captain.'

At weekends sailing races were organised in fishing boats which made William think of home. A letter from his mother worried him about his father's health:

'He is not well these days, M seems worried about him. He worries too much about the war and no doubt about James and I. Poor M what a lot of worries she must carry … found a book of collected O. Henry[1] stories in the Mess today, been reading up about Jeff Peters and Andy Tucker again, took me back to Charlton and Ballywhite with D reading them with such glee. What great characters they are.'

Lieutenant-General Dick McCreery was put in charge of the Eighth Army and came to visit at the end of March. He toured all the companies and managed to talk to most people: William discussed with him the 7th Battalion's arrival in Egypt, specifically about how they were thrown straight into an attack on the front line. 'He bitterly criticised Auchinleck for doing it, saying he and others had told him it was useless and that he must go on the defensive to build up reserves. However Auchinleck had a personal duel with Rommel and insisted on the attack.'

They were moved to Forlimpopoli for the final offensive in Italy. Messages of encouragement came from their leaders, the most rousing of all from Field-Marshal Alexander in a Special Order of the Day:

'Final victory is near. The German Forces are now very groggy and only need one mighty punch to knock them out for good. The moment has now come for us to take the field for the last battle which will end the war in Europe. You know what our comrades in the West and in the East are doing on the battlefields. It is now our turn to play our decisive part. It will not be a walk-over; a mortally wounded beast can still be very dangerous. You must be prepared for a hard and bitter fight; but the end is quite certain – there is not the slightest shadow of doubt about that. You, who have won every battle you have fought, are going to win this last one.'

The attack began on 9th April and William heard the first guns start to fire and bombers going over in the afternoon. They were with the reserve forces and stood back listening to it all going on ahead of them. 'Took me back to Alamein or the opening of the Cassino battle, just a steady rumble of guns – in the distance can see flares and tracer, planes flying around and occasionally the heavy crump of the big guns rattling the windows.'

Success was calculated on the number of rivers crossed and there were four main rivers ahead: the Senio, Santerno, Reno and Po. The 7th Battalion were following the front line action and when they crossed the Senio on the 19th April those at the front had crossed the Santerno. Their next push was to the town of Segni on the north bank of the River Reno: 'All troops quite hopeful, if it comes off it should hasten the end of the war in Italy quite a bit … up at 0530 to see the party off. Fantastic sight in the early light this column moving off. A platoon on each Ark[2] looking like troops on an overcrowded troop ship. Hope no snipers still about, there were some sharpening the road up yesterday evening.' At Segni the locals gave them word of a German presence and skirmishes resulted in casualties and one fatality but they pushed on to Poggio Renatico, which Tim Dewhurst's[3] company successfully cleared of enemy troops. They moved on to St Agostino and took great numbers of prisoners.

Excitement began to mount when the Po was crossed and victory seemed at last in sight. 'Going flat out for Adige Line, little opposition looks as if enemy has lost control. On news says Germans in Northern Italy packing in, everybody racing on.

Looks as if the end is coming, Russians well into centre of Berlin, Hitler still seems to be in command there,' he wrote in his diary on 26th April, adding enthusiastically, 'asparagus in the rations and found a field of strawberries – everything grand.'

They crossed the Po on the morning of 28th April. 'Glad to be on the move as felt we were missing a lot of good loot and fun of the last gallop as Germans are hardly resisting at all … the river looks enormous and fairly full. Quite a few bomb craters but not much sign of fighting or a great deal of defences.' They crossed the Po the same day that Mussolini, who had been captured by partisans, was shot with his mistress and seventeen others and strung up in the square in Milan. 'Probably the best way, especially as by his own people – a little medieval possibly,' William commented. They had planned to wait for the rest of the Brigade to cross but got word to move forward as fast as possible over the River Adige and in the direction of Padua and Udine. They set off with great eagerness having just heard that Himmler had offered an unconditional surrender to the Allies but not Russia: 'Douglas with his horn out blowing away for the last gallop.'

When Padua fell ahead of them it appeared that the war was over and they would not be needed in any push onward. It was a deflating moment having got so far but shortly after going to bed William was woken and told they were moving on at once and in the early hours of 30th April they set off leading the Eighth Army on the road to Udine.

'A strange drive where people turned out in the early light in pyjamas, one man in a beard, pants and shirt; all waving and cheering when we arrived at Zeno Bianco [probably San Zeno], I have never seen such a welcome contrary to all we imagined nobody had been there before and the Germans had only left half an hour before. The whole place was swarming with hysterical crowds – and flowers.' They did not have time to stop; the rush was on to reach Udine, the last sizeable town in Italy on their route: 'we drove like mad through village after village of cheering crowds halting for a bit in Ordeza where the crowds and welcome were staggering.'

In Treviso they met the Americans coming through from the west. There was huge rivalry between the two armies and Colonel Douglas was not about to hand over his lead to them. William writes in his diary, 'managed to beat them off,' referring to the wily way the 7th Battalion stood back and allowed the jostling Americans to pass on ahead of them down the road from Treviso to the River Piave towards a bridge they already knew to be blown. Colonel Douglas maintained the lead by risking heading back into Treviso and finding a more northerly route where bridges were not blown. At this point the battalion had lost radio contact with the Brigade and so Colonel Douglas made decisions and route plans alone.

They crossed the Piave and headed on towards the next river, the Tagliemento, where they ran into some opposition which William's company dealt with: 'Approached fairly gingerly … Germans did not appear to wish to surrender so we

Partisans in Udine

Prisoners of war

Interviewing locals

mortared them first, lot of bombs hit the house where the German commander lived. Put down about 150 rounds on them, ceased fire for a bit to see what would happen, suddenly eight Germans appeared moving through the orchard about 100 yards away. Sent a party after them, as they ran as soon as saw us all disappeared till Sgt Cable eventually located them in a position armed to the teeth, so opened fire on them. Nabbed two and the remainder ran.' They stayed the night in a nearby farm and moved on at dawn.

When all was over William reflected that for him 1st May was the most amazing day of the war. His morning began with some die-hard Germans in an MK IV tank, 'There it was sitting 200 yards down the road beside the river with men passing kit onto it. Couldn't believe my eyes! … it backed away, firing two rounds at us as it went.' This was followed by a burst of fire hitting the house William was in and bringing the ceiling down around him, when it stopped he moved towards an armoured car and asked its occupant if anyone knew where the shots had come from: 'He looked rather surprised and said, 'oh sorry I thought you knew somebody kicked the button on a Browning [machine gun]. Hope it didn't hit anyone!' When the Italians gave the 'all clear' they crossed the Tagliemento and drove on without stopping until Udine.

'Viv and I entered [Udine] in one jeep behind the armoured car having outstripped the other. The approach to the town is a long avenue of trees which was lined with Italians and Partisans getting thicker as one neared the town. Every partisan was letting off his weapon; the noise was appalling and most frightening! As we reached the square it was packed with a howling mob, rifles, pistols, spandaus, Bren all being fired in the air … there was a vast crowd with a line open for vehicles to move through, every vehicle smothered in flowers from previous crowds, one gets quite good at dodging bouquets as they come hurtling in!'

Their role was to hold the town from the Germans who had moved outside and to take prisoners by sending out delegates in armoured cars. While most were more than willing to hand themselves in others proved more determined:

'James Keith going in front with MMG as he came round corner he found four tanks refuelling. Quite undaunted he went up to demand their surrender. He approached the commander and as he was walking up to him he took out his pistol, James thought to surrender it, but he fired at him. Then all tanks started, they dived for cover but the tank got behind them and cut them off and then started off down the road towards B Company. Luckily they had hitched the six pounders behind a white, just got it into action as it came round the corner. They opened fire and knocked it out first shot. Meanwhile James and co cut off. B Company got into defensive position under heavy fire from tanks. That evening patrol out, got six pounder and white back and found one carrier knocked out, one badly bogged by the Germans and the other gone. James Keith, Sergeant

Winterbottom, J's driver and another driver missing. The remainder escaped when our guns started shelling and they swam back over river. Corporal Tyler was badly wounded and he died the next morning[4].'

Two days later he discovered James Keith was alive and in a partisan hospital.

That evening they holed up in a very comfortable house that had been used as a German headquarters and reflected on the huge number of prisoners they had taken and the one hundred miles they had covered in two days. The evening news brought reports that Hitler had killed himself – and Goering, Goebels, Himmler and Kesselring too[5] – and that Admiral Doenitz had taken Hitler's place, but they were too tired to celebrate: 'News affected people little, all taken as a matter of course.'

The battalion moved to Goriza to deal with two rival Yugoslav resistance groups, Tito's Communist partisans and General Mihajlovic's royalist Chetniks. William remained in Udine to set up a Prisoner of War camp. The number of surrendering Germans was difficult to keep up with: he put 800 of them in a local barracks but columns and lorry loads kept on arriving and they all had to be housed and fed. They had to send out troops to bring them in as the Germans refused to pass through countryside likely to be occupied by Tito's partisans whom they feared greatly. When William asked some partisans to help him guard the prisoners it went down very badly. Eventually he got everyone fed with the assistance of the German quartermasters whose efficiency he rated highly. He found a German major and made him run the place himself. He was itching to join everyone at Goriza but equally fascinated by how quickly the camp ran itself.

'Just search them as they come in then hand them over to their own people. Do not know how many we have, estimate about 4,000 including about 60 officers. All easy to handle, though I wish I had no partisans here. Their officers are behaving well, I have them in separate rooms. If anyone wished to escape there is little chance of stopping them, as guards cannot cover all the way round but I told their commandant to warn everyone that I do not wish anyone to go outside as they will be shot for certain by partisans! It is amazing what can be done even if one has not a clue about the job before one starts!'

Churchill chose to support Tito's partisans over the Chetniks and the latter were moved into a concentration area near Palmanova in Italy. The subsequent decision to repatriate the Chetniks is a subject of heated debate as it resulted in their deaths at the hands of Tito's men. Despite British and American support for Tito over other Yugoslav factions there was no support for his forces' behaviour in the region. Amongst the populations of the border regions in Italy and Austria many were Slovenes and Tito claimed the area a Yugoslav territory which put the British in a complicated position. There was no wish to start fighting him and the only solution was to block various roads and rush on to Klagenfurt in Austria, a city that he

Victory at last - 8th May 1945: Klagenfurt

claimed as the capital of the Yugoslav territory of 'Carinthia'.

The 7th Battalion regrouped with the rest of the 61st Brigade close to the Austrian border, preparing to cross at the Tarvisio Pass. On the 7th May an announcement was made that peace had been signed and in the early hours of 8th May – VE Day – the 7th Battalion were the first British troops to cross the Austrian border from Italy.

'I got the company under way in good time for one of our most historic drives … the border marked only by striped pole raised off the road reminding one of pictures of Hitler's original entry into Austria. Here we met our first German troops by the sides of the road, a unique sight to see so many Germans and tanks being driven about and to drive through unmolested!

'On we went at true 7RB pace, Douglas up behind Bill urging him on … the difference in entering Austrian villages to Italian ones was most marked – lines of people and German troops, the civilians waving but scarcely a cheer. In the country occasionally a few flowers were thrown into my jeep, but for the most part a rather doubtful waving and silence.

'We swept through the edge of Villach without stopping and on. Then a lovely sight as we reached the edge of Worther See (lake), sun well up and this lovely lake edged with the tree covered hills and behind by barer and snow capped mountains. Another 15 kilometres and we reached the edge of Klagenfurt, more silent crowds and German troops.'

There they were given buildings to occupy, primarily against Tito's men. They had arrived at last:

'Strange atmosphere, no apparent excitement, people still walking about their business, trams running and no great animosity at us, only our own bustle and hustle. The end is rather an anti-climax. It seems to have faded out, we are still acting as operationally as ever, roadblocks out with six pounders mainly against Tito, though if he comes he is to pass on as are German troops, nor do we disarm them! Got to bed eventually and slept like a log after so many short nights. The first night of Peace!'

Tito's forces were greatly feared by the subdued residents as they were looting farms and generally spreading terror outside the city. The speed of the battalion's advance across the border and subsequent occupation of Klagenfurt had outstripped Tito's men to the city by a few hours: 'an action of far reaching political consequences,' according to a military historian.[xv] On arrival they set up roadblocks to prevent Tito's forces from coming into the towns and set about controlling the flow of German columns coming in to surrender.

Amid all this activity Prisoners of War, mostly Australians taken in Greece, tasted freedom for the first time in four years – some seemed lost while others revelled in it, picking up enemy cars and roaring wildly around Klagenfurt. 'Their joy at seeing us was touching,' William wrote in his diary on 9th May. 'They look fairly well after four years, though all rather starry eyed and slightly strange, especially in their speech which is almost broken English.' The prisoners claimed the Red Cross parcels had saved their lives as otherwise they were fed soup and bread day-in-day-out. William helped close a camp where all the prisoners had worked at a wood-mill: 'One nearly broke down as he said goodbye, they went off on a truck I lent them, others were fairly under the influence.'

William was sent to the banks of the River Drava to disarm a German Corps of 40,000 men arriving from Yugoslavia. The Corps were prepared to surrender to the British but not to Tito's men with whom they were fighting right up to the border. 'Went across to see the German corps commander with Viv, most intriguing to see the German army in battle dress,' William wrote of events on 12th May. 'The bridge [where the Germans had fought Tito's men the night before] was a proper battle scene, dead horses, brewed up tanks and general wreckage … the Corps Commander had been opposite us at Portico and said he was quite prepared to hand over his arms to 6 Panzer Div, but not prepared to mess around with the partisans.' They agreed that the Germans could hand their arms over when they had crossed the river which formed the border and that when they had done so their safety from Tito's men would be guaranteed. The battalion was given some time in a rest area but there was little time to relax thanks to the activities of Tito's men: 'They are like children painting slogans on the walls which they hope people will think the Austrians have put up.' Their behaviour became more and more intolerable, ranging from pulling faces at British soldiers to raping local women.

By June peace seemed more real and a working pattern established itself of two companies on guard duty and two on 'rest and relaxation'. Leave was allowed and officers went either to a villa in Venice or locally to 'the Green Man' which was run by the same man as the Villa Capponi in Florence. Home leave was still a tricky subject and its allocation was determined on the time the individual had served abroad or had left to serve. The news that the 2nd Battalion was being sent to the Far East, where the war with Japan was not yet over, hit everyone hard. All those who had joined the 7th Battalion after 13th July 1943 were expected to change battalions and go with them. William was safe but he saw a number of friends go.

The calmer pace of life in Austria suited William as it gave him the opportunity to set up stables with the requisitioned German horses. He took on 28 horses, called them names such as Torreodor and Felix after his childhood horses, and set about training soldiers and officers who had never ridden before with the help of Colonel Douglas. They arranged a race meeting with the Lancers and set up a Tote for bets and by the end of June organised their own gymkhana and entered races in the 6th Armoured Division Races.

Back at home there was a general election. It was a landslide victory for Labour and on 27th July Winston Churchill ceded his position to Clement Attlee and his promises of huge social reforms. William was not surprised although he was hugely disappointed.

Vivian Street was given command of the 7th Battalion when Douglas Darling returned to England and in August they received orders to move forthwith to the Middle East. The news hit everyone very hard and sitting in a transit camp outside Taranto William wrote glumly in his diary: '… as someone said 'this is where we came in!''

Back in Egypt they guarded official buildings in Cairo or trained at the army garrison in Moascar. They were the only battalion in the region so if trouble flared up in any direction they had to be prepared to get to it fast: 'Ready for anything, from flying to Tripoli to going to Palestine. Palestine's argument is with Jews wanting to get in and getting in illegally in large numbers. Arabs protesting volubly, all well armed and ready for the fray.'

William was very keen to get home in October when Cam and James would also be there but regulations surrounding home leave kept changing and frustrating matters. Eventually it was confirmed that he would not be eligible for home leave until May 1946.

Their free time was spent at the usual haunts, Shepheards and the Turf Club in Cairo, and William celebrated his 24th birthday at the Geneifa Club. He managed to arrange a trip to the Sinai Desert by accompanying Major General Perceval. The journey was fascinating and William was very taken by the rugged mountain

Austria 1945: William on Toreador (left) at Hunter Trials and Col.
Douglas Darling on another of the requisitioned horses.

scenery and the warm sea. They met Bedouins; rode camels; watched fishermen dragging in nets full of sardines; saw porpoises in the Red Sea; and travelled as far as Dahab. The highlight of the tour was a visit to the remote St Catherine's Monastery, built on the site of Moses' Burning Bush in the first century. The monastery meant travelling into the middle of the Sinai desert: 'It is really a fascinating place, quite cut off from anywhere, an ancient civilisation in the wilderness.' They arrived straight from the coast with 14 live crayfish and some mullet, which they shared with the abbot and monks at supper. Otherwise the resident abbot and eight monks lived off what they produced and there were gardens with grapes, pears and peaches growing.

His Regular Commission came through and was published in *The London Gazette* at the end of November. His mother wrote to tell him that he had also been 'Mentioned in Despatches', something he had not seen. Christmas 1945 was the quietest William had known and afterwards the battalion moved to Port Said. His letters from home made him realise how long he had been away – Anne was no longer a child: 'she is talking of face powder and silk stockings,' he wrote in his diary of January 1946, 'shall not know her when I get back.'

When an officer returned from England unexpectedly William learnt that he was free to go home to take up a job at an Officer Cadet Training Unit Colonel Douglas was running. He caught a train to Alexandria and boarded a French boat bound for Toulon, leaving the Middle East for good on 26th January 1946. From there he journeyed by train to Paris and Dieppe. In Dieppe there were no crossings because of storms – he was immensely frustrated and rang the War Office to insist on a 'priority crossing' but the bad weather continued and no boats left. For the first time in years he spoke to his parents at Ballywhite, and to celebrate he drank champagne while doing so. He was forced to spend a few nights in a transit camp before crossing to Newhaven on 5th February. He had been away for almost four years.

1945: General Perceval at St Catherine's Monastery, Sinai

Notes:
1 Pseudonym of W S Porter (1862-1910) American short-story writer.
2 "Armoured Ramp Carrier": military vehicle.
3 He was awarded the Military Cross for his part in operations here.
4 Edwin A Tyler died 1st May 1945 aged 22.
5 Hitler, Goering and Goebbels committed suicide; Himmler followed a few weeks later; but Kesselring died in 1960.

Chapter Sixteen
Mrs White

Agnes around the time of her marriage

WHEN PEACE was declared Agnes was at home with her parents. There were great celebrations on the Audleystown Road where a number of families from the area gathered at the junction with Castle Ward Road. "I played an accordion at that time, and we went up to the end of our road and played music and danced around the three roads."

Later in the summer Frank asked Agnes to marry him. Frank had left his job at Ballywhite in 1942 to manage a potato and soup-canning factory at Ballyfindry, three miles from Portaferry. When he announced his plans to get married an uncle gave him a house on the Abbacy Road, close to the farm he had grown up on and a few miles from Ballywhite. It needed doing up but the building was sound.

Agnes' engagement to Frank made for huge changes in her life. In November 1945 she handed in her notice to Mrs Brownlow working the month out and leaving just before Christmas. For Agnes leaving her job after seven years was not a great severance, she expected to return to work there, "if they had nobody they'd send for you". She arranged for her friend Annie Grey to take on her job and went home to prepare for her wedding. She moved to the Mallard, her parents' cottage, on the Audleystown Road, where she made plans for the wedding, helped her mother and visited her friends. The ceremony took place on 3rd July 1946 in Ballyculter where her parents, cousins, aunts, uncles and members of the Bangor family had married before her. It was not a big wedding, and after the service her family and a few friends attended a reception back at the Mallard. Frank was 37, she was 24 and the last of her parents' daughters to marry. Ida's husband Bob Barrett acted as the best man and their daughter, Jane, was their only bridesmaid. Instead of dressing herself in a white wedding dress Agnes wore a violet blue suit, hat with veil, shoes with bows on them and a rose in her lapel, and Frank put on a dark suit and spotted tie. She had bought it with coupons and couldn't get the material for a proper white dress. The newly weds took themselves away to Belfast for a week's honeymoon where they stayed with cousins of Frank's in the Bloomfield area in the east of the city.

After the honeymoon they started married life at Frank's mother's cottage. Their own house was not ready for them to move in and his mother liked having them with her there. There were four rooms in the cottage and Agnes and Frank were given one of them. His mother was a widow; she and her husband, a seaman in the merchant navy, had brought up six children in the cottage but he had died when Frank was seven. When Agnes and Frank moved in only one daughter, Mary, still lived at home, and another son, Sam, a gardener for Sir Christopher Musgrave who lived near Belfast, came home at weekends. Otherwise, Tommy, the eldest, lived in his house at Ballywhite and Jim had joined the army. Lucy, the youngest, had died from blood poisoning at the age of 13.

The house Frank's uncle gave him had people living in it at the time of his marriage and they had to wait for them to leave. When the house became free Frank and Agnes spent their weekends sorting it out and planning their future there. His mother was not keen to lose them and suggested they returned to her during the week while they were doing it up. This went on for almost six months and by Christmas Frank and Agnes moved into their house properly.

Agnes went back to work at Ballywhite almost straight away after her wedding. She took herself to work by bicycle – it was not a huge distance between the two houses and she had to be up there by 8 o'clock ready to get the house cleaned before the Brownlows came downstairs for breakfast. Her hours became more flexible after her marriage and she tended to escape at about three in the afternoon.

She had remained a central figure in the life of Anne Brownlow who had turned eighteen and was just starting out on the whirl of society parties in London and at home. In 1946 a dance was given by Lady Londonderry at Mount Stewart in aid of the Red Cross: it was Anne's first dance and Agnes was there to help prepare her for it.

"She had a white dress and a red rose in her hair, the dress had hoops in it, it was lovely. We just dressed her and got her on her way," says Agnes. Anne

Frank and Agnes marry, 3rd July 1946

Anne going to a 'Coming Out'
dance

Bob Skillen with Castle Ward maids, Peggy and
Maureen Kane

remembers it well: "It was an 'end of war' ball, everyone wore tiaras and Derek Bury[1] opened the dancing in his Down Hunt coat. I had roses tucking up my dress, it was copied from my grandmother's wedding dress but it was made of crinoline and butter muslin for straining cream because of rationing." William had arrived home in time to accompany Anne to the dance and he writes the evening up in his diary: 'Anne looking very good in white and very excited, she could hardly eat her dinner.' He wore uniform but was pleased to see men in their pink hunting coats – "great to see such colour again" – he barely recognised Anne's friends who had all grown up in his absence. Lord and Lady Londonderry came downstairs at eleven and danced one reel before disappearing. William was astonished that they were not even there to greet the Northern Ireland's Governor, Lord Granville and his wife. The Brownlow party danced all night and William got his sister home at five in the morning.

There were lots of parties at Ballywhite to launch Anne into society, "Suitable people came," recalls Agnes. "There were big dinner parties and all the ages were mixed up." It was not long before Anne met and married Lord Monteagle, an officer in the Irish Guards, and Agnes was invited to join in all the celebrations which were held at home.

The seeds of social change had been sown by the mobilisation of a generation and attitudes towards domestic service altered. A direct consequence of the war was that many who would have naturally gone into domestic service had found a world beyond it and for the employer finding staff became more difficult and expensive. 'The men and women returning from the armed services or factory work had no wish to enter or return to domestic service,' writes the biographer of Lady Londonderry[xvi] reflecting on the reductions of the vast staff at Mount Stewart during that period. Nor did the Labour Government help the financial position of those most likely to be employing substantial domestic staff and the scale of pre-war households was no longer viable.

These changes did not happen at once, and at Ballywhite the Brownlows kept on a similar sized staff in the years after the war. When William returned home in 1946 he noted in his diary how unchanged it seemed: 'Just like pre-war. In the house are Craig, the butler, Lily and Annie, the housemaids, the cook and the kitchen maid. Outside are Curry, the chauffeur/groom, Keogh, Dewberry and the garden boy; Tommy, Welsh, McNamara, Feloona, and one other on farm. So well equipped now, nowhere in England can be as well staffed.' In England far greater numbers had joined up and not all were interested in returning to domestic service. William noted this later in the month after visiting family friends in London: 'Only one servant, so living fairly hand to mouth.'

As the years passed the household slowly reduced in size. The role of the butler disappeared when Craig left, and Agnes took on some of his work. "It was me in charge of the dining room after the war," says Agnes, who had always watched the butlers at work and had learnt much of their work off by heart. "I looked after the silver and put the plates into the kitchen and the Colonel was very particular. He liked to be served from the left and it was all black dresses and aprons then." The changes at Ballywhite were so gradual they went almost unnoticed, especially when figures such as Agnes were prepared to share the work load out between them. Although the number of staff lessened standards did not seem to slip, and 'standards' were of great importance to Elinor Brownlow.

Agnes never worried about work, she enjoyed her job and felt secure in the knowledge that she would always find employment at Ballywhite. Her father did not feel likewise at Castle Ward. He was aware of the financial problems facing large estates and had the vision to understand that increased death duties would ruin some families.

In the autumn of 1950 Lord Bangor died leaving the estate to his son, Edward Ward, who was at the peak of his career as a roving reporter for the BBC. He returned home a short while before his father died and during this time he became aware of the dire situation the estate was in. 'Nothing had been done about making over even a part of the estate to me, so I immediately found myself faced with the prospect of enormous death duties of some £80,000,' he wrote in an autobiography[xvii]. 'I blamed myself bitterly (and still do) for not having taken a more constructive interest in the estate.' While Edward Ward, now the 7th Viscount Bangor, sat in the family church at Ballyculter for his father's funeral he was weighed down by responsibilities he would rather not face.

Agnes watched the funeral procession with her family, "They brought him in the horse and cart to be buried, we watched it from the school and there was a tea in the school for his people – we came out when his coffin passed." While the funeral service was held in the church at Ballyculter, his grave is not found among his forebears in the churchyard – instead he was laid to rest in Strangford Lough. His family thought a sea burial would be the most appropriate for a man so fond of sailing. Edward Ward learnt afterwards that some locals were shocked at the concept of a sea burial, but the Skillens considered it fitting and what he would have wanted.

Her father and a few other estate workers took the coffin out on the boat with Lady Bangor and a minister and heaved it into the lough. It was a lead coffin, but despite its weight it did not sink at once: "it didn't go down very well," Agnes remembers her father describing the actual event. "I think they may have forgotten to put holes in the coffin."

Life at Castle Ward changed at once. There were twelve workmen on the estate and the new Lord Bangor made an attempt to make the estate pay by using them to fell trees and sell firewood, but he had to accept it was futile and that he could not afford to keep them on. His own reflections on this difficult time include his decision to keep on Agnes' father:

'After several months I dismissed all the men except the gardener, Bob Skillen, and a garden boy. Skillen had been very worried about the future after my father's death and had asked me what the prospects were. I told him he would be all right anyway.

"I'm very glad to hear it, Mr Edward," he said, "for let me tell you, I'm a man of apprehension!"'[xviii]

Eventually he decided to give Castle Ward to the nation in order to cover the crippling death duties. Castle Ward went to the Northern Ireland Government who handed the house and estate over to the National Trust with a proviso that the Ward family would be encouraged to look upon it as their home and given space to return to a part of the house for a few weeks annually. Frustrated by his dealings with estate finances and death duties the 7th Lord Bangor returned to his professional life as Edward Ward back in London. In his autobiography Edward Ward reflects on losing his family estate:

'I suppose, in a way that I have been a victim – although I prefer not to look upon it in that way – of the social revolution that has brought about so many changes in our country. All through my life I had passively taken it for granted that I would succeed not only to the title but to a considerable degree of financial security when I inherited Castle Ward and the life tenancy of the Bangor estate. If I had worked hard towards this end, of course, I could have achieved this at least to a certain extent. But the idea of living more or less penuriously in a large house never appealed to me. I had known what it was like to live in a reasonably grand manner at Castle Ward and I preferred to live in my own way in a small house that was really my own than to 'picnic' in a vast mansion that didn't even belong to me but to the National Trust.[xix]'

He stayed in touch with Agnes' parents, sending them a card at Christmas which often included photographs of his children. Eventually the rest of his family moved to England and although they made visits to Ireland, and still come and stay in an apartment in the house today, it was the end of the Wards' days on the shores of Strangford Lough. Their departure had far reaching effects on the families still dependent on the estate for their livelihood and marked the end of a way of life for Agnes' cousins and aunts and uncles who had considered Castle Ward their home.

The National Trust was busy taking over and maintaining houses across the United Kingdom and could only afford to keep on staff essential to the estate's management. When the axe fell at Castle Ward Agnes' father was grateful to find himself still employed and he continued to work in the gardens until he retired. Indeed he was reluctant ever to leave and was well into his eighties when he stopped work, and even then he liked to go down to the gardens and do the odd bit of work, sometimes just wheeling his bicycle down and back.

He loved the estate and his work and as his mind faded towards the end of his life he imagined Castle Ward was still functioning as it once had. "He would say there was her ladyship's car at the door, he thought he was still in Castle Ward, he just loved it there," says Agnes. "He went down to the vegetable garden at the last; he still thought he lived in the lodge and he went across the fields and got stuck in the briars on his way back. They lost him for a night and they found him the next day in these briars, he had gone a wee bit wrong, he thought that was where he lived instead of the Mallard where he had moved there when he retired."

The state of affairs at Castle Ward was by no means unique; across the British Isles a way of life was disappearing. The 1950s saw the owners of numerous large estates forced to cut back or accept they could no longer afford them, and a few years after Castle Ward went to the National Trust Mount Stewart went the same way. Death duties were usually the final blow to estates struggling to survive.

While nothing as drastic as selling up happened to Ballywhite there were many changes to the running of the place. Agnes had gone into domestic service in the final days of grand households but for the next generation the resident gentry did not provide enough work to be considered obvious local employers. Frank saw what was going on at Castle Ward and elsewhere and realised that his decision to leave Ballywhite to find work independently had been a wise one. His job at Stormont saw him through his remaining working years. Despite leaving Ballywhite as an employee he continued to help his brother, Tommy, or nephew, Billy, on the big shooting days, which he loved, and 60 years after he left his official job there he continued to drive the tractor to help out.

Sarah Skillen at the Mallard

Notes:
1 Viscount Bury, the eldest son of Lord Albermarle, who married the Londonderry's youngest daughter, Lady Mairi Stewart, in 1941.

Chapter Seventeen
The Post-War Life

William at a Regimental Birthday Party in 1950

WILLIAM'S BOAT docked in Belfast on 6th February 1946 and his mother and sisters were there to greet him. Despite a few grey hairs his parents had not aged, unlike Anne who had grown up beyond his recognition and Cam who had reached the impressive rank of lieutenant colonel in the ATS. Unquestionably the biggest party during his spell at home was a dance at Government House held in honour of Princess Elizabeth. 'There were vast numbers of people there, nearly all young,' wrote William in a diary. 'The older notables had dined the night before. Princess E. looking very cheerful and dancing every dance, danced mainly with navy or party at Government House … Anne thoroughly enjoyed it and danced away, I danced with her two or three times and mainly otherwise with Jean Graham and Diana Kirkpatrick who was in great form. Finished about 2 o'clock and Princess E thanked the band.'

After the war Cam was demobilised and James left the army, but William had made a decision to stay on and continued to train army recruits in Staffordshire. He enjoyed the different intakes of officer cadets and during his time there as a company commander he met Field Marshal Montgomery and trained his son, David. He was as happy as he could imagine working for Douglas Darling who shared his passion for horses and hunting and had become a true friend.

The course moved from Staffordshire to Eaton Hall in Cheshire, close to where James was working for their mother's family firm W M Christy & Sons Ltd at Droylsden. William was fascinated by James' work and was taken on a tour of the towel making business: 'We have a waiting list [of workers] as opposed to most mills that are short of workmen … all seems very go ahead and cheerful.' The mill had been set up in 1833 by William Miller Christy stemming from a successful millinery business Christy & Co. 'We went round Christy and Co at Stockport which is very old and rather dreary, but the same spirit – I was given a new hat by John Christy Miller.'

There was great happiness in April 1947 when Cam got engaged to David Welsh. Cam rang William in Cheshire who was thrilled: 'He is a delightful person. He commanded the 2nd Battalion, Royal Horse Artillery, who were in support of us in Italy. In fact one of his shells wounded the Colonel!' The wedding was held on a hot day at the end of July at St George's, Hanover Square in London: 'Cam looking well in our Grandmother's Brussels lace which is lovely. D did well giving her away and David looked most calm, cool and collected although all dripping in the heat.'

In June the Allies made a decision to keep troops in Germany until peace was entirely secured, and William joined the Rifle Brigade's 1st Battalion in Minden. Army bases in Germany never became a thing of the past and William spent the majority of his last five years in the army stationed there, firstly as adjutant with the 1st Battalion and later at the British Army of the Rhine headquarters.

As adjutant he worked for a commanding officer who was very keen on the reputation of his battalion. "I was the signals officer," recalls Frank Kitson[1], "and as the wireless sets seldom worked it was usually on myself or the adjutant that the colonel worked off his great excitement." It was the first time William had found himself on exercise since the war and his attitude to such 'practices' was laid back. Frank Kitson paints an amusing picture of their time together at this period: "When things went wrong on an exercise he used to smile happily away and resolutely refused to take it seriously. It did not take long before this realistic approach rubbed off on the colonel who started to cool down. Bill also used to think of distant places to despatch the colonel who would be sent off with the intelligence officer so that we could get a bit of peace. We sat for hours in the battalion headquarters half-track smoking cigarettes, eating compo chocolate or boiled sweets and playing picquet while the signal sergeant encoded and decoded slidex messages for the amusement of the company headquarters. Only if we were obliged to pull down the camouflage nets and drive a few miles to a new position was the even tenor of our life disturbed … until the colonel returned. But by then he was ready for a sharpener followed by his supper."

During his time in Germany he set up a regimental racing stable with ex-German Cavalry horses. 'The Germans had moved all their best horses to Berlin to avoid capture by the Russians, so really our selection was made that much simpler,' he told a sporting magazine[xx] some years later. 'We had two racecourses, at Hanover and Düsseldorf, for the whole of the Rhine Army.' He encouraged young officers to take up racing and one of his most successful recruits was Frank Kitson who had done plenty of riding but had yet to take part in a race. He arranged for both their horses to be taken by a three ton army lorry to a point-to-point at the small spa town of Bad Lippespringe, some fifty miles away. On the journey there the driver turned the truck over and Frank Kitson's horse was badly cut up. "Bill saw that my horse was not fit to compete and decided I should ride his far superior animal which I had never ridden before. About half way round the course something happened and I was unconscious for the next twenty minutes. When I came round I found myself in the First Aid tent unattended as the medical orderlies had all gone to watch the next race. I accordingly got out and went to watch it too. As I approached Bill he said: 'Ah good; you are alive. I was just wondering whether to write a letter to the Admiral (my father) or to send him a signal announcing your premature departure.' As a matter of fact I was nearer dead than he supposed and collapsed soon afterwards with delayed concussion that turned into pneumonia so that it was six weeks before I was ready to renew our partnership in the command half-track."

The following year they rode against each other in the army's most prestigious race. The first post-war Grand Military Meeting was held at Dortmund on Saturday 13th August 1949. William raced on a German horse called Spring and won, as he did again the following year. His 1949 win was only just the case as he was very nearly pipped to the post by his own pupil. "I led all the way," Kitson remembers, "and jumped the last fence well so that I thought the race was in the bag. But just as we were approaching the line there was a noise like an express train in my ears as Bill drove his horse past me to win by a short head. Experience and iron nerve had triumphed over youth and beauty."

The Mounted Infantry Club invited William – as the winner of the Grand Military – to become a member. It had begun as a dining club for those who had fought in the Mounted Infantry in the Boer War, but had evolved to foster equestrian sport throughout the infantry. William had a great uncle who had been a member and whose bravery in the Boer War led to a hill in South Africa being labelled Brownlow's Kopje. William was allowed to return from Germany to attend their first dinner at the Trocadero in London and he was impressed when he found himself sitting between 'Jumbo', by then Field Marshall Lord Wilson, and Major General Sir Hereward Wake.

While he was living abroad Anne became engaged to a young Irish peer, Lord Monteagle of Brandon, who was serving in the Irish Guards and Cam and David had a son, Alexander. William made it back from Germany for Anne and Gerald's wedding in Ballyphillip Parish Church in Portaferry in 1949. The local paper printed a long account of the day's events with every detail from the names of Tommy White's children throwing rose petals at the bride and groom's feet to the 'apt and witty speech'

William wins the Mounted Infantry Cup Race at the Grand Military Meeting, Dortmund, 1949

Back row from left: Lord Monteagle, Anne Brownlow, James Brownlow, Joanie Spring Rice, Mary Marion Kekewich, Mary Lou Pooler, Caroline Stroyan
Front row from left: Rory Annesley, The Hon. James and Tom Joscelyn

William crosses Strangford Lough with his mother, in the days before a proper ferry service. In the background is James McDonald

made by Lord Bangor when raising a toast to the bride. Soon everyone in the family but William was married – James met Susan (Sue) Barnes while he was working in Cheshire and they married there at her parents' home in July 1951.

The only time William was stationed in England again was during his time at the Army Staff College in Camberley. From there he returned to Germany where once again he ran the army racing. He was there when the King died in 1953 and he experienced Coronation Day in Berlin where the British Army put on a huge celebratory parade in an arena last used by Hitler. He described the experience in a letter to his parents:

'On Tuesday we watched the television which was good considering that the nearest relay station is Hamburg. The commentary of course was in German so we turned out the commentary and listened to the wireless which coincided fairly well. They had their parade at 1730hrs in the Mayfield which is the vast place next door to the Olympic Stadium where the polo was played. It was packed with Germans, in addition to the British estimated to be a crowd of 180,000! … Then onto the General's reception where there was a vast concourse of allies including Russians with fireworks and an Elizabethan tableau and the Queen's Speech. We drove round the Old Chancellery and Hitler's bunker area (the real object of going into the sector to satisfy D's curiosity!), the area is desolate; the Chancellery gutted but walls standing and the bunker area is blown up with the bunker itself half on its side. We did not dare get out and walk over to it or I would have chipped off a bit for you!'

Colonel Brownlow's health was not good: he had suffered a number of strokes and when William went home in March 1953 he saw that his father could no longer run the farm alone. For William the time had come to move home but the army kiboshed his first attempt to resign. So William wrote again explaining the circumstances of the farm at Ballywhite which by virtue of its size – 200 acres of beef and arable farming, employing 2-4 men – could not support the services of a land agent: 'This illness of my father is a circumstance which I could not possibly have foreseen when I entered the Staff College, but is one which is now having very far-reaching effects on my family.'[2] He was given permission to resign and in December 1953 he returned to Ireland. He left with the rank of Major and while known to all his army friends as 'Bill' he became known as 'the Major' to everyone back in Northern Ireland. Without continuing his military career he rose to the rank of Colonel in 1973 when he was appointed an Honorary Colonel of the 4th Battalion, The Royal Irish Rangers. Despite this accolade from the Northern Irish Militia few outside it noted his new position and he remained forever 'the Major'.

A lasting legacy of his military career was the great friendship he offered to regiments stationed in Northern Ireland. He entertained generations of officers from many regiments, especially the Royal Green Jackets, very generously at Ballywhite. The Rifle Brigade had merged with the Oxfordshire and Buckinghamshire Light Infantry and the King's Royal Rifle Corps in the 1960s to become The Royal Green Jackets. On one occasion when three Green Jacket battalions were stationed in Northern Ireland he invited them to gather for a partridge shoot at Ballywhite. A lasting memory of one from that day was finding two riflemen in the kitchen listening spellbound to 'the Major' who was recounting some stories from his time with the Regiment. The Green Jackets were finally able to show their gratitude when they invited him to 'take the salute' at a Sounding of Retreat on behalf of all three battalions in 1991 at Omagh where he gave a stirring speech.

When William returned to Ireland it was for good. 'I never looked back,' he told the *Shooting Times*[xvi] decades later. 'After all, I could shoot and ride whenever I wished.' It was all he could wish for and he was happy from the moment he arrived home. His brother and sisters were regular visitors bringing with them the next generation, Cam's son, Sandy, James' children, William, Elisabeth and Joanna and Anne's four, Angela, Elinor, Charles and Fiona. He enjoyed the company of his nieces and nephews and bought them a small blue roan pony, Dinky, and taught them to ride during their stays. He was good at making life fun for children as David Ker, the son of his friends Dick and Bidger Ker, recalls: 'He created excitement for a teenage boy or a child – there was always something going on. Later, when he ran the shooting at Ballywhite he organised boys' shoots – and in many ways the shoot was much more run for boys than grown ups. He was there for my first woodcock, and first pheasant.'

He spent most of his first winter back home out hunting with the North Down Harriers and the following spring racing in point-to-point races. Through hunting he made many friends and his place on the hunting scene became established in November 1955 when the huntsman with the East Down Foxhounds had a stroke and he was asked to step in at short notice. The hounds were kennelled at Seaforde, home to Colonel Desmond Forde whose family had set up the hunt as a private pack a century before. Although Colonel Forde was older than William the two men liked each other immediately and when he retired as Master of Foxhounds he offered the position to William.

The house at Seaforde is a striking neo-classical building erected by a forebear in the early nineteenth century on the site of an earlier house. It is set in parkland and commands impressive views of the Mountains of Mourne. When William met Colonel Forde he lived at Seaforde with his wife, two children and two step-children. He had been married to Lord and Lady Bangor's daughter, Margaret, with whom he had two children, Sylvia and Patrick before marrying Kay Panter, a widow and mother of two children, Michael and Eveleigh. Mrs Panter had lived close by at Enniskeen near Newcastle in County Down. Her first husband, Colonel George Panter, had been some years older than her and had fought and lost an arm in the First World War and she was still young when he died in 1944.

Colonel Forde and Mrs Panter married in 1949 and brought together four children. Michael was 13, Sylvia and Eveleigh were 11 and Patrick was nine. Eveleigh and Sylvia were already boarding together at Manor House School in Co Armagh before their parents' marriage and later they went on to boarding school together in England. The boys also went to school in England. When William became Master he spent a great deal of time at Seaforde. He bought himself a speedboat and kept a Land Rover the Strangford side of the lough to hasten his journeys there, and as a result he often arrived drenched to the skin. While he was busy with the hounds, hunting twice a week, the Forde and Panter children at Seaforde were teenagers and being between-generations in age William did not pay much attention to their comings and goings. In 1957 he bought a house, Derryhill, close to Seaforde, possibly with a thought of living in it as a bachelor, but he let it out shortly after buying it and continued the commute from home.

At Ballywhite he was concerned with the day-to-day running of his father's affairs. Colonel Brownlow's health had continued to deteriorate and in January 1960 he died. His death brought great change to William's world and left him head of the family and responsible for maintaining Ballywhite for future generations. "His father dying probably prompted him to think about marriage," William's widow contemplated 40 years later. At the age of 38 he had only once shown any interest in settling down, with family friend Prue Blakiston-Houston, but nothing had come of it. His cousin Mary Lou Pooler remembers on one occasion a girlfriend of William's complaining he had never given her flowers and witnessing him stooping to pick a dandelion and pass it to her. This independent spirit changed in the spring of 1960 when he began to take notice of Eveleigh Panter. He was not confident of winning her affections because of the difference in their ages.

Eveleigh had always liked 'Major Brownlow'. They used to go to the races and cubbing together and she enjoyed his company. She and Sylvia would watch him going about his business at Seaforde often whistling *Scotland the Brave*, *Bonnie Dundee* and *Yellow Polka Dot Bikini* and joked that when he blew his hunting horn smoke came out the other end as he usually had a cigarette in hand. He taught them how to look after their horses and dogs and was a character everyone enjoyed having about at Seaforde and Sylvia recalls laughing one day when they were out hunting and someone came up to him on foot and shouted, "good morning Colonel, it's great to see you, I heard you were dead." He roared with laughter and replied, 'well I'm glad to be alive on such a fine hunting day. It must be father you were told about'."

When William began to take an interest in Eveleigh their lives were at quite different stages. He was content to be home at Ballywhite while she was enjoying her independence for the first time. In 1960 Eveleigh had just returned from a year travelling around America and was full of plans for a summer of parties in England and Scotland. She had an American friend staying with her at Seaforde that spring and he did not impress her stepfather who called him 'the long streak of American mediocrity,' and hoped she was far from matrimony. The poor American noticed about the time it was dawning on Eveleigh that she had fallen in love with William. "It was in the pouring rain picking up stones before the point-to-point, it would have been March 1960, when the penny dropped that I loved him," she remembers.

Within months William was invited to parties Eveleigh was going to and he joined her in Scotland for the Stirling and Perth balls during the summer. When William's mother had a stroke, a side effect of an attack on her dog by a Rhodesian ridgeback at a local fete, she asked if Eveleigh would like to come over and look after her. Eveleigh went, but everything about Ballywhite, William's mother, and life over on the peninsula was new to her. Eveleigh's stepfather, Desmond Forde, viewed her stay as 'kill or cure' for the burgeoning romance. He was proved right as in October William asked Eveleigh to marry him. Eveleigh knew she was in love but found it hard to ignore the differences in their ages. "He kept asking me and I couldn't commit myself, I was so worried about the 17 year age gap," says Eveleigh. Her mother, whose first husband had been considerably older than her, had no such qualms and quietly explained to William the art of courtship: "Mummy instigated it all," Eveleigh remembers. "She said 'if you want Eveleigh to say 'yes' go round with a huge bunch of roses'. I went over to London to a party and I had a bargain with him – I said 'if you come with me I'll give you my answer' – then he came, arriving at the Gilroy's[3] house in Lyall Mews on Mummy's instigation with a mega amount of roses. We were engaged properly on a day near his birthday and he gave me our engagement ring at the gate, just opposite the Lodge at Ballywhite."

Engaged to Miss Eveleigh Panter

William and Eveleigh on their wedding day, 11th January 1961

The announcement of their engagement took many by surprise. "People did not expect us to get married," says Eveleigh. "When I told David Johnson, who was a sort of manservant at Seaforde, he said 'you must be joking Miss Eveleigh dear'." Their engagement was announced in the newspapers and followed up in the diary columns who found romance in the way they courted: *The Major Calls by Speedboat* ran the *Daily Mail* headline.

Despite a dwindling household life at Ballywhite had not changed greatly since Mrs Brownlow's arrival there in 1938, and Eveleigh was not convinced by her future mother-in-law's suggestion that they all live together there after the wedding. As David Ker remembers, "she was quite a formidable character – easily spotted in her floppy felt hat" – and Eveleigh was a very different generation to her. William and Eveleigh decided they must have a home of their own and began to look for somewhere to live close to Ballywhite. Mrs Brownlow, horrified that they intended to move away from her, suggested she build them a home on Ballywhite land as a wedding present: "My mother-in-law really wanted us to live together. When she realised we really weren't going to live with her she ordered a bungalow to be built," Eveleigh recalls.

The wedding took place at Loughinisland Parish Church, Seaforde on Wednesday January 11th 1961. The rehearsal the day before had annoyed Eveleigh's mother who had disapproved of them going out hunting together that morning and was not amused when they arrived late and used a dog blanket from the car to stand in as a train for her dress. All was well the following day when everyone arrived on time, the Brownlow contingent travelled together in a minibus from Ballywhite and Eveleigh arrived at the church on the arm of her brother, Michael and clad in a Belinda Belville-designed dress. 'The bride, Miss Eveleigh Panter,' wrote the *Daily Mail* reporter 'tall and stately and 23, set a new fashion – she had no grown up bridesmaids … Just child attendants when she married Major William S Brownlow, the Irish racehorse owner.' Her young attendants were mostly relations, William's young cousin and godson Richard Pooler, his three nieces Elinor and Angela Spring Rice and Elisabeth Brownlow[4] and family friend James Mackie. She wore a simply-cut gown of magnolia satin and a train of Brussels lace lent by her future mother-in-law. James was the best man and the ushers were Lord O'Neill, Patrick Forde, Patrick Corbett, Gavin Perceval-Maxwell and William Montgomery. *The Mourne Observer* ran the wedding on its front page 'Wedding of the Year' it splashed, while the Irish magazine *Social and Personal* used a photograph of the newlyweds as its frontispiece and *The Irish Field* pronounced it 'the social event of the season.' They left Seaforde for Madrid and a honeymoon in Tenerife, and they returned home full of the excitement of their trip and their recent wedding. Their mood of euphoria was cut short when only two weeks after their return Eveleigh's stepfather and William's friend, Desmond Forde, died.

Notes:
1 A young officer, five years William's junior, he went on to become General Sir Frank Kitson, GBE, KCB, MC, DL.
2 Letter of resignation: April 22nd 1953.
3 Cousins of Eveleigh's.   4 James & Susan Brownlow's daughter.

Chapter Eighteen
Living at Ballywhite

Jamie and Camilla Brownlow at Ballywhite

THE CONSTRUCTION of the bungalow began during their engagement but it was not habitable for another year which meant Mrs Brownlow got her wish and for 12 months they all shared a home. Eveleigh was used to people working in the house at Seaforde but quite unused to having everything done for her as was the way at Ballywhite. "I never had to wash up," she recalls of the time the three of them shared a home. "They had five staff in the house. I never even had to wash my tights!"

The bungalow stood at the end of the drive at Ballywhite with the exquisite backdrop of Strangford Lough and the Mourne Mountains beyond. William and Eveleigh called it Seaweed Hall in deference to Eveleigh's stepfather who listening to their plans for their new home during their engagement had laughingly labelled it such. It was built over the course of 1961 and his mother, aware that in time she would end up living in the house and they in Ballywhite made sure she had her say in its construction and insisted it was built with bells for servants in it.

They moved in just after Christmas 1961 and in September the following year their first child, a son, James, arrived. Jamie was born in Johnson House, the maternity wing of the Royal Victoria Hospital in Belfast, and afterwards Eveleigh employed a maternity nurse to help her at home. Some were concerned that William would 'bury' Eveleigh away at Ballywhite situated so far down the 20 mile Ards Peninsula. He had been happy at home with his mother and having done his jetting about with the army was content to lead a settled existence, but Eveleigh was "full of go" as Lydia de Burgh, a family friend, recalls. "She really got William back to life again and they went miles to everything and were very happy indeed and had a lot of fun."

Eveleigh saw no need for a large staff waiting on her and William, but Agnes was despatched by her concerned mother-in-law to help with the cooking and cleaning. After the maternity nurse she took on a nanny, but otherwise she ran the house herself.

After Jamie, they had a daughter, Camilla, in July 1964 and in May 1968, a second daughter, Melissa. A year after Camilla was born Mrs Brownlow suggested to William and Eveleigh that they move into Ballywhite as Seaweed Hall was no longer large enough for the family. To house her staff Mrs Brownlow built on another two rooms, a bathroom and a spare room and slowly Seaweed Hall increased in size. She also changed the name to Ballybrack, which means 'place of the seaweed', as she had never quite approved of naming the house Seaweed Hall.

The age difference that had surprised so many when they announced their engagement became less and less relevant as the years passed and they settled into the routine of family life. Their friends came from all age groups and the children's godparents were a mixture of family and friends from both Eveleigh and William's generations. With three children and a wonderful nanny, life in the nursery was happy. Nanny, otherwise known as Rita Connolly, had worked for a number of family friends of the Brownlows. She arrived in her sixties with grey hair and winged glasses and with every intention of working until the youngest Brownlow no longer needed her attentions. She left fifteen years later with brown hair and, according to all who knew her, looking much younger. She retired when Melissa went to school in England: "Dad did not want to become her next charge," recalls Jamie. "I was 17 when she left, she had just about given up trying to influence me!"

She lived in the house and had her own sitting room to which she retired in the evening. She talked nineteen to the dozen and would take the children out for a walk in all weathers, picking up sticks or stripping bushes of fruit as they went and warning her charges not to be too adventurous: 'Don't climb that tree or you will fall down and break your leg. Don't go up the mountain on your own or the foxes will eat you.' They all believe that her philosophy has made them far more cautious than any of their peers. She drove appallingly and the children believed that her magnetic images of St Christopher and the Virgin Mary kept her little Mini on the road. She was a good Catholic attending Mass every week, making pilgrimages to Lourdes and regularly announcing 'oh Jesus, Mother Mary and Joseph' to any drama. When the Pope made a visit to Ireland there was immense excitement and she took herself off to see him. Camilla recalls the event: "While she was waiting she offered a bull's eye sweet to a child who was beside her. The child choked and they had to take it to the first aid post at the moment the Pope passed by."

William teaching Jamie to ride

From left: Melissa, Camilla and Jamie

William takes Melissa (left) and Camilla (right) out cub hunting

In 1969 William and Eveleigh put in a swimming pool at Ballywhite and Nanny's greatest feat was taking the children swimming when she could not even swim herself. William had found a tractor inner tube and she would bob about in it in the pool while the children swam about her.

William was a fair father, his concern was for good manners and he left the discipline to Eveleigh, but on the rare occasion he told the children off they felt his reproach. "He was fair and strict in the old way," says Jamie, "we tended to know what he thought by what was not said." He was good at giving his children confidence, telling them how clever and attractive they were without pushing them and never expressing exasperation when they faced failure in school or university exams. Unlike many fathers he was always at home and consequently spent a lot of time with his children, he was with them for meals and to tuck them up in bed. Every year he dressed in a Father Christmas outfit and put the children's stockings on their beds – nobody ever saw him do this until one year Jamie, then a teenager, woke up and exclaimed 'good god' before returning to sleep.

For his children he was an unflappable figure; if they hurt themselves he would silence them exclaiming 'no blood so you can't cry' and a comforting figure whose happy hum of 'pom, pom, pom' reassured them as he went about the house with a pipe in his mouth and a whistle about his neck. Melissa enjoyed the fact she always knew exactly what was in his pocket: a nutmeg, a pencil and Swan matches. He had become a man of habit and they enjoyed his predictability.

As with his childhood there were lots of dogs about and his children were brought up in the great outdoors. There were terriers, spaniels and Labradors, a hamster, a tortoise, rabbits, budgies, bantams, ducks and a goldfish called Enoch. Dilly the duck became a favourite and travelled in Eveleigh's pocket into Portaferry and once followed her into the polling station on election day – she was loved by the children because she swam with them.

Horses too were a part of life and Camilla first went out on the back of Jackie the Donkey in a wicker howdah. William had already bought a pony, Dinky, for the use of his nephews and nieces when they came to Ballywhite and his own children first took the reigns astride him and a pony of Eveleigh's, Playboy. Dinky first arrived 'on trial' at Ballywhite but proved himself in teaching child after child to ride and died there many years later, aged 40.

William had given up riding by the time they took it up and there was never any pressure on any of them to ride. Jamie's first day out hunting suggested it was something he might enjoy but appearances are deceptive and he did not. The other young boy hunting for the first time that day was Richard Dunwoody – he spent it in tears but went on to become a world-famous jockey. George Dunwoody, the young Richard's father, helped train William's horses. There were gymkhanas and Pony Club events but neither Jamie nor Camilla became passionate about horses.

Melissa's love of riding continued into adulthood although she admits in many ways she rode as a child not to disappoint her father as both Jamie and Camilla had lost interest. "I only carried on as all Dad's horsey friends would ask if any of the children rode and he answered 'one does a little bit'. Latterly I met so many hunting friends of Dad's and called him after every day's hunting, he was delighted and so pleased to hear about it. I think he was finally proud of me riding and certainly very proud of my horse, the Raj, when reports came back."

As a child visiting his grandparents William had enjoyed going out on the lough with Tommy and Frank White. Tommy went on to take Jamie, Camilla and Melissa out fishing for mackerel and there were occasional trips in a large old wooden punt to attempt to net salmon. One day William took them out with nets near Frank and Agnes' house and they came home with 66 mullet and covered from head to toe in mud, having had to drag a sinking friend from the mud. "Nicola Mackie did not want to dirty her favourite jacket so refused to lie on her stomach hence she sank," remembers Melissa. "She was completely stuck so Dad got into our punt-like boat, the *Orange Lily*, to which we tied a rope and he poled himself out to rescue her." The children never became interested in sailing despite doing a sailing course across the lough with the Rowan-Hamiltons at Killyleagh. There was surprisingly little messing about on the lough as children but as adults Melissa and Jamie's wife, Amanda, bought a speedboat to waterski. Jamie was taught to shoot by William at the age of 13, but he was less keen for his girls to take it up despite Camilla professing an interest. She was not encouraged but remained interested and one day when she and Eveleigh spotted a pheasant in a tree in the garden she snuck up on it with a shotgun – Camilla was delighted when the fat cock pheasant fell to the ground but it ended in tears when it was discovered the pheasant was Pedro, a semi-tame bird they had all grown fond of. After much persuasion William did teach Melissa to shoot when she had arranged to take part in a triathlon which included a clay pigeon shoot, and he was amazed when she wounded a rook exclaiming 'good god you hit it!' At the clay pigeon shoot they both achieved the same score: three out of ten.

Jamie, Camilla and Melissa began their education at Portaferry Primary which they travelled to by the school bus. It was a small school with four to a class which were juggled by Mrs Lyttle, who was strict enough to administer the ruler and cane when it was required. Camilla recalls Melissa's arrival: "She spent the first week with her arms outstretched at me and tears streaming down her face, I was very put out that I had to go and sit on the small desk with her while she settled in."

William and Eveleigh arranged for Jamie and Camilla to leave Portaferry Primary and share a governess to help prepare them for boarding school. Jamie spent a term with a governess at Lough Fea in County Monaghan. John and Judith Shirley were distant cousins and great friends and Hugh their son was the same age as Jamie. Together they prepared for Headfort, their future prep school. Jamie was homesick

The Brownlow family pictured in 1962

Back from left: Angela Spring Rice, Charles Spring Rice, James Brownlow, Sandy Welsh, William, Willie Brownlow, Elinor Spring Rice (later Elliott)

Middle from left: Sue Brownlow, Anne Monteagle, Elinor Brownlow with Jamie Brownlow on lap, Nell Welsh (Cam), Eveleigh Brownlow

Front from left: Joanna Brownlow (later Scott) Fiona Spring Rice (later Garber) Libs Brownlow (later Bailey)

leaving home for the first time but he loved the rambling house set in a deer park. He continued to be homesick at Headfort, near Kells, which although small and rural was a tough sort of place with fairly few trips home each term – however he did well there and ended his days as Head Boy and later in life chose it for his own children. William wanted Jamie to go to Eton and despite making very few visits to England he took Jamie there himself for his first day. Jamie found Eton vast and rather a shock after his time at Headfort, especially going with no contemporaries from Ireland.

Camilla left Portaferry Primary at nine and shared a governess for two years with family friends in County Meath. There were four other girls but she was the only one that was effectively a full-time boarder, (the others went weekly or daily), and she was terribly homesick. The governess made them study paintings and plays which was unfortunate for Camilla who was more interested in maths and science. However, the education had its effects and one weekend away a nine year old Camilla impressed her extended family when she recognised the Bruegel prints on her cousin's placemats. Lessons were in the basement and there were a multitude of extra-curricular activities organised – swimming, dancing, drama, nature diaries and gardening. When she left

County Meath she went to boarding school in England, St Mary's Wantage in Oxfordshire, which she enjoyed.

Melissa did not go away to a governess and first left home when she finished at Portaferry Primary at ten. She was very lonely with her brother and sister away and depended on the dogs, the ponies and her much-adored nanny for friendship. At Portaferry she had a very good teacher, Mr Arnold, who saw her through her Common Entrance exam, even helping her to sit a scholarship to St Mary's, Wantage. Melissa did not get the scholarship but she went on to become Head Girl there.

It turned out there were a number of girls from Northern Ireland at the school in Camilla's year and when there were holidays they used to travel to and from the airport together. The girls were happy enough at school, the downside was they were too far away to make it home for weekend exeats or have parents watch them in matches or school plays.

William was not overly concerned about his daughters' education, although he did make one parents' meeting where he was collared by a headmistress and left too bemused to even find Camilla's form teacher. "I think he was of the old school thinking that girls needed to meet nice friends at school and then do a cookery course or something similar, work for a few years and then get married," explains Camilla. "As long as we tried our best that was all that mattered to him," says Melissa. When Camilla got a Sixth Form Scholarship for science, which reduced the school fees by a third, everyone began to notice Camilla's academic capabilities. There was surprise when Camilla suggested she went to university and William discovered there had not been a Brownlow at University since 1710 – and when she disappointed herself by leaving Edinburgh with an ordinary (rather than honours) degree he expressed nothing but pride that she had got that far.

The children's summer holidays were spent at home. It was the best time of the year there and a busy time for the game farm, besides William had lost interest in travelling. The children were used to contemporaries going on hot summer holidays or skiing trips but William impressed upon them they were lucky to live in such magnificent surroundings.

In August the family went to the north coast for the tennis tournament at Ballycastle which was a great social event in Northern Ireland. William would occasionally join them but he hung up his racket after winning the father and Under 10s with Melissa – who was aged 11. Some years they had French exchanges, they all came from the same family and the children took it in turns to go to them, and other years the children were invited on holidays with friends. When Camilla was taken to Greece by her school friend Anna Cadogan, Anna's father, Lord Cadogan, flew his plane into the airport at Newtownards and both families had a seafood picnic at Scrabo. One summer in the Seventies there was a happy family trip to Lough Erne with a family friend Jane Stephens (later Jane Pope) and her son, Sebastian. They hired a boat in fantastic weather and William enjoyed being captain of the boat and waterskiing, and Camilla caught her first fish. From time to time they piled in the car to do a tour of cousins and godparents in England which William had started to consider 'going abroad'. His only other annual trip to England was for the racing at Cheltenham.

His daughters' passion for skiing began when five families arranged a holiday in the 1980s to the Dolomites in Italy – there were thirty-two of them in three chalets. For William it was his first time back in the country since the war and he took his family to Venice on the return journey. His hip hurt too much to ski but he decided to gave it a try. During the first day everyone fell off the ski lifts, landing on top of each other and he decided to retire from the sport! Years later he met his daughters in the Swiss Alps at Verbier when they went to work there.

The biggest surprise came in 1975 when after years of staying at home for holidays Eveleigh told William she was taking him to Kenya, Uganda and Tanzania. It was a shock for William, who had expressed no desire to go abroad, but they both loved the trip. When they returned Eveleigh had a brainwave, deciding that instead of throwing great parties for their children's 18th or 21st birthdays she would take them all to Kenya. It was a much appreciated decision – they rode camels, spent nights in trees waiting for leopards to take bait from beneath them and for three weeks travelled between the top safari lodges as well as making a trip to the coast. As well as the trip being a great experience for the children they enjoyed being together at a time when they were beginning to go their separate ways in life.

For William there was only one thing frustrating about the position of Ballywhite and that was the lack of a proper car ferry over the half mile stretch from Portaferry to Strangford. After the war a privately run landing craft operated as a vehicular ferry for a short time but a craft capsized drowning a man and it reverted to a foot passenger ferry.

William became involved in a move to put pressure on the county council to address the problem of the lack of crossing facilities. In 1958 the campaign for a government-run crossing from Portaferry to Strangford was launched and by 1959 William was on to the case and writing letters to those in positions of power about the necessity of a vehicular crossing. At an early point in the discussion the County Surveyor at Down County Council put forward the suggestion of a tidal barrage across the mouth of Strangford Lough which would act as a road, provide land to reclaim for farming, as well as providing easier access to the lough's islands. His letter to William makes intriguing reading today:

'I know that there will be sentimental objections to altering the character of the Lough … The fact is, however, that the Lough is not a very great tourist attraction at present, and the position is unlikely to improve while it remains tidal. Owing to the tides and mud flats much of the shore is inaccessible at present, and the mud flats do not add to the scenic value at low tide … in my opinion the beauty of the Lough and its attraction to tourists could be considerably increased.'[xxii]

While the suggestion of a barrage did not get far off the ground the idea of constructing a bridge did. Well aware that if you suggest a higher price there is some chance of a satisfactory middle way William backed calls for a bridge and in 1962 he became chairman of the Bridge Committee. Down County Council claimed that a bridge was too expensive and that a council funded vehicle ferry was not an option as they were merely a road authority. The Council's inaction resulted in impassioned speeches from all sides of the community. Edward Bell, the Labour candidate for North Down, joined the committee and made the 'bridge issue' a campaign issue in 1964:

'Unionist politicians in the past have talked about draining the Lough, about dredging it, about encircling it with promenade walks and latterly about bridging it at its narrowest point. It could be the 'Southport' of the North one politician claimed. But still Strangford Lough lies calmly and serenely at ease as it has done for thousands of years smiling contentedly at the vain attempts of these men to conquer it for their own purposes. This stretch of water divides two parts of our country as efficiently as the Irish Sea divides Scotland from Ireland. It has turned the Ards Peninsula into a forgotten backwater … a bridge or tunnel would not be merely joining the two towns of Portaferry and Strangford – it would be joining 100 square miles of what is now virtually an island with the mainland."[xxiii]

In 1964 the costing of a bridge was worked out and dismissed and in 1965 the Council made the monumental decision to operate a vehicle ferry between Portaferry and Strangford. A ferry capable of coping with the strength of the tide was built in Cork and went into operation in October 1969.

During the course of his fight for the ferry William took the somewhat extreme step of proving how much he needed to cross the lough regularly by buying for himself a car that 'drove' on water. The sight of his amphibious car driving into the lough was like something straight out of a James Bond movie and amused everyone who saw it and even drew crowds. It also did the trick and crossed the lough. He had found it in 1963 on a trip to London. While Eveleigh was shopping he decided to entertain himself at the Earls Court Motor Show. There he found an amphibious car which he took for a test drive out of Earls Court and into the River Thames. Duly satisfied with its performance he arranged for it to be delivered to Elliot's, a garage in Portaferry. It was bright red with a soft top and the ultimate in car *chic*. It also worked and he was delighted when it proved capable of dealing with the strong currents in the lough.

The car did have its downsides as William told Bobbie Hanvey who interviewed him about the car for his *Ramblin' Man* programme on Downtown Radio: "It was very difficult parking the car in Belfast because of its propeller." It did not come with a compass, lifejackets or an oar, but William added all these necessities to the car. Not everyone was entirely convinced by their journeys in the car and many recall being terrified when the water lapped at the sides and occasions when with relief they turned back. "If the waves were breaking white you wouldn't go out," William told the listeners on Downtown Radio. "My mother-in-law and Patrick Forde and his wife came out for their first time in the pitch dark and they were distinctly nervous."

His brother once waved off his daughters Libs and Joanna on a trip across the lough with their uncle. No sooner had they set off but they ran out of petrol and were left heading into very strong currents without oars as William had forgotten them. "Luckily we were not too far out," remembers Libs, "and even more luckily Dad was on the shore watching. So he waded out to an anchored boat and rowed out to us and towed us back to safety!"

The car was very expensive to insure and William – who was a Member of Lloyds – was amused to discover that his syndicate was insuring his car, so effectively he was insuring himself. When the ferry came into use he gave the car to Agnes, not to take out on the lough (he had taken the bung out) but to travel on tarmac to and from Ballywhite. In the 1980s Melissa was working for an antiques dealer in Crossgar where she received a telephone call from a man saying he had found Major Brownlow's amphibious car on a scrap heap and wondered if it had any value.

He never lost his interest in the ferry and later in life, calculated that if the council had predicted how much money would be spent on maintaining the ferry route over the years a bridge would have seemed good value: "we could have built a golden bridge."

William's floating car

Chapter Nineteen
Agnes: Family Life

Derek White

FRANK FOUND himself out of work when the potato and soup-canning factory at Ballyfindry closed down. He took another job in the Northern Ireland government buildings at Stormont: "I was responsible for keeping all sorts of machinery ticking over there," he says. With his new job almost 20 miles away the bicycle was not a practical option and he bought an old car from a friend. It was the first time he had commuted any distance to work but car ownership was on the increase and it was becoming more common to drive distances to work. In 1920 half a million people across the United Kingdom owned a car and in 1940 that figure was three million. He had learnt to drive when he was looking after the cars at Ballywhite as a teenager but he had never passed a test as driving tests were not introduced until 1956 in Northern Ireland. Agnes meanwhile had never driven a car and continued to bicycle everywhere she wasn't given a lift.

In 1947 Agnes and Frank had their first baby, a son named Derek. While they had both been born at home Derek's first view of the world was from the hospital in Newtownards. Agnes and mothers of her generation were the first to be encouraged to give birth in maternity units rather than at home. Following Derek's birth Agnes left her job at Ballywhite to care for him, although she went in when she was needed to fill in for others. When Agnes was needed at Ballywhite she left Derek with Frank's mother. In 1952 they had a second son, William, who was born in the same hospital. The five year age gap between Derek and William gave Agnes time for both her boys as well as some part-time work, and she found it helped that Derek was at school when William arrived.

In the mid 1950s they got their first television; it was a black and white one and came second-hand from Frank's sister, Mary. It was still early days for light entertainment on television and the family loved it, especially the boys whose favourite programme was a BBC children's classic, *The Woodentops*.

Derek and William went to the local Abbacy Primary School until it closed down and then a bus picked them up and took them to school in Portaferry. When they were both at school Agnes returned to work more often and in the early 1960s she went to help Mrs Brownlow for a fortnight, because Annie Gray had almost lost her finger in a domestic accident. While she was there Agnes got to know William Brownlow's young wife who was living with her mother-in-law while their house was being built at the end of the drive: "She was about to move into Seaweed Hall and she said to me, 'come down to me for a fortnight when you're finished here'."

Her job at Seaweed Hall may have been intended as a fortnight but in reality it saw her through the next four decades. Eveleigh and William had no grand plans to take on a large staff at Seaweed Hall, and Agnes' new role included cooking and cleaning: "It was different with Mrs Brownlow, because unlike Granny Brownlow[1] she did most things herself. She wasn't too keen on the cooking then, though she's great now."

Eveleigh collected Agnes from her home until William gave her a car: "When I passed my test he gave me Granny Brownlow's car. He kept me in a car for years, before that they picked me up and before that I used to go up on a bike, up to Seaweed Hall every day till about 3 o' clock." The Brownlows encouraged her to learn to drive by offering her a car and with luck she found a friendly police detective who gave her lessons. The detective had accompanied Brian Faulkner, the unionist politician, to Ballywhite and sitting in the kitchen with Agnes enjoying her cooking he heard she wanted to learn to drive. She passed first time and that was the end of her biking days.

At Seaweed Hall the household consisted of Agnes helping out with the cooking and cleaning and a nanny for William and Eveleigh's first child, Jamie. The young Brownlows were choosing to live their life quite differently to the generation before. Agnes remembers the first nanny well: "Nanny Parrot she was called, and her face was blue, she never looked well, she suffered from asthma too. Then one day Mrs Brownlow came to collect me – I wasn't driving then – and she came flying down in a terrible state: 'Nanny Parrot's dead!' she shouted. I said, 'well I'm not going in to see her'. The poor woman had just died; she's buried at the Presbyterian Church." A few years later Camilla was born and Elinor Brownlow moved to Seaweed Hall and Eveleigh and William moved into Ballywhite. Agnes and the new nanny, Nanny Connolly, moved with them to Ballywhite.

Agnes with William

Taking a break at Ballywhite with Nanny
Connolly

Frank and Agnes

Visiting Derek and his family in Persia

The Whites with their grandchildren

When Elinor Brownlow moved into William and Eveleigh's bungalow she required a cook, Pat McGrath, and a housemaid, Annie Gray, to maintain her very rigid standards. Agnes knew those standards only too well: "Granny Brownlow rang the bell between courses and nothing stopped her from eating every meal in that big dining room. Nowadays they would ask 'what did the five of you do in the house, and the seven working outside?' But there was so much to do, fires had to be black leaded. Standards were different then."

Over the course of the following three decades Agnes worked part-time, cleaning and cooking and becoming a huge part of the Brownlows' family life. For Jamie, Camilla and Melissa, Agnes was always there telling them stories about life in the house when their grandparents were both alive. Like her father before her she had found work with one family and lived a contented, settled life alongside their own, and become a much beloved institution within that family. During the course of her lifetime she witnessed domestic service change from a time when you bobbed a curtsey to your employer to today when employers expect to be relaxed with you and want you to call them by their Christian names. The modern way, Agnes feels, for all its advantages has its own effects on the quality of service, for while she was trembling in her boots when she began work that fear made sure she did her job properly. "The young ones coming in [to domestic service today] wouldn't even know how to set a table, would never have learnt how. The girls that come into Ballywhite to help out from time to time put the knives the wrong way turned round, not the blade turned inwards," she comments. "Society has changed so much and the people that are coming in to work are more casual. I have known girls coming into Ballywhite to work and they'd say 'do you want a fag, Major' – that got me, when I heard them saying that I said 'things have changed'. Even in my day when things did relax I wouldn't have been familiar with the Major like that. He'd have made fun with me, but I wouldn't have been like that. In Lady Bangor's time you were bowing and scraping and all that, now you meet the likes of Bill Montgomery [a family friend of the Brownlows] with them in their kitchen. You wouldn't have been introduced to guests in those days, but everyone lives in the kitchen today."

For Frank the changes in four generations of Brownlows at Ballywhite are significant. He knows the changes are a reflection of a different society but he cannot help find strange the casual way everyone gets on with each other today. In his time families in houses such as Ballywhite were employers who lived lives so different to his own it was impossible to imagine a middle ground.

Agnes and Frank's own children had many more opportunities open to them through an improved education system. While it did not enter Agnes' mind not to go into domestic service it did not enter her children's minds to do so. For children of their generation the 'big houses' and the local aristocracy or gentry no longer offered work and a secure life, and with further education more accessible both sons enrolled on practical courses at college after school. For work they both headed to Belfast: Derek got a job at Curry's and William at Mackie's, and as bachelors they lived in flats in the city.

When Derek married he moved to Cloughy and then to Strangford where Agnes gave him the land surrounding her mother's small cottage, The Mallard. Derek built a large bungalow on the land there as a replacement dwelling for his grandmother's cottage. Agnes loves their house and knows that her mother would be proud to see it, and that her father would enjoy the garden Derek and his wife have created on the land. Before Derek and his family settled there he worked abroad as a civil engineer, and was based in Belgium and later the Middle East in Tehran, Riyadh and Oman. His wife, Vivien, returned to Ireland to put their two children, Jamie and Melanie, through school in Downpatrick and later Derek returned and set up his own engineering company, Whites, in Strangford. Like their grandfather, Bob Skillen, Derek and William love to sail and both keep boats. William keeps his near him on the south coast of England and Derek has a yacht on Strangford Lough. Derek's boat sleeps six and with it he has taken his father to Scotland and the Isle of Man. Agnes does not join them on these trips as she has been less than keen on boats since childhood: "My father used to scare us in the boats. He used to take us out every Sunday, he'd jump over board and say 'cheerio' and I was scared."

William settled into a permanent job at the BBC in Belfast and married a nurse. He and his wife, Mary, lived in a house on the Ballywhite estate and later bought a house in Portaferry and had five children, Sarah, Cathy, Lucy, Emily and Philip. From Portaferry William commuted to Belfast to work and until he and his wife separated he had lived on the Ards Peninsula most of his life. After his divorce William moved to Hampshire where he works in the computing world. He returns to County Down to visit but Agnes does not think he will ever return to Northern Ireland to live.

The modern concept of travelling or taking a holiday was not something Agnes and Frank hankered after. The area surrounding Portaferry has always been Frank's home and today neither he nor Agnes have any desire to be anywhere else. Even the suggestion of moving to the other side of the lough, to the area where Agnes grew up, appalls them.

As Derek and William were growing up there were no family holidays. "We never bothered with holidays, maybe a day here," she says. During the boys' childhood Agnes and Frank took themselves away together only once: "We went to Portrush – they had a camping place with so many rooms in it, a marquee thing – the boys were away, we went on our own." Frank's father was a merchant seaman and in the seven years of Frank's life he was alive he impressed on him the excitement of his travels to the Balkans and across the Atlantic. Although Frank enjoyed the thought of his father's journeys to distant lands he never felt any need to travel the world and Agnes even less: "Frank has been to Lough Erne, Donegal, Isle of Man and Scotland – he's been around but I was never one for leaving home. I've been to Dublin once and we went together to Jamie's[2] graduation in Edinburgh. We liked Edinburgh, but didn't think much of Glasgow." Frank's brother, Jim saw much of the world during his time in the army, but Frank did not want such a life. Thus it was a great surprise when, after 30 years of marriage, Frank and Agnes contemplated a trip abroad – to Persia.

It took their son Derek who was working in Persia – modern day Iran – to entice them away from County Down, and even he did not imagine he would succeed in getting them both to come: "They wrote to me from Tehran," Agnes recalls planning their trip, "and said I would be more adventurous than Frank and would I go. When I told him this he said he'd come too." In 1977 they left their son William to look after the house and the dogs and off they went to Tehran for six weeks. "I could have lived there," says Frank. "We'd never been anywhere, we thought it was beautiful. We liked the plane too: I never thought we'd go on an airplane, we flew to Heathrow and we stopped at Damascus on our way back.

"Derek was an engineer. He was in charge of a big project down in the desert, and I went down there from Tehran with him, right through desert. There was one thing about it I noticed, there were no birds about it, never saw a bird about. We were near the Caspian Sea, near where the British made roads around the mountains. We were up there looking down from the road, you would have been sick.

"The back door to their house was on the street and you had to ring the bell and talk before they let you in. They had a good big garden and there was a swimming pool for when you got too warm. We were swimming and next door he thought it was cold, I think it was May. They had a girl in the house working there and if you had a clean shirt and you left it on the floor it was on the line, she thought you wanted it washed. When you went to the market the women were all covered in veils and always walking behind the men."

They both enjoyed themselves so much they went back again the following year, but in 1979 came the revolution in which the Shah[3] and the royal family fled the country and the exiled religious leader Ayatollah Khomeini returned and set up an Islamic state opposed to the Shah's pro-Western policies. Agnes and Frank were happy when Derek eventually settled back in County Down. He set up a very successful business in Strangford and has been a great support to his parents buying them cars, framing his mother's paintings for her, and as they got older arranging for a gardener to come and help them out.

The political troubles in Northern Ireland have had little impact on Agnes or Frank's life and when the Troubles were at their peak, Agnes and Frank felt no political motivation. The reality was their lives were for the main part unaffected by the continuing terrorism. When two bombs went off in Portaferry they were shocked but they knew that worse was happening elsewhere and they were not optimistic of much change. "You never thought about it, you just hear the news and all that, but you don't think about it," Agnes explains. "Peace Process? They're still at it today, it goes on just the same."

During the 1970s they became grandparents and apart from the years Derek worked away in the Middle East they grew up close to their grandchildren, always seeing lots of them. The seven grandchildren have been educated locally, at schools in Portaferry and Downpatrick, but their further education has taken them further afield, to Belfast, Dublin, Edinburgh and London. They have all done well in their studies and grown into able adults with diverse professions. Derek and Vivienne's son, Jamie, got his degree from Edinburgh University and is now a civil engineer and their daughter, Melanie, is studying Geography and the Environment at Trinity College, Dublin. William and Mary's eldest daughter, Sarah, is a nurse specialising in plastic surgery at the Ulster Hospital in Dundonald as well as a mother of two children; Cathy is studying Accountancy at Queen's University, Belfast; Lucy works for the civil service in Belfast and like her sister brings up two children on top of her work; Emily is at university in Ealing studying Nursing and Philip is still at school.

Agnes and Frank take great pleasure in their children and grandchildren's achievements and are delighted to have great-grandchildren who live close by, as both Sarah and Lucy settled with their husbands in Portaferry.

Notes:
1 Elinor Brownlow
2 Jamie White, their grandson.
3 Muhammad Reza Shah Pahlevi, 1919–80.

Chapter Twenty
Politics

William as depicted by local cartoonist, Rowel Friers

ALTHOUGH MANY of William's forebears had stood as MPs for County Armagh he never considered a political career for himself. He did, nonetheless, take an active interest in the concerns of his local community. His freedom from personal ambition meant that when he did enter the political fray he was able to throw himself honestly into what he believed to be right.

His ancestors had allied the Brownlow name with 'liberal' politics. One William Brownlow had been a thorn in the side of conventional unionists in the Irish Parliament of the eighteenth century, and another namesake had allowed Catholics to keep their holdings when the Penal Laws forbade them from doing so by giving them Protestant names in the estate records. During a 17 year allegiance with twentieth century unionism William discovered that he too was more moderate than many of his political colleagues. Lord Mayhew of Twysden, who as Sir Patrick Mayhew had served as Secretary of State for Northern Ireland in the 1990s, recalls that William even in his last decade of life maintained a temperate political outlook: "Although William epitomised what was best in the landed establishment, he was far from conventional in his political perceptions. There was nothing of the 'not an inch' outlook in his political thinking, let alone of any nostalgia for a Protestant supremacy.

He believed in the virtue of bringing people together, and his own relationships with all sorts and conditions of men and women powerfully demonstrated this. What was so manifest was his respect for each of them, regardless of their background or position."

William entered politics through local Ulster Unionist Party branch meetings. He was a straightforward unionist who genuinely believed in maintaining the union with Britain as long as it was the wish of the population of Northern Ireland and he was a natural Conservative (the party linked to the Ulster Unionist Party). In the 1960s the Ulster Unionist Party was used to being in power and had yet to face any realistic political opposition.

He joined his local Portaferry branch of the Ulster Unionist Party when he returned to Northern Ireland. From this connection with the party his involvement snowballed, beginning when Sir Roly Nugent offered him as his replacement as chairman of that branch. William went on to become chairman of the regional office, the Ards Unionist Association. At the same time he had also been persuaded by a delegation from Portaferry to stand for a position on Down Council in 1967. He put a great deal of work into assisting the local community – arranging housing, street lighting, the height of baths in old people's housing, were all part of his daily chores – and he was proud that the local group which approached him to stand for Down Council was predominantly Catholic. Such happy situations were becoming rarer and in an increasing number of areas the local population felt discriminated against by councillors of a different faith to their own.

In the late Sixties and early Seventies he was busy in the local community with his work for the council and his position as a Justice of the Peace. His children remember people from Portaferry and the surrounding area appearing at the house at all hours to ask his advice on a whole range of matters, and he enjoyed being able to help them and penned many letters on their behalf. He had no aspirations to further his involvement in the Assembly that sat in Stormont – Northern Ireland's own Parliament – but an indiscretion by a local unionist colleague meant that at the last minute the Party needed another candidate to stand and to help out he put his name forward.

It was a bold thing to do. The year was 1973 and the Provisional IRA had begun their terrorist campaign four years before. While the majority of the people lived their ordinary lives without any threat to their safety hundreds had been killed and Northern Ireland had become a society where a military presence was needed to prevent terrorism. William was lucky when he was stopped at an IRA roadblock on his way home as from behind his balaclava came, 'oh it's only the Major,' and he was allowed on his way.

In 1921 Northern Ireland was given its own devolved Assembly at Stormont with about 80 Assembly Members.[1] It was taken away when the violence escalated in

March 1972 and direct rule from Westminster was temporarily introduced. A new Assembly was proposed in 1973. "I am not a professional politician, merely a citizen who puts his country above party political gain or personalities," William told journalists when putting himself up for election to the new Assembly. The Proportional Representation electoral system meant that it was worth him standing as even if he was not elected the votes he accrued would be transferable to his colleagues and help their election. While unsure of his future in politics, he stood confident in the knowledge he was doing the right thing for the Party and his colleagues John Brooke[2], Bertie Campbell, Drew Donaldson and Jim Kilfedder in North Down. Despite his diffidence William was elected and on 28th June 1973 he took his seat in the Assembly.

Brian Faulkner, who had been the Northern Irish Prime Minister when direct rule was implemented, became Chief Executive at Stormont and agreed in November 1973 to a joint unionist-nationalist power-sharing Executive. It was the first hands-on attempt to produce some sort of political dialogue acceptable to both sides of a divided community, and, it was hoped, would lead to a cessation of violence. William Whitelaw, the Conservative Northern Ireland Secretary of State, gathered together representatives from the Unionist Party, SDLP, Alliance and others to work out an acceptable deal. He then sat with the Irish Government and agreed to the 'Sunningdale Council of Ireland' which the SDLP had made a prerequisite of their involvement. The result of Sunningdale was that while Britain retained sovereignty over Ulster it was given a consultative assembly – the Council of Ireland – which was made up of members from both Stormont and the Irish parliament. The Council of Ireland proved to be the real bone of contention to unionists.

The 'power-sharing' Executive came into existence on 1st January 1974 but the knives were out for it before it even sat. Many of the unionists who had signed up to it in November regretted doing so afterwards and began to view it as conspiring with Dublin and a step towards a united Ireland. Republicans viewed it as an unacceptable middle of the road solution and Sinn Fein blasted the SDLP for 'colluding' with the British Government. However for the time it lasted William sat as a unionist Assembly Member alongside nationalists such as Gerry Fitt and John Hume, and he was convinced it was the way forward. He was not a politician by nature but he enjoyed the company of some of the very varied characters involved in Northern Irish politics. Eveleigh remembers him inviting Paddy Devlin – a founding member of the SDLP – home to Ballywhite, although she recalls he came to discuss racing not politics.

William was a pragmatist who saw that the Sunningdale Agreement was the only solution to the problem of regaining devolved government. Unionists who felt this way about power sharing were dubbed 'Faulknerites', and critically they were not in the majority in their party. Brian Faulkner could not lead the Ulster Unionist Party with the support of so few and he resigned as chairman of the party a few days after the Assembly sat in January. He went on to take those – like William – who supported power-sharing into a new party, the Unionist Party of Northern Ireland (UPNI) and Harry West replaced him as leader of the Ulster Unionist Party.

In February 1974 there was a General Election and Harold Wilson became Prime Minister. Of direct consequence to Northern Ireland was that Harry West's Ulster Unionists gathered together with the DUP and the Vanguard Party in an 'anti power-sharing coalition' called the United Ulster Unionist Council, and of the twelve MPs sent to Westminster after the General Election 11 were members of the UUUC. It did not bode well for the future of the power-sharing Assembly.

On top of unionist in-fighting the terrorist situation was getting worse and in 1974 the IRA took their bombing campaign to England. The first bomb went off on a coach carrying soldiers on the M62 in Yorkshire killing 11 people, including two children and by the end of 1974 there were bombings in Guildford, Woolwich and Birmingham on top of endless attacks in Northern Ireland.

Hard-line unionists from the Democratic Unionist Party and the Vanguard Party worked at whipping up their supporters against 'the enemy in their midst'. Ian Paisley was good at this and organised rallies and marches and provoked his supporters to stand up for themselves, labelling any unionist who approved of a power-sharing government a 'republican'. William stood against the activities of Paisley and the Vanguard Party's William Craig – he may have shared their desire to keep Northern Ireland a part of the United Kingdom and in the scourge of the IRA, but he did not believe unionists should reduce themselves to such a base level. He also feared that rather than pro-British they were anti-Irish and if Britain did not help them they would work towards an independent Ulster.

The result of a more politicised Protestant working class was an increase in 'loyalist' terrorist activity. In March 1974 Portaferry witnessed a terrorist attack, a 300lb bomb in Church Street. The area had been evacuated before it went off so no lives were lost. The bomb was planted by loyalist terrorists and went off in a stolen Morris car outside a hotel wrecking the premises and a pub opposite. Jamie Brownlow remembers going into Portaferry with his mother and seeing buildings they knew well reduced to rubble. "My knees knocked together, they literally went weak at the sight of the place," recalls Jamie who was only 12 at the time. The attack was condemned by the SDLP who said it was an attempt to violate a mixed community. Bombs and murders had become commonplace and when on 20th April a man was killed in Belfast he became the 1000th person to be killed in Northern Irish terrorist violence since 1969. It was not the last bomb to go off; in Portaferry in June 1976 the Ulster Volunteer Force planted a bomb outside the International Bar killing a 24 year old Catholic[3].

The new Labour Government sent Merlyn Rees to Northern Ireland as Minister of State and Brian Faulkner went to see him and told him that the General Election results proved he could not get unionists to work for him under the Sunningdale Agreement. "I cannot carry it," Rees remember Faulkner telling him. "I have lost my reason to be. I am beaten, overwhelmed by the vote against my sort of unionism, or the unionism I'm trying to carry out[xxiv]." William stood by Brian Faulkner and the UPNI because he believed power-sharing was the only way ahead, but he hated the idea of a split unionist party and unionists standing against each other in elections. In April the Ards Unionist Association decided by a majority vote that Sunningdale was unacceptable. "I had expected to be able to carry the bulk of the constituency association with me into the UPNI but it split," William reflected sadly years later.

In May 1974 the Ulster Workers' Council, a Protestant trades' union in charge of electricity and sewerage, brought the country to a halt with a strike. Across Northern Ireland roadblocks were erected and loyalists used it as an opportunity to wreak havoc. It may have appeared to be an industrial dispute but ultimately 'the Workers' Strike' was co-ordinated to force an end to the sitting Assembly and break the Sunningdale Agreement. There was nothing Rees could do to stop it. The army could maintain some normality by running essential services but it could not intervene on such a scale, and it seemed that the majority of the population believed in its premise: "This was the Protestant people of Northern Ireland rising up against Sunningdale. They could not be shot down," reflected the journalist Peter Taylor.[xxv] William did not see it as a Protestant uprising but as the work of extremists; and recalling the final days of the strike in 1977 he wrote: 'it became apparent that a handful of fanatics might be prepared to sacrifice Ulster through the destruction of power stations.'[xxvi]

William could only get to Stormont from Ballywhite during the Workers' Strike under police guard and Eveleigh recalls being extremely concerned about his journey to and from work. He made an attempt to diffuse unionist fears in a missive to branch chairmen on 15th May, stating categorically that political parties were not in bed together at Stormont: 'SDLP, Alliance and Unionist parties are three different parties of different fundamental policies. We do not hold joint meetings like the UUUC. Our common bond is support of the executive … we are all opposing parties and treat each other as such.' There was no compromising from hard-line unionists, and paramilitary activity both at roadblocks and elsewhere gave the feeling that things were running out of control. On 17th May four loyalist car bombs exploded in Dublin and Monaghan killing 27 people. The strike continued and on 24th May Brian Faulkner resigned, bringing about an end to power-sharing.

The Ulster Workers' Strike lasted 14 days but the limited electricity supply, petrol, food and water shortages and subsequent sewerage problems brought the country to a standstill. The roadblocks and the paramilitary involvement had made it a terrifying fortnight in which most people were forced to stay at home. Despite this it is claimed that the majority of the people supported the bringing down of the power-sharing Executive. When it was over and the Assembly adjourned there were parties to celebrate the strike's success – Merlyn Rees recalls finding the door to Stormont Castle locked the following morning because the doorkeeper had overslept: he had been up all night at what he described as 'the victory celebrations'.

After the strike Paisley spoke out against the violence carried out by Protestants during the Workers' Strike. His hypocrisy infuriated William who wrote letters to the papers stating it was a bit late for Paisley to stand back from the people he had rallied. He felt Paisley and the UUUC had incited this violence by backing the strike and its objectives and that after creating a monster they should not be allowed to disentangle themselves from it so easily.

1974 was the last year to date to hold two general elections. The first had been brought about by the miners' strike, and the second in October was called because although Harold Wilson had the most seats he did not have an overall majority. As a result of the split in unionism William found him in the rather unexpected position of standing for this second election as the Unionist Party of Northern Ireland candidate for North Down. The UPNI was advised by the Conservative Party in Smith Square to field some candidates. Lord Brookeborough was the obvious candidate for North Down but by virtue of his title he could not stand for the House of Commons and William put himself forward in his place.

There was no chance a UPNI candidate was going to get elected to Westminster from North Down, but William believed in supporting the party he had helped form. "I agreed reluctantly … on the grounds that there was no risk of my being elected," he recalled years later. He stood against Keith Jones of the Alliance Party, an alderman of North Down Borough Council and Jim Kilfedder of the UUUC who had been the unionist Member of Parliament for North Down since 1970 when he was elected with the largest majority[4] in the United Kingdom. Although Kilfedder's majority lessened after the split within unionism, he was still ahead by 16,226 votes in the first election of 1974 when he faced unionist opposition from pro-Faulkner candidate Roy Bradford.

In his campaign William put himself forward as an alternative to hard-line unionism. His concern outside party politics was a real one and of vital importance to the farming community he represented: the collapse of the beef industry in Northern Ireland. Kilfedder surprised nobody when he was re-elected to his North Down seat. The results read as follows:

Kilfedder, JA (UUP-UUUC) 40,996[5]
Jones, K (Alliance) 9,973
Brownlow, W (UPNI) 6,037

The UPNI had fielded two candidates, William in North Down and another in East Belfast, and together they received 20,454 votes: 'a record of success which any new party could be justly proud of,' read the UPNI's first annual report.

After the General Election he was ready to take a back seat and keep out of mainstream politics, but his time had not yet come. Merlyn Rees tried again to get the political parties to meet around the table and this time he called an all-party Constitutional Convention to map out Northern Ireland's future. He called elections for the Convention on 1st May 1975 with the hope it may lead to another power-sharing assembly.

With the majority of the unionist vote going to UUUC candidates the UPNI needed all the help it could get and William could not back out. He stood to assist the election of the stronger candidate, Lord Brookeborough. There was no likelihood of two UPNI candidates getting enough votes to join the Assembly for North Down, but one would get a certain amount and the other's would become transferable to him under the proportional representation form of voting. William threw himself into campaigning and Eveleigh assisted him on the trail – one local newspaper reported how the electorate were often muddling her with Lady Brookeborough. His children helped him canvas support by knocking on doors and handing out cards saying 'Vote for Daddy'.

William saw his responsibility as bringing to light the direction unionism was going – if moderate non-sectarian support for the union with Great Britain was trodden down only Paisley's unionism would be left. He argued that the official unionist party was after independence. It had become his great concern and his opinion was reported in *The News Letter* [14/11/1974]:

'As the elections approach, they will assert that their only aim is to ensure that Northern Ireland remains part of the United Kingdom, but behind the scenes they will work for an independent Ulster. Paisley well knows that the Convention will have no power to discuss security or any other matter other than the future structure of government in Northern Ireland.'

There was a wide belief in the weeks leading up to the Convention Election that it could be close and *The Sunday News* reported that the UUUC could only have a one seat majority. Whatever the media was reporting the election produced a triumph for the UUUC which won 47 of the 78 seats and the SDLP 17. As the UUUC were against power-sharing there was no future.

With both hardline unionists and republicans refusing to budge an inch for each other, any future for self-government in Northern Ireland looked bleak and a descent into greater suspicion of the opposition became inevitable. William and Eveleigh's children were growing up at a very difficult time in Northern Ireland's history but even with their father in politics it did not really touch their lives. Camilla remembers going to be a bridesmaid in England at the time of her father's involvement and having to go on her own, it was many years later that she learnt the reason her parents were not with her was because they had been warned not to travel. The activities of the IRA were such a part of the goings-on at the time that once Jamie and Camilla made a plan for April Fool's Day to trick Nanny Connolly into thinking they were under attack.

They put a ladder up to Nanny's bedroom and put tights over their heads but Melissa, scared by the goings-on, had told Nanny who merely exclaimed 'och go away Jamie' when he arrived at the window. They were used to being stopped at army checkpoints, being searched before shopping in Belfast and following military vehicles with soldiers with guns looking out of the back and they accepted this as normal. They all remember being scared at night and searching their bedrooms before going to sleep. "Generally you became used to the Troubles but it did get to you subconsciously," comments Jamie who was once in a subway in Belfast with his mother when a bomb went off; although they were protected from the blast their proximity to it shook him.

"Everyone else was in the same boat and it was very much a way of life," says Melissa. "Certainly we had an idyllic life but you were always aware and sometimes heard bombs in the distance – we definitely varied our route to and from home, checked under cars and we were not allowed to pick up suspicious parcels or letters. Dad was particularly strict about not saying where we were meeting when talking to anyone in the army and to speak slightly in code and not to give precise times."

The police carried out checks at Ballywhite and William kept a pistol under the bed as well as getting an Alsatian dog for the family's protection. Without creating a drama he made sure his children were cautious when answering the door, but it was not until Camilla went away to school in England that she began to understand that Northern Ireland was different to other places. "We used to have the news on in the refectories at Wantage," says Camilla, "and I would dream of hearing that Dad had been shot on the television news." During Camilla's years growing up in Northern Ireland she was only involved in one bomb scare – in Belfast's Marks & Spencer's – and she actually witnessed more as an adult living in London. When Camilla was involved in some television reportage from a troubled area of Belfast she saw the problems and hatreds of inner city Belfast first hand and felt very strongly for the mothers who were trying to bring up their children free from the influence of those about them. Her own experience of a Northern Irish childhood had been worlds apart.

William's niece, Libs Bailey, was the only family member to receive what appeared a straight threat from a terrorist organisation. She was living with her parents near Downpatrick when she experienced the cloud of fear that many in Northern Ireland lived under. Aged 15 she was at home on her own when a door-to-door salesman appeared. She was talking to the salesman when the telephone rang. "The caller claimed to be with the IRA and said that Ballydugan [their house] was next on the list to be blown up because we entertained people in the army and we took them to the races in Downpatrick," Libs recalls. "I got all the information I could from the caller, told the salesman we had just had a bomb scare – he promptly fled – then I rang the police. I suspected that this 'salesman' had planted the bomb while I was on the telephone. The police came out and found nothing so it was only a terrifying hoax.

The salesman called again later that night after my parents had returned and apologised for abandoning ship and leaving me alone."

After the failure of the Convention Election William accepted his time in politics was over. He was depressed by the Ards Unionist Association's decision to remain with the hardliners, and after the meeting that decided this he handed in his resignation. He wrote a letter to Harry McGimpsey the chairman of the Association explaining his reasons:

'It is a hard decision after 17 years of working for a Party, but, though it was suggested to me that one should stay to fight this untidy alliance from within, this is what we have been doing for years – only to see the moderates scared away from meetings in fear and disgust as a result of the disruptive tactics of shouting down and insults by right wing elements.'

Lord Dunleath, an Alliance Assemblyman who was also a good friend of William's living at Ballywalter Park on the Ards Peninsula, told the local press his resignation was the honourable thing to do.

'Major Brownlow had made a genuine attempt to clean up the Unionist Party from the inside but had been frustrated in his efforts by the closed-minded element who had brought about a state of affairs by which in his own words people were 'scared away from meetings in fear and disgust as a result of the tactic of shouting down.'

… Major Brownlow and his liberal-unionist colleagues have been subjected to vilification and abuse from many elements in the party, in that they have been faced with what virtually amounts to fascism in that there is no question of hearing the other point of view but rather is slandered by abuse and insults.'[xxvii]

After his resignation William wrote a letter printed in various local newspapers asking unionists to think before putting all their eggs in Mr Paisley's basket: 'his sole creation was an atmosphere of fear and uncertainty … his ability to destroy seems endless – O'Neill, Chichester-Clark, Faulkner, the Assembly together with its speaker the late Nat Minford and now the convention. … I urge you, my erstwhile colleagues, to break the shackles with this Ulster Frankenstein before he destroys Ulster too.'

William felt convinced he had done the right thing supporting power-sharing but he was not enough of a career politician to continue fighting the increasingly hard-line unionists. Brian Faulkner resigned as leader of the UPNI the following summer and was made a Lord in the New Year's Honours list. William wrote to him after his resignation and received a heartfelt reply from a man worn down by his final years in politics:

'I appreciate it [your letter] much more than I can say in a letter for I know how sincerely you have written. I realise that we did not see (politically) eye-to-eye a few years back. Certainly there were some things I might have done in a different way but I think you appreciate some of the problems I faced.

'For me the only satisfying period since March 1972 was the time of the Assembly and the achievement of the Executive. All the rest has been frustration, mental strain and worry. I suppose we may have to leave it to the historians to recognise that we really did make progress in '73-'74. Our Assembly worked hard and in unity. And I am certain that there is much more satisfaction from doing what you know to be right rather than looking over your shoulder to see what the crowd wishes to hear. It was good to work with you and you were always tolerant and absolutely loyal."[xxviii]

Lord Faulkner was right. When the Good Friday Agreement was ratified in 1998, resulting in unionists sitting in an assembly with both nationalists and republicans, it was the first attempt at political power-sharing since 1974. Seamus Mallon of the SDLP described it as "Sunningdale for slow-learners." Lord Faulkner never lived to see it; he died in February 1977 when he fell from his horse out hunting with the Iveagh Harriers. In a tribute to him William wrote:

'As one who was not always in political accord with him I can most truthfully say that I am proud to have served with a man who had the courage to face almost certain political suicide for what he knew to be right.'

CONVENTION ELECTION
VOTE
UNIONIST U.P.N.I.

Brownlow
Brookeborough
Campbell

VOTE ACCORDING TO YOUR PREFERENCE

Published by U.P.N.I., Mayfair Buildings, Belfast and printed by Newtownards Chronicle Ltd., 25 Frances Street, Newtownards.

Vote Official Unionist
BROOKE
BROWNLOW
CAMPBELL
DONALDSON
JESS
McCLURE

VOTE 1, 2, 3, 4, 5, 6
IN ORDER OF YOUR CHOICE

Bring this card to the Polling Station

Published by Unionist Council, Glengall Street, Belfast and printed by Spectator Newspapers, Bangor.

Notes:
1 The people were also represented in Westminster by 12 Members of Parliament.
2 In August 1973 he became 2nd Viscount Brookeborough.
3 Christopher Byers
4 He finished with 41,443 votes ahead of his nearest rival.
5 Kilfedder had a majority of 31,023 on a 61.2% poll turnout.

Chapter Twenty-One
Field Sports

William with his hounds at Dublin Horse Show

THE PASSION William felt towards field sports had been instilled in him by his parents who understood hunting and shooting to be a natural part of country life. He was indisputably a child of the outdoors and his immense enthusiasm never waned, indeed if anything it increased over the years. When he settled in Northern Ireland in the 1950s he threw himself into hunting and racing locally and later, when the time came to give up the horse, he put his energies into shooting and game bird breeding. As the decades passed and a largely urban public became increasingly opposed to field sports he became a hardworking lobbyist, more than prepared to speak out and act if it helped protect their future. He fervently believed that unless positive action was taken by those interested in field sports, the negative attitude of those against them would prevail.

As early as the 1940s William was aware of the power of negative feeling and when he was still in Germany he set up a region of the British Field Sports Society at the British Army headquarters there. Even then he was aware of the great importance of gathering together those in favour of field sports and making their voice heard above those campaigning against them.

In Northern Ireland he threw himself into racing and became involved in local hunts. He trained his horses on the mudflats at the top of Strangford Lough near Newtownards and he had many racing successes at racecourses across Northern Ireland astride his favourite chaser Chipolata, and in 1956 he became a member of the Irish National Hunt Committee before going on to become Chairman at Downpatrick Racecourse.

His real interest was always the hunt and it was a great joy to him to be made Master of the East Down Foxhounds in 1955. The kennels at Seaforde were of significant historical interest. A report in *The Field*xxix describes their origins: 'These kennels were built in an octagonal shape, a miniature replica of a famous kennel in the Shires of England. They have stood on the Seaforde Estate, the home of Mr Patrick Forde, since his forebear Mr Mathew Forde kennelled his Lecale Harriers here in 1768.' When Desmond Forde was away during the Second World War his sister ran the show and when he returned he changed the hare-hunting harriers to foxhounds. Before the Second World War foxes were only to be found in the Mourne and Sperrin mountains but by the late 1940s it was noted they had begun to forage further afield. There was also a local pack of staghounds but William never enjoyed the thought of releasing a deer to chase it as he felt it was not a 'natural' sport.

Today both the East Down and the Strabane remain the only registered packs of foxhounds in Northern Ireland. For a few years in the early 1950s when Lady Londonderry was made Master she kennelled the hounds at Mount Stewart, but otherwise they have always been based at Seaforde. William loved his six years as Master, as he was doing exactly what he wanted to do. He was good at the organisation that went into it and he enjoyed talking to the local farmers and all the characters essential to the hunt. "He was last of the old school gentleman and he knew how to chat people up – and he remembered every keeper and dogman's name," says David Ker referring to the smoothness with which the hunt ran under his Mastership, "and he was very good with the young, he was encouraging." They hunted twice a week, on Mondays and Thursdays, and a typical meet was twenty or thirty mounted. Aside from the hunting itself there were fundraising events, the Point-to-Point was held annually at Tyrella and the hunt ball at the Slieve Donard Hotel in Newcastle. Billy McCully, who was Master in 1968 remembers watching 'the Major' encouraging the hounds over a fence saying 'over, over, over, over, over' – he says he stopped worrying he would never learn the hounds names as they were obviously all called 'Rover'. William gave his whippers-in whistles to let him know when they were on to a fox, and on a number of occasions Di Kirkpatrick remembers him hearing the whistle and rushing with horse and hounds to the end of a farmer's lane only to discover a surprised looking baker with his delivery van. Bakers announced their presence to farmers' wives with a similar sounding whistle.

By 1961 William's family commitments had increased and he stepped down as

Master and Bidger Ker and Di Kirkpatrick replaced him. On his retirement he took on the less hands-on role of Chairman of the hunt which he remained for the next decade – although the Troubles meant hunting would be cancelled for some of them. During this time he was District Commissioner for the North Down Pony Club, followed by the East Down Pony Club, and he then served as Area Chairman of the Pony Club in Northern Ireland which involved organising the annual Newcastle Show. Inevitably there were pushy mothers with children on swanky horses and he expressed his disapproval of them by making sure that they did not win.

In 1969 he decided he had reached an age to give up riding which he looked on positively as it gave him more time to pursue his interest in shooting. Some found it strange the ease with which he put down his reins and decided the horse must go, but it was possibly the only way he could deal with their departure from his life. His friend Jane Pope remembers him saying, "once you've been a Master you don't want to hunt in other ways." One of Melissa's earliest memories was watching from the rock garden as the horses left the stables at Ballywhite and seeing her mother cry as they were piled into a horsebox and driven away. After that William closed the tack room door and never returned to it, and apart from the odd venture onto a horse to take his children out he barely rode a horse again.

He had enjoyed shooting with friends all over Northern Ireland and when he gave up hunting he decided to arrange his own pheasant shoot at Portaferry Demesne. Lady Nugent continued to live there after the death of Sir Roly in 1962 but without sons alive she was happy to let the shooting. His children used to come to the shoot days and sit in the game cart with Tommy and Frank White. "Frank taught us to make bows and arrows, blow owl noises with our hands and make darts out of rushes," says Melissa. Agnes and Eveleigh would bring the lunch up which they ate in a garage until eventually Eveleigh found a mobile hamburger unit to bring them lunch. When the shooting at Portaferry came to an end William was asked to join a syndicate shooting at Finnebrogue Demesne, a 1,000 acre estate bordered by the Quoile River and Strangford Lough and once owned by Gavin Perceval-Maxwell[1] who had been an usher from his wedding.

When his brother moved with his wife and children to Ballydugan, near Downpatrick, from Cheshire in the early 1960s the opportunity arose to buy some sporting marshland at neighbouring Hollymount. The house at Hollymount was a ruin but the estate comprised of 100 acres of marsh, 120 acres of arable land and about 40 acres of woodland. On top of this the brothers rented some more marshland from Lord Dunleath. For the 15 years James lived at Ballydugan the brothers enjoyed their days out on the marshes together and after James returned to England William continued his days out on the marshes. The Mackie family – who bought Ballydugan from James – were also keen on shooting and for a number of years they organised a pheasant shoot together. The days out on the marshes were a favourite with his children. Camilla's memories are of standing back to back with her father, knee deep in water, trying to spot an incoming duck before they whooshed past: "It was lovely and so peaceful standing there as the sun was going down with a view of Down Cathedral on a hill the other side of the marsh." Melissa loved watching him work the dogs which he had trained himself and understood the great pleasure they gave him.

From his interest in shooting came the idea of experimenting with breeding pheasants and other game birds. A friend of William's, Ossie King, had decided in the late 1960s to set up an Irish branch of Gaybird, the English pheasant breeding company. It proved a success but it was too much work for King and his gamekeeper. William had reared a few birds in still air incubators for stocking the pheasant shoot at Portaferry Demesne and was interested in taking over the game farm when the opportunity arose in 1969. They took on the equipment – a Western five/seven and a battery of Glevum and Gloucester still air incubators for hatching – and during the first season he, Billy and Eveleigh produced about 13,000 birds. It was a family affair and with each season the operation got bigger and the numbers increased until they were dealing were with 50,000 or so eggs.

They put wild birds in pens to lay their eggs and five private shoots did likewise, collecting the eggs twice daily. The eggs took 24 days to hatch and when the chicks were one day old they were put in boxes, 25 to a compartment in batches of 100, "adding two to every box for luck."

Eveleigh's assistance was essential at hatching time. William was insistent that they did not adopt cost- and labour-saving undercover rearing methods feeling that although grass reared poultry are more expensive, they produce higher survival rates in covert. "In other words birds which are not weather-wise before they leave our rearing field have already weeded themselves out at our expense not yours," he wrote in an advertisement. They worked hard and succeeded in keeping their prices well below those of professionally staffed game farms in England.

Jamie, Camilla and Melissa also helped out. "Having nimble fingers we used to set the eggs in the trays," remembers Camilla. "We spent many hours in the pens, putting on plastic bits in the pheasants mouths and catching them for Dad to brail[2] … a very dirty, dusty job when they fly around and when they are bigger they scratch." He taught the children to check the incubators and turn the temperature knobs for him but they were not always helpful and would help chicks hatch if they saw a beak peaking out: "This was very annoying as Dad rightly maintained if they had not hatched by then they would not be strong birds and not worth keeping," says Melissa. "But, oh no, we always picked them out so he then had more to kill later as he always destroyed any weak or abnormal ones."

The summer was the busy time for the pheasants which meant holidays were not

William was Master and huntsman of East Down Foxhounds. Pictured with Hughie Hutchinson (1st Whipper-in) and Brian Fitzsimmons in 1956.

Taking part in Castle Ward's Springer Spaniel Trials

In the pheasant pens at Ballywhite

an option. The elements could be against them – heavy rain could drown the chicks, thunder storms could affect the incubators – and William worried about foxes and badgers breaking in, and pheasant diseases. The children were not concerned about lack of summer holidays but they did not enjoy all the jobs connected with the birds. They tried to avoid him when he was catching the layers to be released as he tended to lose his temper amid the flapping birds if it was not done systematically.

He was soon providing pheasant chicks to shoots across Northern Ireland, and began to wonder about the viability of breeding partridge and setting up a partridge shoot at Ballywhite. There were no partridge shoots in Northern Ireland and so it was an ambitious plan. His friend, Robin Graham, lived in Warwickshire where he had set up a partridge shoot on a small area of land which had encouraged him that he could do the same at Ballywhite. He set up three release sites for the birds on an area of about 60 acres containing winter and spring cereals, oilseed rape and grass. He sought advice on how to organise it and arranged for beaters to go out with plastic bag flags on the end of sticks. At the end of the first year he conceded that their recovery rate was low, about 29%, but that this was not bad for a first year. He told *Irish Hunting, Shooting and Fishing*[xxx] 'The important thing, in this experimental year is that we know that partridges in Northern Ireland are a feasible and exciting proposition.' For over 20 years a partridge shoot continued at Ballywhite, even after William's death, and Ballywhite provided a stunning setting on shooting days with wonderful views of the lough and mountains in the distance.

The game farm would not have been possible without the hours put in by the gamekeeper, William's godson, Billy White, who had worked all his life at Ballywhite helping with the pheasants and horses. Billy was Tommy White's son and William was always fond of him and had taught him how to sail while he was still a boy. It is fitting that with a legacy William left Billy he bought himself a sailing boat.

William and Eveleigh's only other foray into the world of commerce was to import lobsters from Nova Scotia and to grow them on in tanks next to the lough. It had come about when Eveleigh had introduced herself to someone who was planning on setting up the business on their doorstep. She and William were very interested in the idea, both loved lobsters, and they joined them in the scheme growing lobsters and exporting them to Paris. The business lasted about five years but it did not make money and they closed it down.

As the public became increasingly opposed to hunting and field sports William worried that he should be doing more to educate people into understanding the great value these sports bring to the countryside and rural communities. He was a leading member of the Northern Ireland Game Trust and in late 1970 he decided, with Mr Miller of the Ulster Game and Wildfowl Society, to organise a meeting in Northern Ireland to think about a field sports liaison committee. They gathered together representatives from dog clubs, the forestry division, coursing, hunting, fishing, farming, wildfowling, the National Trust and the RSPB. They wrote to the British Field Sports Society in London suggesting they send a representative who would be prepared to talk at the meeting. The point of the meeting was to discuss co-ordinating the efforts of the various sporting organisations and possibly affiliating themselves to a representative body.

William was elected to take the chair, and his address is recorded in the meeting's minutes: 'he explained that there was a growing conviction of the need for a certain amount of organisation to counter the 'anti' feeling currently circulating against field sports, and to this end the Ulster Game & Wild Fowl Society and the Northern Ireland Game Trust had decided to call a meeting of all interested bodies in an effort to arrive at the best solution. There were two sporting organisations which could possibly be of considerable assistance in this connection: the British Field Sports Society and the Field and Country Sports Society (the Irish equivalent).'

The BFSS sent Lt-General Sir Richard Goodwin to the meeting who told them the Society was interested in setting up a regional office in Northern Ireland with a secretary to lead it. The secretary's position was essentially vocational, remuneration would only be £400 per annum plus expenses, and the secretary had to achieve 400 new members in the first year to balance the salary.

Mr Selby of the Field and Country Sports Society explained that they were only a year old and small scale and that as things went though different parliaments it would be better to work in coordination with each other rather than their setting up an office in the North. He said that if the BFSS set up an office in the North they would assist by not canvassing support for themselves there. Everyone agreed that a Northern Irish region of the BFSS was the way ahead and they went away to consider who their secretary should be. The secretary would be expected to attend shows, point-to-points and make the BFSS known to the public, as well as coordinating action on parliamentary lines when necessary. William was more than prepared to put himself forward for something that he really believed and when he was elected to the position he spent two decades energetically campaigning for the BFSS in Northern Ireland and attending their meetings in London.

Delighted with the achievements of this meeting William decided to broach the problem of gun ownership in Northern Ireland in a similar fashion. He gathered together field sportsmen, gun dealers and target shooters to deal with the threats to the use of sporting firearms from the pending firearms legislation at that time. His intention was to create a joint body incorporating all their interests, and in 1973 he succeeded in setting up the Northern Ireland Joint Sporting Shooting Committee of which he was in charge. This idea was quickly followed by the formation of a similar committee in England. These committees have been in existence ever since supporting the individual's right to use sporting firearms.

Eventually William handed his chairmanship of both the BFSS NI region and his Joint Sporting Shooting Committee to John Beach, a local land agent who shared his passion to protect the future of field sports. When he retired the BFSS gave him the less hands-on role as President of the Northern Irish region.

By the late 1990s the BFSS had its work cut out: a Labour government had been elected and made it plain that they intended to outlaw hunting with dogs. In March 1997 William wrote to Robin Hanbury-Tennison, the explorer and chairman of the BFSS, stating that in his view the Society needed to shed its image of fusty army types and foxhunting if it were to attract more members. Later in the month the BFSS wrote to him explaining that they proposed to merge with the Countryside Business Group and the Countryside Movement to prevent confusion and overlapping of the three organisations and to increase their financial position as campaigning resources available to all countryside interests would be amalgamated. They asked if he had any suggestion for a new title which must somehow involve the 'countryside' title. William wrote back, he was excited by the new direction and offered his advice: 'during my long spell of activities, my prime target has been to attack the negative conservation policy of the antis – ban ban ban!: against the positive factor, wherein all field sportsmen have to conserve habitat for their particular quarry – to the benefit of all other wildlife and habitat.' He suggested various names for the society concocted by Eveleigh and himself, the best he felt being the Countryside and Country Sports Society. It became the Countryside Alliance and Dr Goodson-Wickes, an MP involved in the BFSS, became its founding chairman.

There were many angles to William's interest in field sports; he was the recognised link to the Game Conservancy from Ireland until 1984 when they set up the present Irish region; an active chairman of the Ulster Game and Wildfowl Society; and a respected President of Strangford Lough Wildfowlers' Association. His efforts were acknowledged by the BFSS who in July 1980 gave him a certificate 'in recognition of outstanding service given in support of the society,' and in 1991 presented him with the Beaufort Award for exceptional service to country sports. The magazine that so often had his name amongst its pages, *Irish Hunting, Shooting and Fishing* also presented him with the award for the Field Sportsman of the Year as well as a Perpetual Challenge Trophy for his contribution to field sports public relations.

Notes:
1 William had known his brother Robin who was killed at Cassino, Italy in December 1943 aged 20.
2 To stop them flying

Chapter Twenty-Two
Downpatrick Racecourse

William's horse Chipolata in the lead

WILLIAM'S CAMPAIGNING abilities were put to the test when government cuts threatened the future of racing in Northern Ireland. 'If I were a horse I would have been humanely shot years ago,' William wrote to the Minister of Agriculture at Stormont in 1988 'and if I fail after so long to achieve what is reasonable and justified, I agree that I should have been!' It was a fitting description of his resolute approach to solve the problems surrounding racing in Northern Ireland, and came when hope was in sight, thirty-two years after he first began the battle.

After his years racing in Germany he returned to Ireland full of enthusiasm and ready to throw himself into the local racing scene. Astride his well-known grey, Chipolata, he raced to victory in many point-to-points as well as the larger races at Down Royal and Downpatrick racecourses. Typically he was never half-hearted about anything he enjoyed and he became a Steward at Downpatrick in 1956. Even then the club's future, and that of the other Northern Irish racecourse Down Royal at the Maze, was uncertain: 'The position of the Maze and Downpatrick racecourses, which aim to hold four meetings each year, has reached a stage when it is difficult to see how racing can be maintained without assistance of some sort from outside sources' read the two racecourses' memorandum to the Government regarding financial assistance in February 1956. 'The estimated loss on both meetings for 1955 will be over £2000.'

The political divide between Northern Ireland and the Irish Republic did not help the racing scene in the North. For practical reasons the horses trained in the North were entered mainly for races across Ireland rather than in Great Britain and the two racecourses in the North reported to the Irish body governing racing, the Turf Club, which was based in Dublin at the time. The Turf Club behaved benevolently towards Downpatrick and Down Royal and paid travelling grants to those owners going to races in the North and vice versa but the Irish Republic could not regulate betting levies and governmental grants which in Northern Ireland were the responsibility of the British Government.

If this was complicated things were convoluted further by the fact that betting levy arrangements in Great Britain did not apply to Northern Ireland, and therefore the same amount of funding was not available to Northern Ireland's two racecourses.

Downpatrick was Ireland's second oldest racecourse: small and attractive and set amongst the drumlins of County Down, it did not attract huge races or big names but it brought great pleasure to the local community. While low-key it drew a number of royal racing wins – Edward VII's horse, Flaxman, in 1907 and 1908 and later, in 1962, Queen Elizabeth the Queen Mother, who watched her horse, Laffy, run the Ulster National. The latter's visit was organized by William who had known the Queen Mother was going to be in Ireland at the time of the race and suggested to her trainer, Peter Cazalet, that she run a horse.

When Laffy won the National, dramatically after being nearly carried out by a loose horse, it was a momentous occasion in the club's history and one Queen Elizabeth never forgot. 'The memories of Laffy's remarkable victory are as fresh as ever in Queen Elizabeth's mind – and we so often go over every incident of that remarkable afternoon,' Sir Martin Gilliat, the Queen Mother's Equerry, wrote in a letter to William in 1989. 'Whenever I see Willy Robinson [the jockey] we have a good talk about that day. However, as he was semi-concussed from a fall in an earlier race his memory of the race is not too clear.' In the unsaddling enclosure Queen Elizabeth was surrounded by excited well-wishers, which she described afterwards as enthusiastically patting both herself and Laffy, the atmosphere was wonderful. And William remembered one scene especially fondly: "One good lady – popping up from under Laffy's stomach – announced, 'Your Majesty, I have come all the way from Dublin'." The win was commemorated a number of years later when some new rooms in the club were named after Laffy, which pleased everyone and Sir Martin Gilliat wrote to William in April 1968 expressing Queen Elizabeth's delight: 'Certainly, with Laffy's racing plates in position and Queen Elizabeth's racing colours in the background the room must look extremely smart.'

William knew Sir Martin Gilliat from his days in the army and he also knew her Treasurer Sir Ralph Anstruther who had been at school with him. As a result he knew the interest Queen Elizabeth took in the club and kept them informed, and they in turn invited William and Eveleigh to drinks in Queen Elizabeth's box at Cheltenham Races and garden parties in London. Following decades of a happy correspondence with Clarence House William felt moved to ask Queen Elizabeth to become the race club's patron: 'it is perhaps slightly incongruous that, as we seek to relieve senior citizens of a burden[1], I am writing to invite the Queen Mother to be our patron – at least she will not have to attend committee meetings!' She accepted the position in November 1989, nine months before her 90th birthday.

When the Queen Mother died in 2002 some years after William's own death, an interview with him about her involvement with racing was played on the radio. His daughter, Camilla, heard it: "Dad's voice suddenly came on talking about her time at Downpatrick. It was really strange to hear his voice which had obviously been pre-recorded. Everyone kept coming up in Portaferry and saying they had heard the Major on the radio."

William was made chairman at Downpatrick in 1962, and despite the thrill of the Queen Mother's visit the club was not having a good year. It was in dire straits financially, and moves to persuade the government to support the bloodstock industry in Northern Ireland through a grant to race clubs seemed the only possible avenue left if Downpatrick was to survive. With Down Royal they lobbied the Government at Stormont and eventually it paid off and a small government grant of £3000 was made to each racecourse in November 1963. It provoked a small outcry as racing was seen as a rich man's sport and not worthy of Government funding. This response made William very angry and he wrote letters for publication in local newspapers explaining the true nature of racing in Northern Ireland and the money the sport brought the Government:

'Racing in Ireland is not a rich man's sport, the vast majority of the horses and nearly all those from the North comes from small stables of about one to three horses which are mostly owned by farmers ... the grant has come from public funds but how many people realize that the public purse benefits to the tune of about £75,000 a year from racing by way of bookmakers' licenses. Six thousand pounds returned to the source of the revenue seems indeed a paltry sum. How many realize that Northern Ireland is the only major country in the world where no money was returned from betting into the industry, except for a small return from the Tote? ... In England the Racing Levy Board is putting over £1,000,000 per year back into racing, this would average about £20,000 per course. Eire has the Racing Board which puts up capital grants, all the stake money and travel

Opening the new weighroom, Downpatrick Racecourse, 1997

allowances for horses … I can confirm to Dr Nixon that Irish racing is administered from Dublin, but so is the Church of Ireland.'[xxxi]

The grant was meant to be for five years, but it was reviewable annually and following the bad press it was decided in the second year that only Down Royal warranted a grant. This was a bitter blow to Downpatrick – which had just lost out on the Irish Racing Board's decision to withdraw the subsidy for the transport of horses to Ulster tracks – and William knew that they had to fight for the money to survive. The Irish Racing Board were not at fault, they were employed by the Irish Government and were not receiving any revenue from Downpatrick or Down Royal, and had been generous to support them as long as they did. It was a different situation with the British Government and William felt sure he could alter the decision and consequently he approached everyone he could think of from politicians to newspapers.

William talked to Brian Faulkner, himself a horsy man, who thought that the Chief-Whip James Chichester-Clark might be interested in getting the racecourse the grant and he was in a position to make a difference to the views of back-bench MPs. Chichester-Clark was two years below William at Eton and had also been in the army a similar length of time, retiring as a Major. In the Eighth Army they had both fought in Italy where Chichester-Clark was wounded. When he returned to Northern Ireland Chichester-Clark became a Unionist MP for South Derry and was the Chief Whip when William wrote to him seeking his opinion and help. He gave William good advice suggesting he examined the selling points behind racing before going any further:

'When I last discussed this with McConnell, I gathered that further Grants were out – this, however, was in the summer and you may well have changed his mind on it. I hope so!

All I can say is that you will certainly have my support over it and I will have another go at Brian McConnell. I hate to see all the hypocrites getting away with it!

I think if we are to sell this to our MPs and the public we want some pretty solid reasons for doing it and although I do not dispute any of the points you make, I don't think they will sell racing except to the converted. Would it be possible to show that the bloodstock industry in Northern Ireland, provided a worthwhile amount of employment?'[xxxii]

Brian Faulkner was also helpful in talks with politicians and was a part of the decision to transfer racing administration from Home Affairs to the Ministry of Agriculture which meant it became a bloodstock issue rather than a gambling one.

As Chairman William invited dignitaries and politicians to races and hoped they would enjoy it enough to realize its importance. In many cases he was very successful; in the Spring of 1969 he invited the Governor, Lord Grey of Naunton, to a very successful day at the races. 'My wife and daughter and I had the happiest of introduction to racing in Ireland yesterday,' Lord Grey wrote in a thank you letter to William. 'I don't suppose we shall always have such sunshine if we go racing again but yesterday was a memorable day on which to start.'[xxxiii]

His family enjoyed racing and point-to-points, and although they rarely saw him on racing days as he was usually a steward they were very much family days out. Camilla remembers one occasion at Down Royal when her father was standing in as a steward and forced to disqualify a winning horse that did not weigh in. "The racecourse was in uproar, the bookies went on strike … we watched in horror as angry punters and bookies surged towards the weigh in room where Dad and the other steward were with the steward's wife and decided that the steward (a boxer in his youth) would fend them off while Dad could slip out through the back window and run for it."

Forever in the pursuit of an answer that would save Downpatrick Racecourse William turned his attention in 1971 to raising levies on Northern Ireland bookmakers' turnover. He wrote to the Ministry of Agriculture and arranged meetings with the minister, Harry West. He would not give up and following the meeting he harangued them for not organizing a follow up meeting including all the interested parties. Harry West was unimpressed with William's urgency:

'If the racecourses are to receive money from a levy on the bookmakers it is only just, as I know you will readily accept, that the bookmakers should have an opportunity to express their opinions on how the Ministry should use the money. It will therefore be necessary for the bookmakers and representatives of the courses to participate together in some of the discussions so that agreement can be reached about the necessary machine to enable the bookmakers to play their part in any scheme.'

William was irritated by everyone's lackadaisical attitude to the future of the racecourse and felt frustrated in December 1971 when the only way he could see of raising revenue was to increase the price of membership. Things were not good and on 26th August 1972 they worsened when two IRA men accidentally blew up themselves with half the grandstand. The bomb created over £30,000 of damage for which the loss adjusters were prepared to offer only £24,000. By the 1970s any future at all seemed remote. *The Irish Field* ran an article in 1972 expressing the views of an increasing number of politicians that 'there is a powerful sector who believe that the only chance of survival for racing in the North is to scrap Downpatrick and modernize Down Royal.' William was furious with the article and wrote a letter to its author, Valentine Lamb, explaining the situation. Lamb wrote back: 'I am aware of the considerable difficulties regarding financial support but I have been led to believe that it would probably be more forthcoming if there was only one course.'

The early 1970s witnessed the future of the course swing from one extreme to the other. When the new Levy Scheme that William fought so hard for finally made it through at a Parliamentary level it looked as though Downpatrick would get some sort of regular financial backing. Things changed pretty soon after with the publication of a Jockey Club report which came to the conclusion. 'that the continuance of Downpatrick is not essential to the development of horse-racing in Northern Ireland.' This recommendation led the government to decide it would give grants to one racecourse only and that would be Down Royal. In 1978[2] all government funding at Downpatrick would cease. There were many who tried to intervene, including Eddie McGrady, the SDLP Member of Parliament for South Down who appealed to the Secretary of State, but the decision had been made and nobody was for turning.

Rather than despair the race club took its future into its own hands and in 1976 they opened a summer caravan park on racecourse land and organised local sponsorship for races. Local businessman Joe Rea was a guiding force, putting his own money into race sponsorship and persuading others to do so. Unlike other areas Downpatrick was totally dependent on their sponsor's generosity, as can be seen from a letter William wrote to Harp in 1976 thanking them for their sponsorship: 'We owe a very great debt of gratitude to Messrs Harp Lager and the Irish Bonding Co for their sponsorship of racing over the years. One has only to look at racing in England and in the Republic, where millions of pounds are returned to racing in the form of capital grants, stakes etc. from the betting turnover, to realise how great is the value of these generous sponsors in Northern Ireland where grants to racing have been derisory.'

William was prepared to break new ground if it meant raising money for the course and ultimately securing its survival. In 1977 the subject of racing on Sundays was mentioned to him by NITCA. 'I am glad that you raised Sunday racing,' William replied in a letter on the subject, 'I would be keen to try it. As you say we would be a 'first' in the British Isles, and if only to see Paisley's face!' The Royal Ulster Constabulary poured cold water on the idea when in a letter to William they suggested that it was not a good time to further religious controversy on attitudes to the Sabbath:

'Such a venture may be considered by a section of our community to be at variance with accepted Sunday activities and considerable problems could develop in respect of the racecourse itself in that considerable damage could be caused to the course premises etc., which indeed could result in curtailing week-day racing. Harassment to those attending could be so concentrated that the venture would be defeated.

Sunday racing would I believe create civil strife and thereby increase the work-loads and pressures on the already overstretched police service … I have no doubt you may well consider that the time is not opportune for such a venture in Northern Ireland.'[xxxiv]

A strong group of Downpatrick supporters grew and their zeal and energy proved to be the vital element needed to secure the racecourse's future. Downpatrick became best known as a racecourse that succeeded in saving itself through the hard work of local supporters who refused to watch it simply close its gates. 'The original seed for survival was suggested to me by Eddie McGrady, our member of Parliament – get a supporters club going!' William reflected in an article in *The Irish Field* in 1991. 'The seed was planted by Mrs Ann Kerr and Jeremy Maxwell with an embryo initiative.'

Ann Kerr of Corbally Stud invited a group of local horse breeders to a meeting to discuss the possibility of sponsoring a meeting at Downpatrick and discovered local enthusiasm was extremely strong and realised there was enough support for an official 'supporters club'. Jeremy Maxwell became the first chairman in 1977 and together this team of supporters committed themselves to raise funds to help the race club survive. The supporter's club got to the bottom of problems such as the bar not making money, arranging charges for horses to gallop at the end of races (which was common practice elsewhere) and putting up advertising bill-boards for local businesses. In less than a year they had raised £4,500 for the club. Their work was relentless and by 1983 the club turned over its first small profit. The Northern Irish press championed Downpatrick:

'They are the people who were told Downpatrick was written off and they refused to accept that premise. The result is a race-horse trainer's wife cooking a *Cordon*

Bleu lunch for more than 100 sponsors and influential backers – and the wife of a retired Army Major, (her husband is a Steward and Chairman of the Racecourse) washing up the dirty dishes.

It is volunteers manning the bars and turnstiles, offices and even helping to tidy up the litter after a meeting. And it is a story of the whole of County Down points to with pride.

It's the Story of the Racecourse That Refused to Die!

After the government withdrew its support, in favour of a metropolitan racecourse at Down Royal, local people, townsfolk, farmers and punters rebelled and proclaimed: 'we'll keep Downpatrick racing'.'[xxxv]

William's children were there on race days and they helped out behind the bar or with the washing up after the lunches in the Box. "Primitive facilities and rotting floors made it exciting," says Jamie, while Melissa admits it nearly put her off racing for life. Their early induction into the racing world gave them independence – their father was always stewarding and their mother helping with the lunches – and an early taste for gambling as Melissa recalls: "At home we used to go to Patrick Trainor, the bookie from Portaferry, and put on 2p – we often won 10p and that was so exciting."

Josie, who worked for the family, would often come racing with them – on one occasion when the family had grown up and Melissa had just got her driving test she and Josie passed a man at the race club gates who flashed at them. Later Melissa and Josie recounted the story to Nanny Connolly who was visiting Ballywhite, 'Sure what's wrong with that?" said Nanny imagining somebody had a flashed a torch at Melissa and Josie. When it was explained that he had exposed himself Nanny clutched her chest with horror and exclaimed, "oh my good Father that happened to me once and I grabbed the steering wheel and drove for my life – och Josie stop laughing you a married woman and all, poor wee Melissa."

While the Supporters' Club continued with their fundraising William battled with the powers-that-be at Stormont concerning the setting up of a mini Levy Board for Northern Ireland which would raise funds to support racing there.

Iain Duff [who became the course Registrar] remembers a meeting with Lord Lyell, the Minister for Agriculture, in which William, realising things were not going well, turned to his Lordship and said "You are wet, Lord Lyell!" In fact William sensed that Lord Lyell understood the logic behind uniformity with Great Britain on Levy Board lines and consequently he pursued him in an attempt not to let the subject drop. He was right to have felt Lord Lyell shared his line of thinking and in August 1988 he received a letter explaining that in principle he was prepared to agree to extend funding to Downpatrick once more. This time, perhaps because of their fight for survival, nobody seemed opposed to Downpatrick getting the money. The racing correspondent in *The News Letter* wrote in September 1988: "I heartily agree with South Down MP Eddie McGrady's sentiments about Lord Lyell's and the Government's decision to restore Government funding to Downpatrick Racecourse – if ever a racecourse deserved support it is Downpatrick, confidently written off by the ignoramuses of mainland racing and the Dept. of Agriculture a few years back.' A local paper added its voice: 'the wrong of removing state funding almost 12 years ago has now been righted.' By the end of 1990 the storm had been weathered and Downpatrick was once again receiving grants. Its survival during this difficult period was entirely due to the Downpatrick Supporters' Club and William's own dogged determination with Government officials. With this achieved William announced his retirement.

Before he left his post in January 1991 he made a few last efforts on behalf of the future of the club and racing in Northern Ireland. He pointed out to Peter Bottomley, the new Northern Ireland Minister for Agriculture, the Irish Government's decision to allocate a proportion of betting tax revenue to the development of horse and greyhound racing. Bottomley's office was not impressed by William's optimistic suggestion that something similar be proposed north of the border: 'There is, of course, no prospect of that happening in the UK, either on a national or regional basis. Furthermore, there can be no question of adjusting support levels or structures in NI to match the financial provision or arrangements in the Republic,' replied Aidan Cassidy, Bottomley's private secretary. 'The arrangements which have been devised for NI were framed to meet the particular local circumstances. The Department of Agriculture will continue to apply the limited resources available to assist the racecourses to meet essential race day costs.'[xxxvi]

In the last months in office he attempted to arrange for the Queen's Plate - a Down Royal racing prize contributed by the Queen and taking the form of a piece of china bought locally with prize money she donated - to be changed to a perpetual trophy. He wrote to Buckingham Palace in November 1990 and received an immediate reply from the Queen's Keeper of the Privy Purse, Sir Shane Blewitt[3]: 'Her Majesty would be happy to present a perpetual challenge cup for the Queen's Plate as you have requested, and I enclose a photocopy of the trophy Her Majesty has in mind to present … Perhaps you would be kind enough to let me have the details you would wish to have inscribed on the trophy itself.' William was surprised by the speed of Buckingham Place's consent to his idea and embarrassed when he discovered the Down Royal Corporation of Horse Breeders did not like his suggestion of a perpetual trophy. He was forced to accept his idea was unpopular locally and admit as much to Buckingham Palace.

When he did retire it was after 27 years as chairman and naturally he did not give up his association with the club. A post-script on a letter to Jeremy Hughes, the new chairman, pointed out his desire to remain linked with the racecourse: 'Incidentally, I notice that my name is still shown on the race card as a Steward.

When I gave up Chairman I also retired from the Board. If the Board wants, as I do, to keep my contact with the club alive, I suggest that some honorary role be invented – rather than false pretence!'[xxxvii]

On his retirement he was Northern Ireland's most senior member of the Turf Club which, with its 104 members, had governed racing in Ireland since 1790, as well as a member of the Irish National Hunt Steeplechase Committee. *The Down Recorder* reported his retirement describing him as 'the area's foremost gentleman of racing.'

In summer 2001 the William Brownlow Trophy race was run at Downpatrick in his memory and Eveleigh was surrounded by their children and grandchildren for the event. Three years later Eveleigh was invited to become the Patron of the Racecourse, replacing the late Queen Mother.

William's family with the winners of his Memorial Race held at Downpatrick Racecourse, 2001
Back from left: Paddy Benham-Crosswell, Camilla Benham-Crosswell, Melissa Brownlow, winner, Eveleigh Brownlow, Jamie Brownlow, Amanda Brownlow, Elinor Brownlow, winner.
Front from left: William Brownlow, Aidina Brownlow, Tom Benham-Crosswell, Freddie Benham-Crosswell

Notes:
1 He was trying to retire as chairman of the club.
2 They were given two years grace when they were paid grants at the increased level of £6000.
3 The author's father.

Chapter Twenty-Three
Agnes Retires in her Eighties

Agnes

OVER THE years Agnes' role at Ballywhite evolved and to William's children she is best known for her amazing baking skills and her story-telling of life in their grandparents' day. For Melissa a strong memory of waking at home was the smell of her baking as she always came in early on baking days and got straight on with it. An average baking day would see Agnes cooking twenty scones, two cakey breads, a chocolate cake, a plain sponge, shortbread, chocolate squares and 30 meringues – and then there was lunch, a favourite of hers was cheese and potato pie and gooseberry fool. If there were dinner parties or shoot days she would pull out all the stops and there would be a vast array of recipes including a much-loved chocolate bomb and an equally-favoured syrup tart.

With Agnes at the stove teas at Ballywhite were legendary and many questioned how the Brownlow family remained so slim. The Brownlow children took back to boarding school tuck boxes filled with Agnes' delicious chocolate squares which other children would try to beg or buy from them. The children enjoyed helping her cook, and were particularly partial to cleaning up the bowls of cake mix, but try as they might they found it almost impossible to get a recipe out of her as her cooking is almost instinctive. She never uses a recipe or scales. Melissa explains: "to

Agnes revisits the gatehouse at Castle Ward where she was born

Celebrating their Ruby wedding anniversary with nephew Billy, (left) son Derek with wife Vivienne (right)

One of Agnes' watercolours. Scene overlooking Strangford Lough where William proposed to Eveleigh.

get a recipe you are told a 'blob of this, a splash of that and well you just know by how it looks or feels'. Top tips were to sieve the flour, lift the mixture so as to give it plenty of air and do not over-knead the pastry."

She was hugely inventive when it came to making birthday cakes: "I had a rabbit, a horse, a hedgehog," says Melissa, who has never forgotten a cake. The one she remembers most especially was the one Agnes made for a family friend Sebastian Stephens when they were both very young. "Best of all was his train. They were just leaving Ireland so he had his party with us. It had *Wagon Wheels* for wheels, *After Eights* for the carriages, chocolate swiss roll for the body and chocolate fingers for the funnel." William's favourite cake was a chocolate and almond one which he always asked Agnes to make for his birthday. The Christmas cake and Christmas pudding were made in November and Agnes ensured that William was around so that he could stir the cake; he only did two stirs but Agnes felt his input brought luck.

When Frank retired from Stormont he occupied himself with his garden, his role as church warden and his shooting and fishing. Over the years Agnes' work at Ballywhite continued and even when she decided to stop working there she found it was not possible to break away from what had been a lifetime's involvement with a family. When she gave up the housework she continued to bake for them and remained cooking the shoot lunches given by William and then Jamie until 2002 when she was 81. She and Frank had helped out on the shoot days since they began at Portaferry Demesne and Eveleigh recalls how her eye became attuned to a good or bad shot: "She once said that some chap out with us at Portaferry 'couldn't hit a bullock on the bum with a baking board'!"

Beyond the world of Ballywhite Agnes was known for her artistic and musical talent. "During my time at Ballywhite I was always painting, then when the boys were all away I took myself to Glastry once a week to the Tech. to learn." Her painting is of wildlife and local scenes – the lough and the wildfowl. In Portaferry a group of artists gathered together for painting evenings and Agnes joined them, as did Jamie's wife, Amanda. Their work was put up for sale in an annual exhibition held in a gallery in the town. Derek takes her paintings and has them elegantly framed and they sell for a respectable price.

Music has always been important to her, right from the start of her life when her musically-inclined father showed her different instruments and encouraged her to try and make them play. She sings in the choir, remembers all the ditties, and plays the fiddle, the spoons, the black notes on the piano and the accordion. If she is given a new instrument she tinkers with it and can usually play it without any training. She is obviously musically gifted and as she watches her grandchildren going off to university to study all manner of different subjects she admits she wishes she had nurtured her musical talent through study. "I would love to have studied music as I can play every instrument by ear. I often thought I should have done it later but I never got round to it."

It is over 60 years since she first pedalled her hired pushbike up the hill to Ballywhite and told her stories to a young Anne Brownlow tucked up in bed while her parents dined in style downstairs. In the intervening years she has attended family weddings and funerals and become a part of life at Ballywhite. In more recent times the Brownlows have given parties for Agnes, firstly for her and Frank's Ruby Wedding Anniversary and then later to celebrate the Sixtieth Anniversary of the auspicious day she arrived at Ballywhite in search of work.

It is a tribute to her light-hearted and generous approach to life and her own unquestioned loyalty that every generation of the Brownlow family at Ballywhite has taken her to their heart. 'Aggie' is already a firm family fixture to the youngest generation of Brownlows growing up at Ballywhite today. There are few in a position to tell them: "Aidina's[1] more like Granny Brownlow."

Agnes teaching Anne's grandchildren how to bake

Notes:
1 Jamie and Amanda Brownlow's eldest daughter

Chapter Twenty-Four
Public Duty

William as Lord Lieutenant with Diana, Princess of Wales

IN 1985 with the political situation in Northern Ireland entirely desperate Sir George Clark, president of the Ulster Unionist Council at Unionist Headquarters in Glengall Street, Belfast wrote to the members. 'If you share the general concern about the present situation, would you consider writing to the Prime Minister giving her your views about the harm of the continuing state of uncertainty in the Province.' William took Sir George Clark at his word and his letter prompted the following reply from Tom King, the new Secretary of State for Northern Ireland:

'I know that our talks with the Irish Government have caused concern and that some people have tried to exploit this. The Prime Minister and I would clearly like to set that concern at rest and explain our talks in detail, but we cannot sensibly do so until we know what the outcome will be. Talks between Governments must inevitably take place in confidence until they reach a conclusion. No one should, however, be in any doubt that the Government remain committed to the maintenance of the constitutional status of Northern Ireland as part of the UK for as long as the majority of the people of Northern Ireland so wish. I hope too that people recognize, as we have already firmly stated, that ideas like joint sovereignty cannot be accepted. … Until the outcome of the talks, you will understand that it would be impossible for the Prime Minister to make any statement as you suggest.'

Without any official political position William felt able to speak his mind as an individual who cared very deeply for his country and understood that politicians needed all the help they could get. In April 1986 he heard that Harry West, the leader of the Unionist party, may meet with the Taoiseach and that it may even lead to an Anglo-Irish Agreement. William was impressed by this step forward and wrote to Garret FitzGerald, the Taoiseach, on 14th April 1986 giving his own feelings on flashpoints in the Northern Irish problem and explaining the irony that it was West who had stood in the way of any such agreement in 1974. The Taoiseach wrote back to his letter on 23rd June 1986:

'I am grateful to you for letting me have your views on the matter and I appreciate the supportive attitude you have taken. I recognise the widespread concern about the Agreement in the unionist community. This not so much due to the actual content of the Agreement but rather to the way in which the unionist people have been misled by their own politicians. I wish to get across to unionists that the Agreement is also designed to protect their interests. In this context, it is most significant that the Irish Government, in an international agreement, affirm that any change in the status of Northern Ireland would only come about with the consent of a majority in Northern Ireland and we formally recognise that the present wish of a majority in the North is for no change in that status.

'It is my hope that in due course unionists will come to appreciate that, far from depriving them of their rights, the Agreement provides significant reassurances about their future.'

William wrote letters where he felt he could help or to congratulate people who may need the encouragement of approval. To Austin Currie, a founding member of the SDLP who had served with William in the power-sharing executive and had since moved into politics south of the border, he wrote to congratulate him on his initiative in getting British-Irish talks arranged. 'What a tragedy that the cover was blown on your talks and I write to congratulate you on the initiative and your handling of the subject since. I hope that the damage is not permanent,' he wrote in February 1989. 'There are advantages to being party-free, normally I would now support Alliance but in the EEC election I gave John Hume first vote, I hope he will remember that if *Field Sports* matters come up in Brussels!' Austin Currie went on to become a member of the British-Irish Parliamentary Body, 1991-1994.

When John Major began his effort to tackle the problems in Northern Ireland William backed him wholeheartedly and in a letter of February 1996 he wrote to encourage him despite an outbreak of violence:

'The horror about the resurgence of bombing is very widespread throughout the whole community over here – even in much of the traditional republican areas.

My hope is that it may further isolate the terrorists within all the nationalist areas and prove how right you were to stand firm on your conditions for talks … I do not envy you in your search for a balanced and fair policy, Patrick [Mayhew] well knows what a difficult lot we are and you are fast finding out – in your devotion to getting to know the problem. At least Patrick has the advantage of having an Irish grandmother!'

Over the years he wrote letters to many of the Northern Ireland Secretaries as he felt it was his duty to support them in dealing with their most difficult task. Lord Mayhew, as Sir Patrick Mayhew went on to become, remembers being offered, "a kindly welcome and at the same time some fatherly advice. He was good enough to say that reports he had had of me were favourable. Nevertheless I recognised well enough that for some time I would be on fairly sceptical probation." In May 1997 he wrote his final such letter to New Labour's Mo Mowlam:

'I will pass on the one piece of advice which I have tendered to all Secretaries of State since Willie Whitelaw, which is that – you will sometimes think 'the logical answer to a problem must be …' my advice is that 'there aint no logic in Ireland – so forget it!!' Happily, County Down must be unique – anyway since Partition – in having a Lord Lieutenant and current High Sheriff who are both members of the Roman Catholic Church.'

When William became Lord Lieutenant he seemed a natural choice, he had been one of a number of Deputy Lieutenants since 1961, but he had been sure that his friend Dick Ker would get the top job. Dick Ker took himself out of the running by moving to England and in 1990 William became Lord Lieutenant. His role as the Queen's Representative in County Down was one he carried out with utter scrupulousness and enjoyed wholeheartedly. Lord Mayhew, who was serving as Secretary of State for Northern Ireland during his incumbency, remembers him as entirely suited to the position of Lord Lieutenant: "He brought to his duties as Lord Lieutenant the self discipline and thoroughness of the natural soldier, and the tactful solicitude of the Christian gentleman for those in trouble, need, sickness or any other adversity … When he retired from the Lieutenancy I gave a luncheon party in his honour at Hillsborough, and in a speech I described William as '*a varray parfit, gentil knight*'.[1]"

The most noticeable role of the Lord Lieutenant to the public is his presence on every royal visit to the county and as most royals would stop at Hillsborough Castle which came under his jurisdiction they kept him busy. In one ten day period there were six royal visits. On a visit made by the Queen in June 1993 the heavens opened for the duration of the Secretary of State's annual Garden Party. The Queen's Private Secretary, Sir Robert Fellowes, wrote to William after the visit, 'to be greeted by you, cheerful as always, added much extra pleasure.' *The News Letter* reported that Ian Paisley had told the Queen at the garden party that the showers kept the grass green, before quipping, "but I couldn't get the word 'orange' in."xxxviii

In his position he also saw great sadness brought about by Northern Ireland's political problems. In an official capacity he attended funeral services for every RUC officer killed during his time in office and Eveleigh remembers how the funerals really wore him down. Lord Mayhew remembers the impeccable way he continued to carry out his duty even with failing health. "He was particular about attending those funerals at which his presence would be a supportive symbol. Too many were those of RUC officers. Walking behind him through pouring rain, when he seldom wore his cape, I more than once felt tempted to fall out, as he would have put it, and I perhaps would have yielded had it not been for the uncomfortable thought of later suffering William's quizzical reproach. He had been left for dead, I knew, on the battlefield in North Africa, and he now was increasingly in frail health – yet ramrod straight when on parade."

With such a public position came the threat of terrorism and Ballywhite was kitted out with bullet proof glass and security cameras and the car was fitted with bomb detectors. The terrorist threat was something his family had become quite used to living with and they looked upon these security measures as run of the mill, if not advantageous. "The glass kept the house much warmer," jokes Melissa, "and we could see people coming on the cameras and decide if we wanted to see them or not!"

As the Queen's Lord Lieutenant William took it upon himself to keep her informed of the feeling on the ground in Northern Ireland as he saw it and other matters which might provoke her interest. "It was common practice in the eighteenth century to write about the state of the county to the monarch and it was wonderful that William did it," says David Ker, Dick Ker's son. "I know that Robert Fellowes, the Queen's Private Secretary, used to look forward to getting his letters."

'I am sure that the Queen is deeply concerned about our problems here,' William wrote to Sir Robert Fellowes in November 1993. 'There is undoubtedly a great deal of fear on all sides but I do not think it will escalate totally out of control. … As an example – in our own area which is 90% Catholic but where all work together in harmony, the Sunday Masses were put off till Monday in fear of UVF action designed to stir up trouble where it does not now exist. … The Down Royal meeting on Saturday, including the Queen's Plate (represented by a salver) which I presented on behalf of Her Majesty, went off well with only a few absentees. I very much hope that we will still get a good number of Royal Visits, for they are undoubtedly good for morale.'

William was Lord Lieutenant when the Princess of Wales flew into Northern Ireland just days after dramatically announcing her withdrawal from public life. It was her seventh visit to Northern Ireland and the *Belfast Telegraph* ran the headline 'Is this our last glimpse?' She had come to open a new child development centre at the Ulster Hospital and met schoolchildren as well as representatives from Home Start and Relate at Hillsborough. After the visit William wrote a letter to her Private Secretary, Patrick Jephson, wishing the Princess 'a happier new year' and commenting that his own children's nanny – Nanny Connolly – had watched the visit on television and had been amused to see he could keep up: 'I must admit that I could no longer win the Mile at Eton.' Patrick Jephson wrote back: 'She has asked me to remind you that even present day Eton athletes might have trouble contending with sword and spurs.'[xxxix]

The work was interesting and he enjoyed the wide variety of people he met through it. In describing the lesser known aspects of his role on local radio[xxxx] William explained: "You chair the JP Committee and put forward names to the Lord Chancellor to organise the one hundred birthday telegrams. I try to get a personal note into the letter … You'd be surprised how many make 100 birthdays and Diamond weddings (about 3 a month)."

At the age of 75 William stepped down as Lord Lieutenant – "put out to grass" was how he described it - and he handed the mantle onto one of his deputies, Bill Hall.

William with his successor Lord Lieutenant, Bill Hall.

Notes:
1. From Chaucer's *Canterbury Tales*

Chapter Twenty-Five
Ballywhite: 'A Home Away from Home'

William with a statue of Master McGrath

THROUGHOUT WILLIAM and Eveleigh's marriage their children, and later their grandchildren, brought them their greatest pleasure. After completing degrees, agricultural college and skiing seasons they all found work in London and lived together in Battersea – Jamie was employed by Bonham's Auctioneers, Camilla by SKY News and Melissa set up her own company, Mountain Beds, organising skiing holidays.

On one occasion Camilla's work took her to El Alamein for a Poppy Appeal and for the first time she asked her father about his experiences there. Melissa organised her work so that she could spend her summers at home in Ballywhite and succeeded in having the best of both worlds. Her father was surprised by Melissa's choice of name for her company but he supported her all the way – once wearing a hat with her company logo on it to the tennis tournament at Ballycastle.

Ballywhite was more than home to William, Eveleigh and their children, it was home to all Brownlows. Anne remembers how Eveleigh would always put her in her childhood bedroom when she stayed and for William's nieces and nephews it has childhood memories as their Granny's home. "I can't remember how old I was when Granny moved out of Ballywhite and Uncle William moved in, but, to me, the house kept its magic," says Libs Bailey, James' daughter. "Uncle William and Aunt Eveleigh were absolutely wonderful to us all – it was always an open house for cousins." When Libs' first marriage came to an end she faced her first Christmas without her children and rather than spend it with anyone else's she turned to Uncle William and Aunt Eveleigh: "Ballywhite was almost a home from home – and to Ballywhite I went!"

William never teased his children or even questioned them about boyfriends or girlfriends and like most parents his greatest desire was for them to be happy. Melissa was not the sort to rush home and discuss boyfriends but when a great romance came to an end she did tell her father how heartbroken she felt. In return he admitted how devastated he had been when Prue Blakiston Huston had rebuffed him but how lucky it was that these things happened because as a consequence he had married Eveleigh.

Camilla met her future husband, Paddy Benham-Crosswell, when he was serving with his regiment in Northern Ireland and he came to Melissa's 21st birthday party. There was no romance at first but they became friends and he eventually wooed her three years later with a plate of oysters and a bottle of champagne. For Paddy it was strange to return to Ballywhite as the boyfriend after so many years as 'the friend' and he found the experience awkward. When he proposed to Camilla they kept their engagement secret for six months while she worked out how she would cope with army life and he made arrangements to visit Ballywhite to ask William's permission. When they did get there William sat down with Camilla and said "What is this Miss CJ Brownlow engagement in the newspaper for?" – Camilla's heart leapt as she thought Paddy had lost his nerve and just put an announcement in the paper. It turned out to be the engagement of a second cousin. When Paddy did summon the courage to ask William's permission for Camilla's hand he responded with, "you are brave!" while Eveleigh and Melissa dissolved into tears.

They married in Portaferry on 31st July 1993. One of the problems of living in Northern Ireland was getting permission for army officers to come to the wedding. In the end William wrote to the Queen saying it would be a sad day if his daughter could not marry an army officer with his friends there in a part of the United Kingdom and permission was granted. The bridesmaids and pages included a godchild but were otherwise related and mostly grandsons and granddaughters of Nell, James and Anne. William carried out the only *faux pas* on the day; his friend Thomas Stoney, a retired archdeacon, was marrying the couple and pointed out how rude he considered it when a bride arrived late. As they pulled up outside the church William told Camilla she had five minutes to arrange herself as it was not yet 4pm. Camilla panicked – the wedding was 3.45pm. William had never taken note of the time on the invitation and they walked down the aisle to stony looks from Eveleigh and the Archdeacon. The party afterwards went on all night and at 2am William told Camilla she really must go as the older folk were keen to leave. Camilla and Paddy settled in Hampshire where Paddy's family came from. It amused William that Paddy's prep school was the building opposite Twyford House, his home as a child.[1] Life was starting to come full-circle.

Jamie met his future wife with Camilla in London in 1989. He asked Amanda Watson to marry him when she was staying at Ballywhite for New Year, proposing on the mountain behind Ballywhite on 30th December 1993. They married in July 1994 at her parents' home in Churt in Surrey. In September 1995 they had a daughter, Aidina, named after Amanda's grandmother. The following year they moved from London to Ireland and made their home at Seaweed Hall. For William, now in his seventies, it was time to start handing over: Jamie had come home to learn about the responsibilities of Ballywhite just as he had done almost forty years before. Jamie and Amanda settled into family life in County Down – their second child was born in the Ulster Hospital in Dundonald in 1997 and they christened him William.

William had been lucky to leave the desert alive in 1943 and in later life Eveleigh wondered about the long term effects such a great physical trauma had on his body. "He got headaches, he was not robust enough and the headaches did not get better latterly." It was not until 1997 that his health really became a cause for concern when his cough, the side effect of a lifetime smoking, became more accentuated. Eveleigh remembers in June that year noticing that the emphasis of the cough had changed and she worried about it. In November William was diagnosed with cancer of the lungs and by Christmas he was being operated on in the Ulster Hospital. "He had not been great for ages" Jamie recalls, "and one sensed something was up." Melissa did not know what to say when she heard her father was ill, but he said the right things and put her at ease. In truth she did not understand the gravity of the situation but she came home as did Camilla and they were all together for a harrowing supper the night before his operation. Camilla had spoken to a doctor friend about lung cancer and understood the seriousness of the illness and she stayed with her mother while he had the operation.

After the operation he was very ill and his health deteriorated further when he got an infection which resulted in septicaemia. Despite the seriousness of his condition he remained in good spirits as Lord Mayhew remembers: "William never lost his great sense of fun … even when near the end and in hospital, he was vastly amused and delighted when a piece of shrapnel acquired at Alamein was extracted from him. It should become, he agreed, an heirloom." Eveleigh recalls how cheered both he and the nurses were when Lord Mayhew – who was the Secretary of State for Northern Ireland at the time – sat on the hospital floor chatting away during a visit. He went home in the New Year and seemed much better and was even well enough to do a bit of shooting despite needing to stay in bed in the morning.

He was excited at the thought of the Countryside Alliance's protest march in London in March and he and Eveleigh planned their trip. 'The Countryside March' through central London was planned to express opposition to the government's

1993: Camilla marries Paddy Benham-Crosswell
From left: Melissa Brownlow, William, Paddy Benham-Crosswell, Camilla Brownlow, Eveleigh Brownlow, Jamie Brownlow

1994: Jamie marries Amanda Watson
From left: Camilla Benham-Crosswell, Paddy Benham-Crosswell, Eveleigh Brownlow, Jamie Brownlow, Amanda Watson, William, Melissa Brownlow

Three generations of William Brownlows – William with his brother James' son, William and his grandson William, Jamie's son.

attitude to rural affairs. It had been prompted by the threat to the future of hunting and was a cause that could not have been closer to William's heart. It passed off good-naturedly and without incident and was the sort of event William would have been proud to be associated with, but sadly he was not there. On the Monday before the Countryside March his doctor had said he was fit enough to travel, but as Eveleigh remembers "by the Thursday he wasn't going anywhere and on the Sunday we watched it on the television."

At Easter the whole family was at home, including all the grandchildren, even the latest addition, Tom Benham-Crosswell, Camilla and Paddy's eight week-old son. William was happy surrounded by his expanding family – Amanda and Jamie were expecting another child[2] – but he was very weak and it was obvious he had little time left. A few weeks later everyone was back at Ballywhite when William was taken into the Ulster Hospital in Dundonald. He died on April 30th 1998 aged 76, with Eveleigh and his sister, Anne, by his bedside.

He was buried close to his parents in the graveyard of the Abbacy Church near Ballywhite. He had requested that his friend Bill Montgomery 'blow gone away' and then 'gone to ground' on the hunting horn. In the July following his death a thanksgiving service was held in Down Cathedral in Downpatrick with a reception afterwards at the Racecourse. His friends came from far and wide and some recall bumping into each other on the aeroplane to Belfast. His friend from the shooting field, Archdeacon Thomas Stoney, gave an address in which he described William: "*A man greatly beloved* because he was deeply trusted and widely respected."

Celebrating his 75th birthday with Eveleigh

Notes:
1 Camilla and Paddy's son Freddie has gone to the same school.
2 Elinor Brownlow was born in August 1998.

For Aggie

1

How do you start to write a verse
On someone that you know,
Whose abilities are endless
Who'll give anything a go?

2

She'll tackle any task you throw,
No way would she give up.
To me she is incredible
– A genuine "Super-pup."

3

Some call her Aggie Baby,
Some say Agnes – Mrs White
She's guaranteed to make you smile
– An absolute delight.

4

When young she worked at Ballywhite
As Maid – her skills did hone
And one day in the garden
Overheard a manly tone

5

She could not see across the wall
To know from whence it came,
But being full of devilment
Joined in his sweet refrain.

6

He'd sing "Little sir echo"
Then went on … "how do you do"
Whilst Aggie, still obscured from sight
Replied "Yoo hoo, Yoo hoo!"

7

Frank was beguiled by Aggie's charms
Her devilment and fun
And Aggie found her Mr White
They wed and were as one.

8

To Major Brownlow and his clan
Our Aggie played her parts
By spoiling them with gorgeous bakes
Her cakey breads and tarts

9

Her talents, well they're endless
They could fill so many books
The one that makes me giggle
Is the way in which she cooks.

10

No weights or scales impede her space
- No recipes in sight
Just handfuls of ingredients
That come together right.

11
She once made Christmas puddings.
You'll not believe what she did wear,
An apron with inflated boobs
And antlers in her hair!!

12
I've heard she plays piano
(Strictly ebony for tunes)
And also plays accordion,
The fiddle and the spoons.

13
At art club she was mustard
All the laughter – 'twas insane
I left each week in stitches
Not a painting to my name

14
And sometimes when I looked at her
She'd pull a funny face

And all ideas I had of work
With laughter were replaced

15
Her paintings are a sheer delight
Attract the keenest buyer
Another talent that she has
Is singing in the Choir.

16
She really is like yummy jam
I'd like to spread around
An antidote to anyone
Who's feeling low or down.

17
Agnes, you're superbulous
Fantastical, such fun
A mix of everything that's nice
Humdinger – Number One

– Caroline Reid

Bibliography

Suggested Further Reading:
The Imperial War Museum Book of the Desert War 1940-1942. Editor Adrian Gilbert
Editor in Chief: Field Marshal Lord Bramall.

Bombs on Belfast: The Blitz of 1941
Introduction by Christopher D McGimpsey
Pretani Press.

Northern Ireland in the Second World War
Brian Barton, Ulster Historical Foundation.

Jackets of Green
Arthur Bryant, Collins.

The Rifle Brigade
Basil Harvey, Pen and Sword.

Ike and Monty
Norman Gleb, Constable.

El Alamein to the River Sangro

Field Marshal Sir B L Montgomery
Printing and Stationery Services, British Army of the Rhine. 1946.

The Rifle Brigade Chronicle
From the year 1942.
From the year 1943.

The Royal Green Jacket Chronicle
From the year 1996.

Rommel
Desmond Young, Collins.

The Italian Campaign
G A Shepperd 1943-5, Arthur Barker Ltd, 1968.

I've Lived Like a Lord
Edward Ward, Michael Joseph, 1970

Number One Boy: An Autobiography
Edward Ward, Michael Joseph, 1969.

We Wrecked the Place
Contemplating an end to the Northern Irish Troubles
Jonathan Stevenson, The Free press, 1996

The Provos, the IRA and Sinn Fein
Peter Taylor, Bloomsbury 1997.

The Chronicle of the World
Editor in chief: Derrik Mercer
Dorling Kindersley 1996.

The Bangor Family Papers
The Brownlow Family Papers
Public Records Office, Northern Ireland.

Castle Ward
National Trust Publications

Lurgan: An Irish Provincial Town 1610-1970
Francis X McCorry, Inglewood Press

Circe, The Life of Edith, Marchioness of Londonderry
Anne de Courcy, Sinclair Stevenson

The Londonderrys
H Montgomery Hyde, Hamish Hamilton

Bibliographical References:

i Public Records Office, NI. D/1928: Brownlow Papers.
ii Radio Ulster: History of Lurgan. The Lough referred to is Lough Neagh.
iii Public Records Office, NI. D/1928: Brownlow Papers.
iv *Shooting Times & Country Magazine* November 7-13 1991
v Public Records Office, NI. Castle Ward Papers. Castle Ward Papers.
vi Letter to Rev Canon WH Good, 25/6/50 Public Record Office, NI, Castle Ward Papers
vii *I've Lived like a Lord*, by Edward Ward.
viii P16 *Northern Ireland during the Second World War*

ix From Report 49. 27/10/41. Canadian Military HQ, London.
x Arthur Bryant, *Jackets of Green*
xi *El Alamein to the River Sangro* by Field Marshall Sir BL Montgomery
xii *Ibid*
xiii by Adrian Gilbert
xiv p 64 Report in Rifle Brigade Chronicle 1943
xv Arthur Bryant, *Jackets of Green*
xvi Anne de Courcy, *Circe*
xvii *I've Lived Like a Lord* by Edward Ward
xviii *Ibid*
xix *Ibid*
xx *Shooting Times & Country Magazine* Nov 7-13 1991
xxi *Ibid*
xxii Letter from County Surveyor to William Brownlow, 29th July 1959.
xxiii *The Newtownards Chronicle*, 4th September 1964
xxiv *Provos* by Peter Taylor
xxv *Ibid*
xxvi A tribute to Lord Faulkner by W.S. Brownlow, 3rd March 1977.
xxvii from local newspapers in William Brownlow's files.
xxviii Letter of 25th October 1976.
xxix *The Field* 13 January 1982.
xxx Vol 3, No 4
xxxi Letter from *Belfast Telegraph* and *News Letter*, November 18th 1963
xxxii Letter from Major J D Chichester-Clark, Jan 11th 1965
xxxiii Letter from Lord Grey of Naunton, 6th March 1969
xxxiv Letter from the Chief Superintendent, Newtownards, 28th Oct 1977
xxxv The *News Letter*, 22nd March 84
xxxvi Letter to WSB, 25th February 1990
xxxvii Letter from WSB 19th May 92
xxxviii Edition of 12th June 1993
xxxix Letter of 14th December 1993
xxxx In conversation with 'The Rambling Man', Downtown Radio.